Minds and Bodies

Minds and Bodies: An Introduction with Readings is a concise, accessible introduction to the mind–body problem. It requires no prior philosophical knowledge and is ideally suited to those coming to philosophy and philosophy of mind for the first time.

Written with the beginner in mind, Robert Wilkinson carefully introduces the reader to the major issues in the philosophy of mind: Descartes' dualist account of mind and body as separate substances; together with other types of dualism; recent monist views including functionalism and eliminativism; computer science and artificial intelligence. Each chapter is helpfully linked to a reading from key thinkers in the field such as Descartes and John R. Searle. With the use of exercises, readers are then encouraged to think critically about the readings themselves.

By the end of the book students will be able to:

- understand and evaluate for themselves the major options in the philosophy of mind
- confidently discuss some of the writings on the mind philosophers such as Descartes, John R. Searle and Thomas Nagel
- understand proposed solutions to the mind–body problem and the major objections to them.

Key features also include activities and exercises enabling readers to monitor their progress throughout the book, chapter summaries and guides to further reading.

Robert Wilkinson is Head of Philosophy at the Open University. His previous publications include *Fifty Eastern Thinkers*, Routledge 2000.

Minds and Bodies

An introduction with readings

Robert Wilkinson

London and New York

First published 2000
by Routledge
11 New Fetter Lane, London EC4P 4EE

Simultaneously published in the USA and Canada
by Routledge
29 West 35th Street, New York, NY 10001

Routledge is an imprint of the Taylor & Francis Group

© 2000 the Open University

This updated and revised version is based on a coursebook previously published by the Open University.

Typeset in Perpetua by Taylor & Francis Books Ltd
Printed and bound in Great Britain by TJ International Ltd, Padstow, Cornwall

British Library Cataloguing in Publication Data
A catalogue record for this book is available from the British Library

Library of Congress Cataloging in Publication Data
Wilkinson, Robert, 1948–
Minds and bodies: an introduction with readings / Robert Wilkinson.
p. cm.
Includes bibliographical references and index.
1. Mind and body. I. Title.
BF161.W465 2000
128'.2–dc21 00–030595

ISBN 0–415–21239–1 (hbk)
ISBN 0–415–21240–5 (pbk)

Contents

Acknowledgements

I have benefited greatly in preparing this book from the comments of Dr Michael Clark of the University of Nottingham. I would also like to record my gratitude to Dr Nicholas Nathan (now of the University of Liverpool) who, many years ago, showed me what was involved in reading a philosophical work.

Grateful acknowledgement is made to the following sources for permission to reproduce material in this book: Haldane, E.S. and Ross, G.R.T. (trans.) (1931) *The Philosophical Works of Descartes*, Vol. 1, Cambridge University Press (for Readings 1, 2, 3 and 4); Shoemaker, S. 'The mind–body problem' in R. Warner and T. Szubka (eds) (1994) *The Mind–Body Problem*, Blackwell Publishers Limited (for Reading 6); Churchland, P. (1981) 'Eliminative materialism and the propositional attitudes', *Journal of Philosophy* 78(2): 67–76, February 1981; The Journal of Philosophy, Inc., by permission of Professor Paul W. Churchland (for Reading 7); Searle, J. R. (1990) 'Is the brain's mind a computer program?', *Scientific American*, January 1990, pp. 20–5 (Reprinted with permission. Copyright © 1990 by Scientific American, Inc. All rights reserved) (for Reading 8); Nagel, T. 'Consciousness and objective reality', in R. Warner and T. Szubka (eds) (1994) *The Mind–Body Problem*, Blackwell Publishers Limited (for Reading 9).

1 | Introduction

This book is intended to be of interest to beginners or near-beginners in philosophy, and it has two main aims: the first is to introduce you to the mind–body problem, a central question in the branch of philosophy called the philosophy of mind; the second aim is to show you, by means of guided reading of primary source texts dealing with this problem, what is involved in reading a text from a philosophical point of view.

Let me say something about the second of these aims before getting on to the main business of the book. Reading a text from a philosophical point of view is somewhat different from reading it as would a student of literature or a student of history. Philosophy is the study of our most basic and general concepts and beliefs: the whole edifice of human thought rests on such concepts and beliefs that serve as its foundations, and it is the business of philosophy to identify and analyse them in a particular way, which we will see exemplified in what follows. The principal techniques used are the analysis of concepts and the deployment and evaluation of arguments – there will be many examples of both these techniques in this book, so I will not attempt here to define them – it is, in any case, much easier to grasp what is involved by means of examples. The point to fasten on for the moment is that, when reading a text philosophically, the aim is precisely to evaluate the arguments and conceptual analyses in it. Accordingly, reading a text philosophically is not reading *about* philosophy but in a real sense *doing* it. Indeed, critical reflection on written philosophy is one of the principal ways in which the subject proceeds, though it is not the only one. I doubt if many philosophers would disagree with the view that 'live' debate with other philosophers is equally important. These activities are indeed two sides of the same coin. As we will see repeatedly in what follows, philosophy proceeds by dialogue: by the advancing of an argument or analysis; by the putting forward of objections, and then (if possible) of replies to these objections, and so on. Accordingly, knowing how to read a text philosophically is an essential skill for any philosopher.

As a key means to fulfilling this second aim, exercises have been included throughout, and you should try to resist the temptation to skip them. They have a number of functions: to reinforce your understanding of the most important of the concepts and beliefs discussed; to give you practice in the close reading of a philosophical text, and to consolidate your grip on the fundamentals of philosophical reasoning. You will benefit much more if you try to do these exercises yourself before reading the specimen answers and/or discussions provided. To repeat: reading in this way is not just reading about philosophy but doing it.

It is important to note that reading philosophy in this way is not quick: philosophical texts are much more like dense plum cakes than soufflés: a little goes a long way and takes a while to digest. All philosophers, however expert, find the same. To my knowledge, nobody has yet devised a way of skim-reading a philosophical text and understanding it properly, so do not be either surprised or depressed if you find it takes you some time to understand this material – this is a good sign!

We can now turn to the substantive business of this book, a consideration of the question philosophers term the mind–body problem. In the remainder of this introduction I want to set out some basic considerations which will allow us to state the mind–body problem in a preliminary way, and to begin to see why it is a real problem.

In fact, it is not too much to say that the mind–body problem is one of the most intriguing in the whole of philosophy. Typically of such philosophical problems – for example, concerning the nature of time or the source of the power of music – the mind–body problem arises when we reflect philosophically on features of the world which normally we take for granted and hardly notice in the ordinary course of life. The mind–body problem arises when we begin to pay attention to what is in fact a most remarkable feature of human beings (and indeed a number of other forms of life as well), namely, that we are conscious or, as we usually say, that we have a mind as well as a body. When you really stop to think about this, it rapidly comes to seem much more puzzling than you might expect. We all have an intuitive understanding of what material objects or bodies are like; but if you ask yourself the question: Is my mind the same sort of thing as my body or not? – in other words: Is the mind an effect or property of the body or at least significantly like it? – then we are liable to stop short at once and be stuck for an answer. Perhaps many people would accept, for example, the view that the mind must at least depend on the body in some way, on the ground that there are regular (or as philosophers sometimes say 'law-like') correlations between states of my body (like putting my hand on a drawing pin) and states of my mind (a sharp pain). Again, bodily disorders often result in predictable mental disturbances: the fever brings on the delirium. Yet the fact (if it is a fact) that the mind might depend on the body in some way yet to be fully specified does not entail that the mind cannot be a quite different type of thing from the body. Dependency is logically quite compatible with distinctness. Informal reflections of this kind will start us off on our inquiry, but we find rapidly that they will not take us far along the road. In order to think about this matter to some purpose we need to do some philosophy.

We will begin our investigation in this Introduction with two steps: first, I will ask you to work out where you stand at the moment with regard to a basic question; and then I will set out some basic philosophical considerations about minds and bodies that will allow us to state the mind–body problem in a more detailed way and show why it is so intriguing and genuine a problem.

Put at its simplest, the question we are going to investigate is: What is the mind, and how is it related to the body? I now want you to work out roughly where you stand on this question at the moment, before you have investigated it from a philosophical point of view: to repeat, everyone has a basic intuition about this, and it is interesting, as a starting point, to tease it out. So, let us proceed by identifying your present basic idea about the mind–body question. Let me sketch out two different points of view, towards opposing ends of the spectrum of opinions which are taken on this issue.

POINT OF VIEW 1

The mind must be a very different sort of thing from the body. Many religions include the doctrine that it can and does live on, in some way, after the death of the body, and for that to be true minds[1] have to be very unlike bodies. After all, everything that is a material thing above the level of elementary particles is made of parts, and there is no material thing whose parts stay the same, or stay organized in the same way, forever. All material things change and decay, and all the living beings we know on earth — vegetable, animal and human alike — are mortal. They change and eventually they die. And so, if minds do not die, they must be very different sorts of things from bodies.

Again, you don't have to be religious to believe this. People have out-of-body experiences, and these are so well attested they just can't be ignored. Here is a typical report of such an experience:

It was a hot day and the air conditioner was on. After taking a shower I stretched out on the bed to cool off before dressing to leave the house. I did not fall asleep. I was not in the habit of taking naps in the afternoon and was very alert but thinking of nothing in particular that I could recall later. One moment I was on the bed, the next I was standing away from the foot of the bed. The mirror of the dressing table was in my line of vision and I saw myself. The reflection looked like me, yet it did not. … It was as if I looked like myself but that I had been refined and my features made more regular ... I was aware of the body on the bed but not interested in it ... I was not a 'body' such as was on the bed; it was something I wore, in the same way that one wears clothes. I did not want to go back to my body and felt a sense of heaviness in relation to it.

I have met only one person who was able to verify such an experience. Her name is ... When she was so ill she was not expected to live, she thought she had left her body and was looking down at the house (of course, much more details to it) and saw a garden hose on the roof. It was a flat-topped house they had just bought so that when she came to herself she knew that if there was such a hose up on the roof that she then had actually seen it. Not telling her husband why, she asked him to go up, and there was a hose to his surprise (a new one the last owners had forgotten).

(Tart in Ramakrishna 1993: 127–8)

In the light of experiences like these, it just isn't plausible to say that the mind is in some way a material thing, because material things just don't act like this. No other aspects or properties or bits of me can act in this way, so my mind must be a very different sort of thing from the rest of me.

POINT OF VIEW 2

The best guide to the way things are in the universe, in all its aspects, is science: it has worked better than any other method human beings have yet devised, and has made more true prophecies about the future than all the prophets there have ever been. What science has discovered is a universe of material things and forces in which extremely simple basic elements, like sub-atomic particles, have, over the unimaginable stretches of cosmic time, combined to form the extremely complex and richly varied universe we live in. Now, no scientific theory to date has included the idea of something so different in nature from matter that it escapes the conditions, like change and decay, which have been found to affect all complex material things. Even if we don't know yet how the brain generates the mind, it's a safe bet that it does generate it in some way, and that minds will turn out to be – in any sense of the word that is significant – material things. The peculiar out-of-body experiences just described are not enough evidence on their own to justify believing in minds that are not matter-dependent in some important way. After all, these experiences are really only like having a body that can do odd things such as flying: the people who have them always report visual sensations for instance, and if you really were detached from your body it isn't likely that your experience would be anything like having sensations at all, because you would not have any sense organs. We don't yet know how odd experiences like those described in Point of View 1 are to be accounted for, but the most probable assumption to work on is that some day we'll find a neat biochemical explanation for them – maybe the wiring in a key bit of the brain goes haywire for a while, or the electrochemistry malfunctions. After all, the human brain is the most complex entity in the known universe, with literally billions of connections and very complex processes going on in it all the time: small wonder if some of them go wonky now and again. One day we'll work it out. You won't get anywhere with this problem unless you take a scientific point of view, and that means not assuming there are ghostly things in the universe without much better reason than we've found so far.

EXERCISE 1.1

TWO POINTS OF VIEW

The first question to answer is this: To which of these alternative points of view are you broadly sympathetic at the moment, or are you currently a 'don't know'? Please note down your present point of view and keep it handy. We shall return to it at the end of the book.

DISCUSSION

I am not going to comment on the assertions in these points of view here: in a sense, everything we are now going to do for the rest of this book will be a commentary on these opposing outlooks. If you take the view, inherent in Point of View 1, that minds and bodies are very different sorts of thing, then you probably take some form of the point of view philosophers call dualism, and we will be looking closely at this in the next chapter. If, on the other hand, you are more sympathetic to Point of View 2, which includes the assertion that minds and bodies are fundamentally the same sort of thing, then you will believe a version of the view philosophers call monism (in this case materialistic monism), and we will spend some time investigating some versions of that outlook in Chapter 3, where all these technical terms are explained. However, you may – very reasonably – take the view that you are not sure about where you stand on this question at the moment. It may well appear to you – and you are by no means alone if this is so – that there is merit in both these points of view. This is a position in which many people find themselves when faced with this problem for the first time. The only way to proceed in such a case is to do what we are about to do, namely examine the arguments on both sides.

What we are going to do in this book is to take both these points of view very seriously indeed, and subject them to philosophical investigation. It is worth mentioning the point that philosophical studies of this kind are not, as they are sometimes alleged to be, ivory-tower pastimes – clever games for idle people in warm libraries or university departments, with no practical implications whatsoever. Take the following examples from our present area of study, the philosophy of mind. The first is as follows:

Over the centuries, human beings have given a number of different answers to the question: What are we to count as sentient beings – i.e. beings with some form of consciousness – capable of feeling, for example, pain and fear? What you believe about this question, together with your moral beliefs about rights and about obligations to minimize suffering (for example) has direct implications for the way you behave in treating the rest of the universe. Descartes – whose philosophy of mind we will come to presently –

believed that, so far as life on earth is concerned, consciousness is a property only of human beings, and that other animals are automata, no different in principle from clockwork dolls. A direct consequence of this view is that there is no moral ground on which to disapprove of vivisection or hunting since automata do not feel pain: the rabbit I infect or blind with cosmetics or agonize with electrodes, or the fox torn apart by dogs, is no more the subject of pain and fear than a car disassembled by a mechanic.

Second, many philosophers have thought that only if dualism is true can human beings be said to have freedom of the will: the material world (it is argued) is a realm of inexorable causal sequences with no room in it for freedom of choice in any meaningful sense – if what I experience as my choices are just neuronal functionings, are they not just as rigorously determined as the boiling of a kettle of water over a flame? If the mental is a distinct realm from the physical, outside the network of physical causes (it has been argued), perhaps this rigorous determinism can be avoided. (I should add that though this is a widespread view, it is by no means universally held: other philosophers hold that the question of free will is logically independent of the question of the nature of the mental.)

My final example is less controversial and it is simply this: what you believe about the nature of the mind or soul has a very direct bearing on how it is rational and moral for you to behave. If you believe in the immortality of the soul, and that this life is merely a prelude to a timeless life after death, then it is quite possible for you rationally to take a very different attitude to setbacks in this life from that of someone who believes this life is all there is. On the other hand, for those who believe in the mortality of the mind or soul, the quality of life here and now is, quite rationally, a matter of consistent urgency.

MINDS AND BODIES: SOME BASICS

One of the most difficult things which everyone finds when beginning philosophy is to understand what the given problem is: in our case, the question of the nature of the mind and its relation to the body. We can add a supplementary question here as well, one which has been debated, literally, for centuries: Why is it, apparently, so hard to settle? In a sense it will take the whole of this book to answer that question. However, we can begin to see why there is a deep problem here if we start by getting clear about some of the basic features or properties of the two terms of the problem – the mind (or the mental) and the body (or the material or physical, which are synonyms, and used interchangeably). I want now to reflect on a few basic features of each, in a not too technical way. We can refine our understanding of these ideas as we go along, but we need to get a basic grip on the ideas which follow now, as they are taken as read by all the philosophers whose ideas we are going to consider.

As I have said, like many philosophical questions, the mind–body problem arises when we begin to reflect in a philosophical way on some concepts which are entirely familiar to us: namely, those concepts in which we in daily life describe our mental life and those we use to describe the material universe. We will begin with the mind, and return to the material world presently. We can profitably begin our investigation of the mind by reminding ourselves of some facts about daily human mental experience. Human mental experience in our normal waking state consists of self-conscious awareness of the different types of phenomena which philosophers refer to as mental contents. (In one way, this is an unfortunate term since it might be thought to imply that the mind is some odd sort of container, but that is not the intention at all. Mental contents are just the sorts of things we are ordinarily aware of in ordinary daily conscious life. The term implies nothing about the nature of these contents or the mind.) First, we are aware of the sensations furnished by our five senses which inform us of some feature of the world other than our own bodies – sights, sounds, smells, tastes and sensations of touch. There are also bodily sensations which inform us of our own physical condition, from intense pleasure to a generalized sense of well-being, through all the vast array of disagreeable and painful sensations of which we are capable. Second, we are aware of the state of our emotional life via consciousness of moods and emotions. These fluctuate, as do sensations, but generally over rather longer periods, from hours to years, and have a marked bearing on that mysterious condition we call our happiness (or lack of it). Third, we are aware of thoughts; we have beliefs, opinions, wishes, desires, goals, wants and needs, most of which are subject to change over time. Fourth, we have memories, of varying degrees of vividness and accuracy, of the events of our own lives or of things we have learned. Fifth, we have imagination: we can imagine things and situations which have not happened to us. Our imaginings can be more or less vivid, more or less valuable, but everyone has this ability to some degree. Sixth, we perform what are called mental acts: we take decisions to do certain things, and so forth. Finally, we assume that, in normal health and in all but a few special cases (e.g. reflexes), our bodily movement is under our control: if we want to move a limb or (more unusually) make a deliberate conscious decision to move it, then the limb moves. This is a feature of the mind philosophers call mental causation.

Further – to make a point which is less commonsensical but no less obvious when pointed out – we experience all these types of mental content as ours; this is a way of saying that we are not just conscious but self-conscious. The experiences I have are all experienced as mine: for any mental content you name – sensation, thought, memory, and so on – it is always the case that when I am aware of it, I am aware of it as my sensation (etc.). I never have to try to work out, for any mental content, whose it is. Any such content is always experienced as mine. Our minds are not at all like mirrors, which just reflect passively and unpossessively what is before them. Human experience is, save for a few quite exceptional cases, experience which is always the experience of an individual – or, as philosophers often say, of a subject. To say that something is a subject in this sense is to say that it is such that it experiences the world from a unique point of view.

This idea of being a subject in this strong sense is worth dwelling on for a little longer. Associated with it are a number of features of our mental life we need to keep in mind as we go along. The most important of these is that there is something odd and special about the way I am aware of my own experience as compared to the way in which I am aware of anyone else's. The point is often put quite graphically as follows: there is in the universe only one person whose experience I can be aware of from the inside, namely myself. My awareness of the experience of every other being in the universe is from the outside. This feature of our experience is reflected in the way we understand our own states of mind as opposed to the states of mind of others, even those few other persons whose mental life we know well enough to be able to predict many of their reactions. For example, I never need to work out by observing my own behaviour what my feelings or beliefs are: I am aware of these aspects of my mental life directly by self-conscious awareness. I have no comparable way of being aware of the mental life of any other person, no matter how close I may be to them. In order to understand what someone else is experiencing, I need, as we say (and the form of words itself makes the point), 'to put myself in their place'; I must try to imagine what they are going through and perhaps empathize with them – and we can become quite good at this with people we know well. But what I am doing, in every case, is imagining what it would be like for me to go through what they are going through. My imaginings and empathic feelings remain my mental contents and not theirs: there is a certain type of solitariness and isolation built into the framework or constitution of human consciousness. The point to hang on to is that the way in which anyone is aware of their own mental contents is unique in their experience. In a very strong sense of the term, our awareness of our own mental contents is private to each individual. A number of other phrases are regularly used by philosophers, including those we are to read in this book, which make much the same point – for example, that we have privileged access to the contents of our own minds or that we have immediate awareness of them. We will meet such turns of phrase fairly often in what follows. Behind all these technical phrases lies the extremely important set of related features of human mental life we have been discussing which centre on the concepts of privacy and subjectivity. Whenever you meet these terms in writings on the philosophy of mind, bear in mind that they are being used in these very strong senses.

To recap then: our ordinary mental experience is a ceaselessly changing blend of the elements we have called mental contents, unified by their being our experiences, the experiences of a subject or self which is constant through the changes of mental content. Moreover, these experiences are private to each individual, in the special sense just outlined. The next step is to look at our ideas about matter or the material world, and compare it to the world of the mental.

As revealed by the methods of empirical science, the material world has a number of important properties. All material things or objects exist in the framework of space and time (space–time, as one has to say in the post-Einsteinian world, but relativistic effects are not relevant to the phenomena we are considering). Indeed, this is in effect a definition of what a material thing is: it is something which occupies a position in space and a position in time. (Quantum effects are not relevant in the present context.) Anything which exists in space has a location which can be specified, and has dimensions which can be specified.

Again, so far as is known, all material things have a time at which they begin to exist, and none endures forever. Material things are subject to the forces which have been discovered in the universe, and obey the laws of physics, chemistry, the life sciences, and so forth, as is appropriate to their constitution.

Very importantly from our present point of view, the phenomena studied by science are public and objective; that is, all these phenomena can in principle be studied by all observers in the same way. Any experiment to test a particular hypothesis can be carried out by any competent observer. In principle, there are no data which are not available to all observers, and no observer occupies a point of view with regard to the data which is not available to all other observers. For example, all the data collected by neuroscientists about the fantastically complex physical structure and electrochemistry of the brain are public and objective in exactly this way.

Broadly, then, the universe revealed by science is a vast web of forces and material entities which stand to one another in causal relations. All the phenomena thus revealed are public, observable in principle in the same way by all observers. Moreover, the application of scientific methods to these phenomena has been startlingly successful in allowing us to understand, predict and in some cases modify to our benefit some features of the universe in which we have evolved. I don't mean to imply by this last statement that all is well with regard to human applications of science and technology – far from it; only that empirical science, of the human intellectual tools so far devised, has the highest success rate in enabling us to understand our own nature and our environment.

SUMMARY

This chapter introduces you to some of the most important properties of each of the terms of the mind–body problem: the mental and the material. In respect of the former, we have seen that our mental life in normal waking states consists of self-conscious awareness of our mental contents: we are, in the sense explained, subjects of experience. Moreover, our awareness of these contents is private in a very strong sense of the term: we have a mode of awareness of our own mental contents which is unique to us and which is in principle unavailable to others. These properties are in contrast to those of the material world as revealed by the empirical sciences, the realm of matter moulded by forces and following strict causal sequences. Importantly, all material phenomena are in an important sense public. All material phenomena can in principle be observed by any observer: none are subject to any special mode of access and none are in principle private, and it is important to note that this conclusion applies to any brain state. It is this very striking asymmetry of properties between the mental and the material realms which gives rise to the mind–body problem. If it is so strikingly unlike the material realm, what can the mind be and how is it related to the body?

CONCLUSION

If we now put these basics about mind and matter together what emerges is both a contrast and, on the face of it, an anomaly. Among the most important features of human mental experience are what we have called subjectivity and privacy: each individual has a special way of being aware of their own experience which is unique to them and which no one else can share. Put in the language I have just used to describe science, no other observer can be aware of my experiences as I am aware of them. Note that it is no objection to this assertion to point out that all observers (me included) can be aware of my brain states as manifested on devices which record changes in the electrochemistry of the brain, because my experiences are not experienced by me as brain states: they are of what we have called mental contents – sensations, emotions, thoughts, and so on. I am (it seems) no more aware of brain states by introspection than I am aware of the chemical processes of digestion.

Many philosophers, when faced with the considerations I have set out in this chapter, have concluded, not at all unreasonably, that what follows is that the mind must occupy a unique and anomalous position in the scheme of things; nothing else studied by science is like it; nothing else has this special property of subjectivity. Further, many thinkers from science and theology as well as philosophy have concluded on grounds such as these (there are more, and we will notice them in detail as they come up in the course of reading) that minds really must be very different from bodies or material things, and these thinkers take up some version of the view of the mind called dualism: that is, the view that there are two irreducibly different sorts of things in the universe – minds and bodies. Dualism is one of the most important types of philosophical position proposed as a solution to the mind–body problem, and it is with a consideration of four dualist views that we begin our philosophical investigation of the nature of the mind and its relation to the body.

NOTE

1   Or souls: in this book these terms will be used interchangeably.

FURTHER READING

On the mind–body problem:
Churchland, P.M. (1988) *Matter and Consciousness: A Contemporary Introduction to the Philosophy of Mind*, 2nd edn, Cambridge, Mass.: MIT Press.
Warner, R. and Szubka, T. (eds) (1994) *The Mind–body Problem: A Guide to the Current Debate*, Oxford: Blackwell.

On out-of-body experiences:
Green, C. (1968) *Out-of-the-body Experiences*, London: Hamish Hamilton

2 Dualism

INTRODUCTION AND BACKGROUND TO DESCARTES' PHILOSOPHY

In this chapter we are going to investigate four forms of dualism in the philosophy of mind. What all forms of dualism have in common is an acceptance of the view that the universe – all there is – is composed of two irreducibly different sorts of stuff, the material and the mental. They all construe the material in much the same way, as outlined in the previous chapter; but, as we will see, they differ in the way in which they construe the mental, and in the way in which they regard the mental as related to the physical. In the history of modern philosophy, undoubtedly the most important thinker to adopt the basic dualist premise was René Descartes, and we will devote most of our investigation of dualism to a consideration of his version of it. Though he does not use the modern terminology I have just used to describe the nature of our mental lives, he was perfectly aware of the apparently anomalous position of the mind in the material universe. He also had religious reasons for adopting dualism – he was a sincere Catholic; but he had other reasons too. He was a scientist of some note, as well as a philosopher, and was well aware, in his own terms, of the features of the mental and the physical we noted in Chapter 1. We are now going to look in detail at how Descartes answers our basic question on the nature and relation of mind and body using the basic assumption that minds and bodies are irreducibly different in nature.

CARTESIAN DUALISM

In this section, we are going to examine in detail one strand of argument from *Meditations on First Philosophy* by Descartes, first published in Latin in 1641. I stress *one* strand of argument advisedly: the *Meditations* is one of the richest texts in modern Western philosophy and we simply do not have the time in the present context to examine it all. The arguments we need to focus on are in *Meditations* II and VI, together with four Articles (i.e. short sections) from a later work by Descartes, *The Passions of the Soul* (written in the winter of 1645–6, but not published until 1649). The additional articles from the later work are necessary because they provide the fullest statement of a crucial point in Descartes' philosophy of mind, furnishing more detail in that area than the text of the *Meditations*.

If you have glanced at any histories of philosophy or articles about him in encyclopaedias, you will probably have found Descartes described as 'the father of modern philosophy', or in some similar way. If you were to penetrate further into what has been written about him – and the bulk of the secondary material in European languages alone is now awesome in its extent – you will have discovered a variety of opinions: from those which portray his ideas as being unprecedented, the product of pure original genius, to those which find extensive antecedents for them in the earlier philosophical tradition known as scholasticism. There is some truth in all these approaches; what is beyond dispute, however, is that Descartes changed the direction of Western philosophical thought decisively and irrevocably. No one after him could ignore what he had said or escape the influence of the change he had brought about, and that is a sure sign that we are dealing here with a thinker of world class.

Descartes was not only a philosopher and an empirical scientist but also a mathematician of considerable stature, and even if he had not written one word of philosophy he would still have a place in the history of mathematics. He is generally credited with inventing the discipline of co-ordinate geometry, and this branch of the subject is named after him. Nor is it an irrelevance in the present context to mention this fact, since it leads directly to the identification of one of the most important assumptions Descartes makes about how to do philosophy, and what it can achieve. Perhaps the best known of Descartes' works is the

Discourse on the Method of Rightly Conducting the Reason and Seeking for Truth in the Sciences (1637), usually referred to as *The Discourse on Method*. This was, in fact, Descartes' second important work: before the *Discourse* he had written another essay concerned with method, the *Rules for the Direction of the Mind* (1628) (in commentaries on Descartes you will often find this work referred to by the first word of its Latin title – the *Regulae*). Even the titles alone prompt one to ask why Descartes should have been so concerned with the right *method* to use in philosophy, and what he thought that method was. The answer lies in the influence of mathematics, an influence which not only affected Descartes but was also one of the major factors shaping philosophical thought in Europe throughout the seventeenth century.

The seventeenth century was without doubt one of the most spectacularly innovatory in the history of mathematics, due partly, of course, to discoveries made by Descartes himself. Now, when any intellectual discipline begins to deliver significant results, when major discoveries begin to be made, when human knowledge grows rapidly in a given area, the thought naturally occurs that we must be doing something right. Equally naturally we ask: What are we doing right, and can we do the same thing in other areas of thought and make the same sort of advances? This is precisely what Descartes asked himself about mathematics, and he decided that what was right about mathematics was what he took to be its method, which he believed he could reduce to simple rules. Hence the subjects of the two early works just referred to. He believed that the method he had identified could be applied to any area of human knowledge, and this he set out to do. Consistently, his approach to philosophy employs this method.

To digress briefly: this phenomenon – that of trying out the method and concepts of the most powerful and successful contemporary discipline elsewhere – occurs quite regularly in human thought on large and small scales. For example, in eighteenth-century Europe (roughly speaking) the most powerful intellectual model was supplied not by mathematics but by what we would now call an empirical science. Newtonian mechanics and its method then came to be applied to many other areas of culture. Later in this book we will look at another if less grand contemporary example of the same thing, the belief that some discoveries from computer science can help us to understand the human mind.

The next question, obviously, is this: What is it about mathematics, and particularly its method, which so impressed Descartes and others? The easiest way to answer this question is to look briefly at some basic features of the *Elements* of Euclid, the greatest single work of Greek geometry, dating from around 300 BC. Book I of this work begins with a few brief *definitions* – for example, a point is that which has no part; a line is a length without breadth; an obtuse angle is an angle greater than a right angle, and so on. These definitions are accompanied by what are termed *postulates* – for example, that all right angles are equal to one another – and by *axioms* (also called *common notions* – remember this phrase). Examples of axioms are: things which are equal to the same thing are equal to one another; if equals are subtracted from equals the remainders are equal; or: the whole is greater than the part. Definitions, postulates and axioms are all types of fundamental assumption. Every area of thought has to make some basic assumptions in order to get off the ground, as it were, and Euclid takes care to spell them out. The differences between definitions, postulates and axioms need not concern us here. Think of them as the assumptions Euclid believed he had to make in order to do geometry at all.

What so impressed Descartes about this method was the following: first, it begins from fundamental assumptions – the definitions, postulates and axioms – which are of the greatest simplicity and clarity: they appear to be beyond the range of the doubtful. Second, it uses strict deductive reasoning; and third, it is able, from its fundamental assumptions and using strict deduction only, to generate a comprehensive and complex geometry which appeared at the time (and long afterward) to describe actual space. So, by using a few very simple fundamental assumptions and deductive logic, it appeared possible to construct a body of knowledge of unparalleled clarity, certainty and rigour and which described the real world. Small wonder, then, that Descartes should have been so keen to apply this method in other areas of thought, philosophy included. Small wonder also that those who shared these same beliefs about the power and applicability of the mathematical method should have genuinely expected real benefit for humankind as a result. Later in the century, the philosopher and mathematician Leibniz (1646–1716), who also took mathematics to be the model for all human knowledge, hoped by the use of its method to be able to resolve finally not only problems in metaphysics but also (for example) issues in ethics. As he put it:

> The only way to rectify our reasonings is to make them as tangible as those of the Mathematicians, so that we can find our error at a glance, and when there are disputes among persons, we can simply say: Let us calculate, without further ado, in order to see who is right.
>
> (*The Art of Discovery* (1685) in Weiner 1951: 51)

And this is the voice of genuine conviction, not propaganda.

One last point about terminology before turning to Descartes' text to see what the application of this method to philosophy looks like. The full title of the text is *Meditations on First Philosophy*. As with so much of the terminology of Western philosophy, the phrase 'first philosophy' begins its life in the works of Aristotle (*Metaphysics* E, 1, 1026a, 23–32), and common to all its uses is the notion that this is the area of philosophy which deals with those assertions that are the most fundamental, and on which all other branches of the subject rest. Descartes' use of the term is entirely appropriate: his aim here is no less than to establish with mathematical certainty the foundations of all human knowledge, including centrally our knowledge of the nature of mind and body.

DESCARTES' ACCOUNT OF THE NATURE AND RELATION OF MIND AND BODY

In this section, we will examine Descartes' philosophy of mind, using methods which are applicable to any philosophical position. The first step will be to break down the text into the individual arguments of which it is composed; then, for each argument, we shall make sure that the meaning of any technical terms is clear; then we shall set out the argument as a series of premises and a conclusion or conclusions, examining it for validity and soundness. If it is invalid or unsound, we need to work out where the problem lies. Quite often, the fallacies of a great philosopher are instructive, revealing some unapparent aspect of the problem in hand. Finally, we will also look for important presuppositions and consequences of the argument. Unnoticed presuppositions are often the root causes of philosophical difficulties; and, of course, if an argument entails a consequence which is false, it must contain at least one premise which is itself false.

For the rest of this section on Cartesian dualism, we are going to examine in detail the arguments in the second and sixth *Meditations* dealing with mind and body, and will look only as is necessary at the other major issues which Descartes raises, notably the nature of sense perception and the nature of knowledge. Though split into six individual *Meditations* by Descartes, the *Meditations* as a whole is a very fine example of a single sustained chain of philosophical arguments. To try to give a flavour of this without distracting from our main focus of attention on the mind, I have summed up the omitted *Meditations* in the head notes to the texts printed in the readings at the end of the book. Please be sure you read the head notes as well as Descartes' text: in what follows, I am going to assume that you *have* read them, at the appropriate point.

In our investigation of Cartesian dualism, the arguments in *Meditations* II and VI are broken down into stages: we have to investigate the trees before we can generalize about the wood.

STAGE 1: *MEDITATION II*, PARAGRAPHS 1–3

Now read paragraphs 1–3 inclusive of Descartes' *Meditation II* (Reading 2) in conjunction with the summary note at the start of *Meditation I* (Reading 1). (Note that *Meditation I* is optional reading.)

Reading
pp. 149, 155

Two points are raised by the title of the second *Meditation*: 'Of the Nature of the Human Mind; and that it is more easily known than the body'. The first is that we can expect there to be two major stages in its argument, one concerned to establish the nature of the human mind (I will drop the qualification 'human' from now on, and take it as read), and a second concerned to show that the mind is more easy to know than the body, and this is indeed how the piece is structured. The second point is more complex: when Descartes speaks of the *nature* of the mind, he is making a more precise and technical claim than the use of this innocent-looking word suggests. In order to understand Descartes' argument, we need to spend a short time alerting ourselves to the framework of basic technical terms he is going to use, and which he could assume his contemporary readers understood. The most important of these terms are: substance, attribute, mode and essence.

SUBSTANCE

Descartes' view of mind and body is properly and more fully referred to as two-substance dualism, and obviously we need to be clear what he means by the term 'substance'. His own most helpful definition of it does not occur in the *Meditations* but in a later work *The Principles of Philosophy* (1644), where he writes:

> By substance, we can understand nothing else than a thing which so exists that it needs no other thing in order to exist.
>
> (*Principles* I, 51; Haldane and Ross 1931, vol. I: 239)

The contrast presupposed in this remark is between substance on the one hand and qualities or properties on the other: a property is that which cannot exist on its own, but has to be a property of something, and that something is a substance. This is a point Descartes goes on to make – note that he uses the phrase 'common notion', which we noticed above in Euclid, and, as in Euclid, Descartes is here using the term (as he always does) to mean 'axiom', a fundamental and unquestionable assumption:

> it is a common notion that nothing is possessed of no attributes, properties or qualities. For this reason, when we perceive any attribute, we therefore conclude that some existing thing or substance to which it may be attributed, is necessarily present.
>
> (*Principles* I, 52; Haldane and Ross 1931, vol. I: 240)

In other words, substance is that which qualities qualify: wherever there are qualities we always assume there must be a substance of which they are the qualities.

ATTRIBUTE AND MODE

These are different types of property. An attribute is an invariant property, a property uniformly present in a substance – for example, all material things have the attribute of duration or existence in time; a mode is a property which is variable – for example, cats may be tabby, ginger, black, white (and so on), and tabbiness (etc.) is a mode in this usage of the term. Having some colour (i.e. being coloured) is an attribute of a cat; having a particular colour is a mode.

ESSENCE

This concept has one of the longest and most complicated histories of all philosophical concepts, starting (once again) in the works of Aristotle. It is one of those concepts which should put any reader of philosophy on the alert, since it has been used in a number of different if related senses, right up to the present century. Descartes is using the term in a sense drawn from the earlier scholastic tradition of philosophy. In the present text, we can think of what he is driving at in the following way: the essence of any thing is that which makes it what it is; or, put another way, to state the essence of *x* is to specify the property or properties the loss of which would entail the loss of *x*'s identity. Accordingly, to state the essence of *x* is in effect the same as defining *x*, or saying what its *nature* is. For example, it is an essential property of a chair that it is an artefact suitable for human beings to sit on. If any artefact lacks or ceases to have this property, then it is not or ceases to be a chair. By contrast having four legs is not an essential property of a chair: chairs can have three legs, or more than four, or indeed be one continuous piece of steam-bent wood and have no legs (properly so called) at all. Again, chairs can have plain wooden seats, or cane seats or upholstered seats, and so on. Properties like these – i.e. having a certain number of legs or a certain type of seat – are called in this terminology *accidental* properties of chairs: objects called chairs can either have or lack these accidental properties and still be chairs; but if an object loses the essential property of being an artefact suitable for human beings to sit on, it ceases to be a chair. Thus when Descartes claims to identify the essence or nature of anything he is making a powerful assertion: he is claiming that whatever property he picks on as the essence of *x* is such that the loss of this property entails that *x* ceases to be *x* at all.

We can now return to the second point raised by the title of *Meditation II*. To repeat: it is important to note that for Descartes 'essence' and 'nature' are inter-changeable terms. Accordingly, when he says he will discuss the *nature* of the mind, Descartes is making a weighty philosophical claim. He is claiming to be able to establish which property or set of properties constitutes the essence of the mind, the property (etc.) which makes the mind what it is.

EXERCISE 2.1

DESCARTES AND DOUBT

Write a summary of paragraphs 1–3 of *Meditation II*, including in it an answer to the question: What does Descartes believe he cannot doubt?

SPECIMEN ANSWER

Descartes resolves not to accept as true any belief he can find the least reason to doubt, and in the light of the dream and evil-genius arguments, rejects all beliefs derived from sense perception, including the belief that he has a body. However, he finally reaches a belief which he cannot doubt, and which is true even if the whole fabric of his experience is a deception woven by the evil genius: it is absolutely indubitable that he himself exists, at least every time that he thinks, since in order to be deceived, he must exist.

DISCUSSION

This famous assertion raises a number of interesting philosophical issues, and it is well worth dwelling on it for a short while:

1   In *Meditation II*, Descartes states his indubitable belief in these words: 'This proposition: I am, I exist, is necessarily true each time that I pronounce it, or that I mentally conceive it'. You have probably come across another, better known, formulation of this proposition, 'I think, therefore I am' (in Latin, *cogito ergo sum*).[1] This formulation, which Descartes uses in the *Discourse on Method* and in works written later in his life, does not occur in the text of the *Meditations*. For ease of refer-ence, it is always referred to as the *cogito*, and a great deal has been

written about its unusual logical properties. One question which is raised is whether it is necessary, as the formulation *cogito ergo sum* seems to imply, to *deduce* the notion of existence from that of thought, since, as Descartes seems to realise in the formulation he uses in the *Meditations*, the bare proposition 'I exist' is indubitable in the way he needs it to be. However, though interesting, this point is not of great significance. Descartes can deduce existence from thought, since whatever thinks exists. Much more important is the fact that Descartes has here hit on a type of statement with an unusual logical property, namely that of being self-confirming: both 'I think' and 'I exist' have the odd property that in order to be formulated at all they must be true. Descartes has accomplished his purpose of finding a statement which is immune from doubt.

2   Descartes describes the proposition 'I exist' as 'necessarily true' and you may well have found this puzzling in the light of the way the phrase 'necessarily true' is now used in philosophy. In current usage, necessary truths are those whose denials are self-contradictory, such as 'all bachelors are unmarried males'. This usage of the term 'necessary truth' post-dates Descartes' time, and he is using this form of words merely as his way of indicating the logically unusual property of the *cogito* I have mentioned.

3   As we have seen, the *cogito* is intended by Descartes to be the indubitable starting point for the programme of reconstructing the whole of human knowledge on logically unassailable foundations, foundations which do not involve the assumption of the truth of anything at all doubtful. A number of his contemporaries objected that, covertly, Descartes is in fact taking for granted much more than the *cogito*. Another way of putting their objection is that the *cogito* takes for granted the truth of unstated presuppositions which Descartes has not argued for, and the objection is an example of a standard philosophical technique, that of unveiling or making explicit the unstated presuppositions of an argument.

Descartes is in fact taking for granted much more than the truth of the *cogito*. He is assuming that we know what the terms he is using mean (notably 'doubt', 'certainty', 'think' and 'exist'); that the rules of logic are acceptable, and that our memory of all these things is to be relied on. Descartes was well aware of this objection, and gives his reply to it in his later work *The Principles of Philosophy*:

> I do not here explain various other terms of which I have availed myself or will afterwards avail myself, because they seem to me perfectly clear in themselves … when I stated the proposition *I think, therefore I am* is the first and most certain which presents itself to those who philosophize in an orderly fashion, I did not for all that deny that we must first of all know *what*

is knowledge, what is existence, and what is certainty, and that *in order to think we must be*, and such like; but because these are notions of the simplest possible kind, which of themselves give us no knowledge of anything that exists, I did not think them worthy of being put on record.

(*Principles of Philosophy* I, in Haldane and Ross 1931, vol. I: 222)

Descartes in effect admits the force of the objection, but argues that a number of concepts and presuppositions must be taken to be true in order for there to be thought at all, or put another way, for thought to be possible. Precisely which concepts these might be has been the subject of prolonged and continuing debate – it is a major theme in the philosophy of Immanuel Kant (1724–1804) and is also present in the work of the linguist Chomsky, for example – but that there are such unavoidable basic concepts few philosophers would deny.

4   You will notice that in the passage just quoted, Descartes states that he does not trouble to explain things which are perfectly *clear* in themselves; and elsewhere, in many places in the text of the *Meditations* he speaks of ideas or beliefs being 'clear and distinct'. Again, and very importantly, at the opening of the third *Meditation* he says that anything he clearly and distinctly perceives is true: in other words, clarity and distinctness are Descartes' *criteria* of truth. He has discovered in the *cogito* a proposition he cannot doubt, and as he makes explicit later in his argument in the *Meditations*, he considers that what marks it out from other propositions is that when he thinks of it, he does so with absolute clarity and distinctness. He further feels justified in assuming that whatever has these properties of clarity and distinctness must also be true, and he makes use of this principle to guarantee the truth of some key assertions he needs in his overall argument to reconstruct human knowledge on foundations as secure as those of geometry.

It would take us too far from our focus on Descartes' philosophy of mind to consider all that can be said about the satisfactoriness or otherwise of clarity and distinctness as criteria for truth. They were objected to, for example, by Descartes' contemporary Pierre Gassendi (1592–1655) in the fifth set of *Objections* published at the time to the philosophy put forward in the *Meditations*, and by Leibniz (in many places but principally *Meditations on Knowledge, Truth and Ideas*: see Leibniz (1969)) as merely psychological and subjective: how do I tell if my ideas are conceived sufficiently clearly and distinctly for me to be able to assume they are true? (See section 5 below for more on the *Objections* to the *Meditations*.) Put another way: clarity and distinctness are of no use as criteria for truth until we have objective criteria for clarity and distinctness. There has been a good deal of debate among philosophers as to what exactly Descartes means by the terms 'clarity' and 'distinctness' (see, for example, Gewirth (1943)) and further debate on the issue of whether he uses them in such a way as to make his argument in the *Meditations* circular. (A good place to start on the investigation of the question of Descartes' alleged circularity of argument is Loeb (1992).) The problem is that Descartes appears to need to be able to assume the truth of the clarity and distinctness principle in order to prove the existence of a non-deceiving God, while at the same time only the existence of a non-deceiving God will guarantee the truth of the clarity and distinctness principle. This issue is referred to as the Cartesian circle. For the moment, it will be enough to remember that these innocent looking words, 'clear', 'distinct' and their cognate forms, are technical terms in Descartes and are his criteria for truth.

5   Another point it is important to be clear about is what Descartes regards as covered by the terms 'thought' and 'think'. One might easily assume that he might be referring only to what we ordinarily call abstract thought, but he is careful to point out in a number of places that he uses these words in a much broader sense. Descartes' friend Fr Marin Mersenne (1588–1648) circulated the text of the *Meditations* to a number of theologians and philosophers who made comments on Descartes' arguments. At the end of the replies he made to the second set of these objections – there are seven sets in all – Descartes adds a summary of his argument set out *more geometrico*:[2] that is, in the manner of geometry – highly formalized, beginning with definitions, postulates and axioms, and proceeding to formally laid-out versions of the arguments in question. The first definition he gives is of the term 'thought':

> Thought is a word that covers everything that exists in us in such a way that we are immediately conscious of it. Thus all the operations of will, intellect, imagination, and of the senses are thoughts.
>
> (*Reply to Objections II*, in Haldane and Ross 1931, vol. II: 52)[3]

EXERCISE 2.2

DESCARTES AND THOUGHT

Look back at the description of the types of mental content on page 7. How inclusive is the term 'thought' in Descartes' usage?

SPECIMEN ANSWER

Very inclusive. Anything immediately present to the mind is a thought in his use of the term, not only beliefs or abstract ideas, but also all sensations, memories, imaginings and mental acts.

Accordingly, when Descartes says 'I *think*, therefore I am', *any* mental content counts as a thought in his usage of the term.

6   A further important distinction, one regularly used in the philosophy of mind, is made by the use of the innocent-looking adverb 'immediately'. Descartes is here making a point about sense perception. At the stage in the argument of the *Meditations* we have now reached, Descartes will accept only those beliefs which he has shown so far to be immune to doubt, and he has at this point found only the self-verifying *cogito*. He has as yet no reason to accept the existence of an external world, i.e. of anything beyond his own mind. Yet, as we have seen, he wants to include sensations in the class of thoughts (= mental contents). Now the function of sensations is precisely to give us information about the state of our bodies and the external world and so, in order to be able to speak of them consistently without begging the question as to whether there is an external world, he makes a distinction between what we are immediately aware of in sensation, and what we can infer from that about the state of the external world. Normally, when we report our sense experience, we assume that it tells us about a world existing independently of us, and our reports assume this – for example, 'I see the sun in a cloudless sky': in making statements about what we perceive, we take it for granted that, by and large, our perceptions report accurately the state of the world around us whose existence we take for granted. If I do not want to assume that there is an external world, I must restrict myself to a report of what is immediately present to my mind, in Descartes' sense, and I will say: 'I am visually aware of a yellow disc against a blue ground'. Statements of this kind make no assumptions about the existence or nature of an external world. We will have more to say about statements of this form in other contexts as we go along. For the moment we can note that they are logically very different from the corresponding statements which take it for granted that our sensations are accurate reports of something out there. Immediate sensation statements, it is widely held, when formulated in the first person, have an unusual logical feature called *incorrigibility*, i.e. they are such that the utterer of such a statement sincerely made cannot be wrong about what is asserted. (Ask yourself: What would count as showing that such a report was a mistake?) So long as I restrict myself to talk of what is immediately present to my mind I am immune from error. Descartes assumes that these assertions are true.

7   Last among this selection of issues raised by the *cogito* is a serious objection raised by the English philosopher Thomas Hobbes (1588–1679) and developed by the contemporary philosopher Anthony Kenny. Descartes defines thought as anything of which we are immediately *conscious*. This is equivalent to the claim that consciousness is the defining property of the mental: for any *x*, if *x* is mental, then I am conscious of (or aware of) *x*. Hobbes raises the question: If I am conscious or aware of a mental content, is this consciousness identical

to the content or is it different from or additional to it? He then casts his objection in the logical form called a *dilemma*. The aim of a dilemma is to show that a given philosophical assertion can be construed in only two ways (called the horns of the dilemma) and that both ways are logically untenable. In the present case, the horns are these: if consciousness of a thought is identical with that thought, then it is no different from the thought itself and so cannot be used as a defining property of the mental. Alternatively, if consciousness of a thought is different from that thought, then what is termed an infinite regress of thoughts is generated. Hobbes puts the second point this way:

> it is not by another thought that I infer that I think ... we cannot think that we are thinking, nor similarly know that we know. For this would entail the repetition of the question an infinite number of times; whence do you know, that you know, that you know?
>
> (*Objections III*, in Haldane and Ross 1931, vol. II: 62)

In other words, if consciousness of *x* is something different from *x*, then to have the thought *x* I must be conscious of *x*; but this consciousness of *x* is also a thought, and so there must be a further thought, that I am aware that I am aware of *x*, and so on, *ad infinitum* (cf. also Kenny 1968: 75 seqq.). There is something suspect, then, about trying to use the concept of consciousness to define the mental; we can keep this in mind for the moment.

We can now return to the text of the second *Meditation*. Though he has found a proposition he cannot doubt, Descartes has a long road to travel before he can claim to have reconstructed the whole of his beliefs on this secure foundation. He cannot doubt the proposition 'I exist', but what does he know about the 'I'? He now has to try to discover what sort of thing this 'I' is. In so doing, he will claim to establish by argument the nature of the mind.

STAGE 2: *MEDITATION II*, PARAGRAPHS 4–6

These paragraphs contain some of the central arguments about the mind in the text of the *Meditations*, and we need to go through them carefully. It is much easier to grasp what is going on if we adopt one of Descartes' own rules of method and break them down into smaller units: he resolved to

> divide up each of the difficulties which I examined into as many parts as possible, and as seemed requisite in order that it might be resolved in the best manner possible.
>
> (Second rule of method, *Discourse on Method*, in Haldane and Ross 1931, vol. I: 92)

 Reading
p. 156

Now read paragraphs 4–6 inclusive of Descartes' *Meditation II* (Reading 2).

EXERCISE 2.3

DESCARTES' METHOD

After reading paragraphs 4–6, answer the following questions:

1   What principle will Descartes adopt in his attempt to discover more fully what he is (paragraph 4)?
2   What did he assume himself to be before he adopted the method of doubt?
3   After adopting the method of doubt, what can he now accept as indubitably true of himself?

SPECIMEN ANSWERS

1   Descartes will assent only to those beliefs about himself which, in the light of the sceptical arguments he has brought forward so far, are 'absolutely certain and indubitable'. (He is simply reminding himself of, and at the same time reaffirming, his resolve to follow his avowed method.)
2   He formerly adopted what we might call a reasonably common-sense view as to what sort of being he is: namely, a being with a physical body with a mind or soul whose relation to the body he thought of rather vaguely as like a subtle ether spread throughout it. This body experienced sensations and could perform actions.
3   He can no longer accept any of the beliefs summarized in the answer to Question 2.2. They are ruled out by the dream and evil-genius arguments. However, when he arrives at the notion of thought, he asserts that this cannot be separated from him.

DISCUSSION

The last part of paragraph 6, from the words 'What of thinking?' contains the first stage of Descartes' argument about the nature of the mind, which we can now examine in the standard philosophical way. The first stage is to set it out in a slightly more formal manner so that its structure becomes more evident.

Premise 1	I accept only what is necessarily true. (NB: this is Descartes' own sense of the phrase 'necessarily true' which we came across earlier in our discussion of the *cogito*.)
Premise 2	It is necessarily true and so certain that I exist.
Premise 3	I exist only when I think, since if I ceased to think, I might cease to exist.
Conclusion 1	Therefore thought alone cannot be separated from me. Put another way: thought alone is an attribute of me. (This is Descartes' technical sense of the term 'attribute', meaning invariant property.)

Conclusion 2   Therefore, all I can say of myself with certainty is that I am a thing which thinks. (This last phrase, 'I am a thing which thinks' is another which commentators almost always refer to in its Latin form, *sum res cogitans*.)[4]

Before we can assess this argument for validity, we need to be absolutely clear what the conclusion means. We have already come across instances of innocent-looking words which are used by Descartes in a precise technical sense, and this is the case here with what must be the most seemingly innocuous of all terms, namely, 'thing'. This term is always used by Descartes as a synonym for substance: i.e. an individual entity which has qualities. Accordingly, it follows that what Descartes is claiming to have proved in the above argument is that there is one continuously existing thing which thinks, which exists through time and which is the subject of all the thoughts he has mentioned. He makes this point explicit a little later in paragraph 9: 'it is so evident of itself that it is I who doubts, who understands, and who desires, that there is no reason here to add anything to explain it'. By the term 'I' here he means 'one and the same I which exists through time and has various thoughts'.

A number of philosophers have objected that Descartes has not yet proved enough in the argument of the *Meditations* to establish this conclusion. The point was most famously stated by Immanuel Kant in a section of the first edition of his *Critique of Pure Reason* (1781) called the 'Paralogisms of Pure Reason' (a *paralogism* is a special type of fallacy). Kant objects that it is being *assumed* here and not *proved* that there is one and the same I which is the subject of many experiences through time. It is possible that there are many short-lived I's with illusory memories that they have had a long sequence of experiences through time, and nothing Descartes has said so far proves that this is not so. All that Descartes has shown so far is that sometimes something thinks.

EXERCISE 2.4

KANT ON DESCARTES

Is Kant claiming that Descartes' argument is invalid or unsound?

SPECIMEN ANSWER

Kant is claiming that Descartes' argument is invalid. The final conclusion Descartes wants to establish can be stated: 'I can say of myself with certainty that I am a thinking substance, a continuously existing subject of mental experiences'; but nothing in the premises establishes that the subject exists *continuously*.

STAGE 3: *MEDITATION II*, PARAGRAPHS 7–9

You will recall that the title of *Meditation II* includes the phrase 'the *nature* of the human mind' (my emphasis), and that for Descartes the terms 'nature' and 'essence' are synonyms. He is now going to move on in his argument to try to show something about the nature of the mind. As we have just seen, he believes he has proved that he is a *res cogitans*, a thing which thinks, meaning that he is a continuously existing subject of experiences. He is now going to try to show that thinking is the *essence* of the I, and this needs a separate argument. He begins by clearing the ground.

Now read paragraphs 7–9 inclusive of Descartes' *Meditation II* (Reading 2).

Reading
p. 157

EXERCISE 2.5

DESCARTES ON IMAGINATION

From your reading of paragraph 7, why does Descartes here reject the imagination as a source of possible extra knowledge about himself?

SPECIMEN ANSWER

Descartes equates imagining with having a mental image of a physical thing – 'corporeal' is a synonym for 'physical'. Since he has not yet established any reason to believe in the existence of the physical world – he has yet to refute the dream and evil-genius arguments – he cannot use any ideas furnished by his imagination as a source of knowledge about his own nature. This is because the imagination only uses ideas derived from the physical world.

DISCUSSION

Descartes concludes Paragraph 7 with an exhortation to himself to avoid using ideas derived from imagination in his quest for knowledge of his own nature. He then asks himself, in the very short eighth paragraph, what he can say about himself: what is a *res cogitans*? – 'It is a thing which doubts, understands, [conceives], affirms, denies, wills, refuses, which also imagines and feels'. (The square brackets around 'conceives', and elsewhere, indicate only that this word was added by Descartes to the French translation of the text, and doesn't appear in the Latin version.) Without using his imagination, Descartes can amplify his notion of what he is by listing the modes (in his sense of the term) of thought, and what he produces is a list of mental acts and states.

He then goes on to ask, in paragraph 9, whether these mental contents pertain to his nature, and that is equivalent to asking whether his essence is thinking. The argument he puts forward here to prove that his essence is thinking is not as easy to follow as it might be since, for rhetorical purposes, he casts the premises as questions. It is easier to see what is going on if we turn the questions into statements:

Premise 4   Even if I am dreaming or deceived by an evil genius it is certain that I doubt, deny, etc. (i.e. because I cannot be wrong about the contents of my own consciousness: I am incorrigibly aware of them).

Premise 5   None of these attributes can be distinguished from my thought or, put another way, separated from myself.

Premise 6   It is self-evident that the doubting, affirming, and so on, is done by me (i.e. a continuously existing subject of experiences).

Conclusion 3   Therefore, my nature or essence is to think.

What we have now to ask is whether this argument is valid. A number of philosophers make the following point (most recently Cottingham 1992): Another way of putting Premise 4 is:

Premise 4A   All I am incorrigibly aware of is thought.

The question is: Does this entail the conclusion Descartes wants? That conclusion is:

Conclusion 3   My nature or essence is to think.

Regrettably, it does not. The reason is that Descartes has assumed, without argument, that his essence is something he must be aware of. He has not countenanced the possibility that his essence might be something he is not aware of. Another way of putting this point is to say that the argument, as Descartes has presented it here, is an enthymeme: it is valid only if we assume the truth of the suppressed premise that Descartes' essence is something he must be aware of, and he gives us no reason whatever to suppose that this is true.

Though this is an important objection, it is not at this stage fatal to Descartes' enterprise in the *Meditations* as a whole. In the *Synopsis* which precedes the work, Descartes is careful to state that his argument concerning the nature of the mind or soul is not completed until *Meditation VI*, and that he needs a number of additional premises before he can establish his conclusions finally. Accordingly we will suspend judgement for the moment. Before approaching the text of *Meditation VI*, there are a few other points to consider.

The first of these, and the most important, is to be clear about exactly what is implied by Descartes' claim that he is a *res cogitans* and that his essence is to think. We have seen that Descartes believes he has proved that he is a continuously existing I or subject of experiences. Another way of putting this is to say that he believes he has proved that his mind is a mental substance. If you look back to his definition of substance in Stage 1 above, you will note that a substance is the subject of properties. He takes himself to have proved so far that he is a mental substance whose essential property or principal attribute is thought. He is taking it for granted that you also know one further important property of mental substance, and that is that it does not exist in space, and it is important to have a firm grasp on this notion since it has major philosophical implications which we will take up as the argument proceeds. Let us for the moment concentrate on coming to grips with why he believes this. The way to understand that is to return to the list of mental contents which we noted in Chapter 1 – perceptions, internal sensations, emotions, mental acts, memories, imaginings, and so on – and to contrast them with material or physical entities and events. We noted above that if anything is a material object, then it has a size and a position in space, and so it follows that, for any physical entity, it always makes sense to ask the questions: Where is it located? or What is its position? What size is it? and What shape is it? (I am aware that there may be some fairly recondite physical entities postulated in particle physics to which these questions might not easily apply, but these entities raise deep philosophical questions of their own, and we can quite safely leave them out of account here.) These are questions which can always be asked of a physical entity: to repeat, they are simply another way of saying that a physical entity by definition exists in space. Descartes' way of saying this is to state that the essence of material substance is extension, and by 'extension' he means simply 'having three dimensions in space'. Now what happens if we try to ask these questions of mental contents? Can we meaningfully ask questions such as: What shape is your belief that the world is more or less round? Where is your feeling of love/hatred/despair/joy? What size is your decision to take next week off? The answer is manifestly that such questions are senseless, and they are so for a logical reason: mental contents are just not the sort of things which have spatial properties of this kind. They do not have shape, size or position. Hence, Descartes (and many others) assume, they cannot be spatial entities at all. Accordingly he concludes that mental substance and its properties are non-spatial. The mind, in Cartesian dualism, does not exist in space at all: it has no position, shape or size, and this philosophical conclusion appears to follow directly from the purely logical considerations just outlined.

The other points we need to glance at are raised by the wax example.

STAGE 4: THE WAX EXAMPLE: *MEDITATION II*, PARAGRAPHS 10–16

We noticed above that the title of the second *Meditation* indicated that in it Descartes will try to establish two conclusions: first his view of the essence of the mind (namely, that it is thinking); and, second, that the mind is more easily known than the body. The wax example (as it is always called and which you should now read) is designed to prove the second of these propositions. This second conclusion is not as central to our concerns in this book as the first, so we will not consider these paragraphs in as great detail as we have those we have already looked at. However, this argument does raise a number of philosophical questions which it is appropriate at least to be aware of.

Reading p. 158

Now read paragraphs 10–16 inclusive of Descartes' *Meditation II* (Reading 2).

The argument of the wax example can be summarized as follows:

Premise 7	When I heat the wax before the fire, those properties of it which I am aware of by means of the senses change;
Premise 8	yet none would deny that what remains after heating is the *same* piece of wax.
Conclusion 4	Therefore I must be aware of this sameness by some means other than the senses.
Premise 9	The only other possibility is that I am aware of this sameness as a result of an operation of my mind.
Conclusion 5	Therefore perception must involve an intuition of the mind.
Conclusion 6	Therefore there is nothing which is easier to know than my mind.

It would regrettably take us too far from our central interest in this book to investigate in detail all the assumptions and assertions Descartes makes here concerning sense perception.

However, I doubt if any philosopher since Descartes would deny that Conclusion 5 is a truth of some importance. What he is saying is that sense perception is not merely a matter of passively receiving data provided ready finished, so to speak, by the world. Sense perception undoubtedly involves a number of complex operations of conceptual processing which no one would deny can properly be called mental in nature, though it has to be stressed that to say that these operations are mental in nature need not involve a commitment to Cartesian dualism. What is far less clear is the assertion that Conclusion 5 can be said to entail Conclusion 6, which is the overall conclusion Descartes wants to establish here. The thesis that sense perception involves mental processes (Conclusion 5) just does not entail that mental operations are more easily know-able than any other objects of knowledge (Conclusion 6).

We can now move on to read the text of *Meditation VI*, where Descartes concludes his arguments about the mind. As with *Meditation II*, I have broken his arguments down into stages, and for ease of reference I have numbered the stages covered in this section to follow consecutively from those used in our reading of *Meditation II*.

Reading p. 163

Before reading Stage 5 below, be sure to read the head note to the text of *Meditation VI* (Reading 3).

One point about the title of this *Meditation*: as we noticed in connection with *Meditation II*, Descartes' titles are precise synopses of the contents which follow them. Accordingly, in *Meditation VI*, we can expect two major arguments, one to show that material things *exist*, and another to identify what he calls the 'real distinction between the Soul and Body of Man'. This difference in nature between soul (i.e. mind) and body is such, he will argue, that the former can exist disembodied, without the latter.

STAGE 5: *MEDITATION VI, PARAGRAPHS 1–3*

Now read paragraphs 1–3 of *Meditation VI* (Reading 3). Then write short answers to the following three exercises, 2.6a, 2.6b and 2.6c. My answers and discussion follow the third exercise.

Reading
p. 164

EXERCISE 2.6A

IMAGINATION AND ABSTRACT THOUGHT

How does Descartes describe the difference between imagination and 'pure intellection', or, as we might say, purely abstract thought (paragraph 2)?

EXERCISE 2.6B

IMAGINATION AND ESSENCE

What reason does he give for not regarding imagination as part of his essence (paragraph 3)?

EXERCISE 2.6C

EXISTENCE OF MATERIAL THINGS

What conclusion concerning the existence of material things does Descartes draw from his analysis of the imagination (paragraph 3)?

SPECIMEN ANSWER 2.6A

In imagining something, in Descartes' sense of the term, I always have a mental *image* of something before my mind; in abstract thinking, I merely grasp the *concept* of whatever it is I am thinking about.

DISCUSSION

The example of the various types of polygon makes this clear: there is a fairly low limit on the types of polygon most people can inwardly visualize in anything like an exact way: triangles and quadrilaterals are usually not a problem, nor usually are pentagons, but beyond that we generally hit trouble, and certainly no one can visualize a chiliagon, a figure with a thousand sides. We can however conceptually grasp what a chiliagon is, deduce the size of its angles, and so on.

SPECIMEN ANSWER 2.6B

The reason Descartes gives for not regarding imagination as part of his essence is that his identity would not be affected even if he did not possess it.

DISCUSSION

I have laboured this point and the previous one because the nature and status of the imagination is a more significant element in Descartes' view of the mind than might first appear. As we have seen, Descartes is consistently very careful to define imagination as the capacity to entertain mental images. Now images can only be images of things which are physical – shapes, colours, sounds, and so on – and so it follows for Descartes that the imagination is a mental ability or faculty which invariably draws its subject matter from the material world. Granted this view of the imagination, Descartes has to argue that this faculty is *not* part of his essence, since this is the only view compatible with his view that the soul can exist disembodied. It is worth spelling out why this is so; the reason is as follows.

To repeat, for Descartes, the imagination always takes as its subject matter mental images based ultimately on physical objects or phenomena. If he were to adopt the view that the imagination were part of his essence, i.e. were such that if he lost it he would lose his identity, then he would have allowed as part of his essence an ability which depends on existence in the material world. This would not be compatible with his view that his soul or mind can exist without the body, since in the disembodied state the soul has no experience of the material world: the disembodied soul does not exist in space at all.

One could well object here that Descartes has made life difficult for himself by restricting his definition of the imagination to the ability to entertain mental images of items from the material world, whether as they are experienced or recombined in some way, as when we combine the bodies of a human and a horse in the image of a centaur. It is perfectly possible to argue that imagination is necessary in mathematics, philosophy and other disciplines which employ predominantly what Descartes calls pure intellection, or in other words that his notion of the imagination is too narrow.

SPECIMEN ANSWER 2.6C

From his view that the imagination draws all its objects from the realm of material things, Descartes concludes that it is *probable* that material things do exist. However, he cannot derive from his clear and distinct idea of the essence of the nature of material things – i.e. that they are extended – any argument which will allow him at present to prove with certainty that they exist.

One further detail before moving on to the next stage: you may wonder what Descartes means when he says in the first paragraph considered in this stage that he knows that physical objects may exist 'in so far as they are considered as the objects of pure mathematics, since in this aspect I perceive them clearly and distinctly' (Haldane and Ross 1931, vol. I: 185). All he has in mind is that many of the properties of physical objects can be described in mathematical terms: their dimensions, speed of motion, relative positions, and so on. Since mathematical propositions are for Descartes the paradigms of clarity and distinctness and so of truth, it follows that it is at least possible for physical objects to exist in so far as they can be mathematically described.

STAGE 6: *MEDITATION VI*, PARAGRAPHS 4–7

Descartes here begins the argument which he hopes will both prove that material things exist and show that mind and body are so different in nature that the former can exist without the latter. In these paragraphs he examines the nature of sense perception to see whether any proof of the existence of material things can be derived from it.

Now read paragraphs 4–7 of *Meditation VI* (Reading 3).

Reading
p. 165

EXERCISE 2.7

SENSE PERCEPTION

In paragraph 6, Descartes gives two main reasons why, in the period before he adopted the method of doubt, he regarded sense perception as an indicator that the external world existed. What are they?

SPECIMEN ANSWER

First, that sensations are not under the control of his will, i.e. he could not decide what he perceived in any non-trivial sense: of course he could decide what to look at, for example, but could not control how the selected object looked. Second, the experience of sense perception is much more vivid and intense ('lively', as he puts it) than any experience furnished by introspection ('in meditation'), i.e. experiences remembered or imagined: a remembered or imagined experience, he claims, is never as vivid as the real thing. So much more vivid are sense perceptions than the experiences of introspection that Descartes concluded that the former cannot be produced by the mind alone.

However, these considerations were overridden by the dream and evil-genius arguments, which he sums up once more in paragraph 7.

Descartes has recapitulated these points yet again because he is now finally about to produce the arguments which will override them. This key passage takes up the next three paragraphs.

STAGE 7: *MEDITATION VI*, PARAGRAPHS 8–10

Reading
p. 167

Now read paragraphs 8–10 of *Meditation VI* (Reading 3).

The short eighth paragraph refers to the conclusions Descartes has so far reached which have withstood the method of sceptical doubt introduced in the first *Meditation*. These conclusions are: (a) the *cogito*, (b) the belief that he is a *res cogitans*, and (c) his belief in the existence of God. In paragraph 9, he sets out his key argument for the real distinction of soul and body, and in the course of it he uses one important concept we have not so far met, namely omnipotence, an attribute of God. Dictionaries usually define this term as 'all-powerful', but Descartes is using it in the more precise sense which it has in philosophy. Omnipotence is the power to do anything the description of which does not involve a self-contradiction. Thus even an omnipotent being cannot make a triangle which has four sides, since this involves a self-contradiction. An omnipotent being can do anything the description of which is self-consistent.

It is as usual much easier to understand and assess the argument if we set it out somewhat more formally than Descartes does here:

Premise 1	All things which I clearly and distinctly apprehend can be created by God as I apprehend them.
Conclusion 1	Therefore, if I apprehend clearly and distinctly that one thing can exist apart from another, then I may be certain that they are different, since they can be made so by God's omnipotence.
Premise 2	I know with certainty that I exist (the conclusion warranted by the *cogito*).
Premise 3	I do not remark that (= I am not aware that) anything necessarily pertains to my essence except thinking.
Conclusion 2	Therefore I conclude that I am a thing whose essence is to think.
Premise 4	I have a clear and distinct idea of myself as a thinking thing.
Premise 5	I have a distinct idea of body as extended and unthinking.
Conclusion 3	Therefore I can be certain that soul [i.e. mind] and body are distinct.
Conclusion 4	Therefore I can be sure that soul can exist without body.

We need now, as usual, to assess this argument for validity and soundness. An appropriate way to do so is to consider some of the objections raised by Descartes' contemporaries in the *Objections* to the *Meditations*. Here is a point raised by the eminent thinker Antoine Arnauld (1612–94) in *Objections IV*:

> The problem is: how it follows, from the fact that one is unaware that anything else [except the fact of being a thinking being] belongs to one's essence, that nothing else really belongs to one's essence.

> (Haldane and Ross 1931, vol. II: 81)

EXERCISE 2.8

ESSENCE

Put Arnauld's objection in your own words, showing to which stage of the above argument it applies and whether it is a claim of invalidity or unsoundness.

SPECIMEN ANSWER

Arnauld is making the claim that there is an *invalid* step in the argument. He is claiming that Premise 3 does not entail Conclusion 2. Descartes has made a logically invalid step from the premise 'I am not aware that anything except thought is essential to me' to the conclusion 'Thought alone is essential to me.' There may, for all Descartes has proved, be something essential to me of which I am unaware.

DISCUSSION

This point raised by Arnauld is enough to show that the present argument is invalid. However, he has some more illuminating things to say. In our terms, his remarks bear on Conclusion 1, Premise 4, Premise 5 and Conclusion 3. Descartes asserts in Conclusion 1 that in order to be certain that one thing is different from another it is sufficient that I am able clearly and distinctly to conceive of the one apart from the other. Arnauld points out, however, that this follows only if the conception I have of each thing is

> held to refer to an adequate notion of a thing [i.e. the notion which comprises everything which may be known of the thing], not to any notion, even a clear and distinct one.
>
> (Haldane and Ross 1931, vol. II: 82)

One can put Arnauld's point another way: once again, Descartes has stated his argument as an enthymeme, and the unstated premise is highly suspect. The unstated premise is that all clear and distinct conceptions are also *exhaustive*, i.e. that they express the whole truth concerning their object. The contemporary Cartesian scholar John Cottingham puts Arnauld's point as follows:

> my ability clearly to perceive X apart from Y (e.g. mind apart from body) cannot, since my intellect is limited, rule out the possibility that there is a chain of necessary connections, *unperceived* by me, which would reveal that Y is after all essential to X.
>
> (Cottingham 1992: 245)[5]

This argument, then, is doubly invalid and so cannot be taken to have established the distinction Descartes wants between mind and body.

STAGE 8: CONCLUDING REMARKS ON *MEDITATION VI*

Reading
p. 169

Now read paragraphs 11–24 of *Meditation VI* (Reading 3).

Having to his own satisfaction proved the distinctness of mind and body, Descartes goes on in these concluding paragraphs to establish the *existence* of material things by relying on the notion that God is benevolent and so not a deceiver: since God is not a deceiver, I can rely on the accuracy of my sense impressions provided I consider them with due care. As Descartes has already stated:

> I do not see how [God] could be defended from the accusation of deceit if these ideas [i.e. sense impressions] were produced by causes other than corporeal objects. Hence we must allow that corporeal things exist.
>
> (*Meditation VI*, paragraph 10)

You will notice that in these paragraphs, apart from establishing our belief in the existence of material things on a logically secure foundation, Descartes' other chief preoccupation is with giving an account of delusory sensations, e.g. when we desire things which do us harm or due to some malfunction in the nervous system have inaccurate perceptions. He needs to do this at length because the belief he relies on so heavily – that God is benevolent and so not a deceiver – is in danger of proving too much. If God is benevolent (etc.) how then is it possible for us to be deceived in these ways? Is it not possible so to have created us, for example, such that we always and only desire what does us good? Descartes is here in fact tackling a version of what is termed the problem of evil, a problem generated by the apparent incompatibility of the properties attributed to the Christian God with certain manifest facts about the world. If God is both omnipotent and benevolent, how does it come about that the world contains any evil? This is a huge and difficult question, and it would deflect us greatly from our present subject to investigate it here.

Having shown the existence of material things, he has arrived at the end of his argument, with the whole of human knowledge now resting on foundations of axiomatic simplicity and certainty. One of the principal views Descartes regards himself as having established is that of the real distinction of mind and body. He believes he has shown that there are two types of substance in the universe: mental or non-extended, and material or extended. We have seen in the course of our investigation that some of the arguments he deploys are logically suspect, but it is important to be clear what the objections so far considered establish concerning the viability of Cartesian dualism as an account of the mind. What we have established so far is only that the arguments in the *Meditations* do not prove what Descartes wants them to prove. Nothing said so far has established that no such arguments could be mounted, or – to put the same point in another way – that two-substance dualism is faced with objections which are unanswerable. In the next section, we will look at three of the most serious philosophical difficulties involved in this account of the mind.

THREE OBJECTIONS TO CARTESIAN DUALISM

1 THE PROBLEM OF MIND–BODY INTERACTION

You will recall from the section 'Minds and bodies: some basics' in Chapter 1 of this book that one of the major features of the mental realm — which, accordingly, any answer to the mind–body problem has to accommodate — is mental causation. That is, any satisfactory philosophy of mind has to be able to give a coherent account of the way in which mind and body mutually affect each other. For example, if I decide (a mental event) to move part of my body then, unless hampered by illness or external forces, that part of my body will move as I intend it to move, and the movement will be an event in the material world. Conversely, certain physical events — the stimulation of the appropriate nerves by light or sound (and so on for the other senses) — will, with the same provisos, result in my having visual, auditory (and so on) experiences, and these are mental events. The topic we have now to consider is this: Can this interaction be coherently described within the conceptual framework Descartes has set up?

We have seen in our consideration of *Meditation VI* in particular that Descartes has tried to show that mind and body are entirely different in nature. However, in order to do justice to the common facts of our daily experience of what it is like to have an embodied mind, he has also to allow that mind and body are intimately related.

EXERCISE 2.9

MIND–BODY INTERACTION

In one of the paragraphs you have just read in connection with Stage 8 of the argument, Descartes puts this in his own words in a simile. Which paragraph is this, and what is the image in question?

SPECIMEN ANSWER

In paragraph 13, where he says:

> Nature … teaches me by these sensations of pain, hunger, thirst, etc., that I am not only lodged in my body as a pilot in a vessel, but that I am very closely united with it, and so to speak so intermingled with it that I seem to compose one whole. For if that were not the case, when my body is hurt, I, who am merely a thinking thing, should not feel pain, for I should perceive this wound by understanding only, just as a sailor perceives by sight when something is damaged in his vessel.

DISCUSSION

Descartes is contending that were mind and body not 'very closely united' (as he puts it), then I (the *res cogitans*, the mind) would merely *observe* that injuries had affected my body in exactly the same way as a sailor observes when damage has occurred to his ship. What actually occurs, of course, is that I experience injuries to my body *as mine*, i.e. from the standpoint of a subject. Descartes is therefore fully aware that he has to do justice to this feature of ordinary experience.

It is easier to see why Descartes has a problem here if we remind ourselves of some of his basic concepts.

EXERCISE 2.10

TWO KINDS OF SUBSTANCE

(a) What do you understand by the concept of substance in the context of Cartesian philosophy?
(b) What are the terms Descartes uses for the two fundamental types of substance into which he divides all the created universe?
(c) How does Descartes define the essence or nature of each of these types of substance?

SPECIMEN ANSWER

(a) Substance is that which needs no other thing in order to exist. It is contrasted with qualities: qualities must be qualities of something, and cannot exist on their own, and substances are what qualities qualify.
(b) Mental substance and material substance.
(c) The essence of mental substance is thought; the essence of material substance is extension. Mental substance exists in time only, not in space. Material or extended substance exists in both space and time.

If his philosophy of mind is to be satisfactory, Descartes must say exactly how mind and body interact.

 Reading
p. 177

Now read the four Articles from *The Passions of the Soul* (Reading 4).

Note that in this context, Descartes (like many other thinkers of his time) makes use of a now discredited theory of neural transmission whose central concept is that of animal spirits. It was known at the time that sensations were conveyed to the brain via the nerves, but in the absence of knowledge of the electrical aspects of this process, the received view was that messages were transmitted along nerve fibres by the agitation of an extremely fine fluid, the animal spirits.

EXERCISE 2.11

MIND–BODY INTERACTION

How, according to Descartes, do mind and body interact?

SPECIMEN ANSWER

Descartes claims that, though the soul or mind is 'joined to the whole body' (*Passions*, Art. 31), yet there is one place only in which interaction between mind and body (in both directions, as it were) occurs, namely a small gland in the brain. (In modern terms, this is the pineal gland.) Descartes thinks this must be the seat of interaction because it is the only component of the brain (so far as he knew) which is not duplicated.

DISCUSSION

There is something very odd about Descartes' assertion that, though the soul or mind is 'joined to the whole body', yet there is one place only in which inter-action between mind and body occurs (*Passions*, Art. 31), which becomes clear when we spell out the picture to which Descartes is committed. As the contemporary philosopher Bernard Williams suggests (1978: 289–90), it is very hard to make sense of the assertion that the mind is both joined to the whole body and yet only causally interacts with one part of it: Descartes' model is that the mind causally interacts only with the pineal gland; all other interac-tions take place solely in the realm of the material. Thus, for example, when I decide to move my arm, my mind interacts with the pineal gland, and the rest of the causal sequence is taken care of by the animal spirits. Yet one is bound to ask: if in one place why not in others? The point that the pineal gland is not duplicated has no logical weight whatever. There is, however, a much more serious objection to Descartes' view here, spotted at once by his contempo-rary, the philosopher and scientist Pierre Gassendi (1592–1655), in *Objections V*. Gassendi puts the objection as follows:

> we cannot grasp how you impress a motion upon [the animal spirits] ... unless you are really a body ... How can there be effort directed towards anything, and motion on its part, without mutual contact of what moves and what is moved? How can there be contact apart from body, when (as is so clear by the natural light) 'Apart from body, naught touches or is touched'.[6]
>
> (Haldane and Ross 1931, vol. II: 199–200)

Gassendi's point is this: how can the mind, which is not in space, causally interact with the body, which is in space, whether at the pineal gland or anywhere else?

This is an immensely powerful objection, and it is worth pausing to consider it fully. Put in the terms introduced in the first chapter, Gassendi is asserting that Descartes' philosophy of mind cannot accommodate one of the key features of mental experience, namely mental causation. The first point to note is that this is a logical objection, not an empirical one. Gassendi is indicating a problem arising from the basic framework of concepts which Descartes is using, not from the details of his now discredited beliefs about human physiology. A modern Cartesian, using the same notions of substance, but equipped with the latest data on the structure and functioning of the brain, would be open to precisely the same objection: how can non-spatial and spatial substances causally interact with one another?

The second major point of philosophical interest arising from Gassendi's objection is that the objection itself relies for its force on the truth of a presupposition which Gassendi himself makes explicit – namely, the way in which he understands the concept of causality. So far we have not raised the issue of precisely how this notion is to be understood, and it would take us too far from our present subject to consider it in depth. However, we can note that for Gassendi the kernel of the notion of causal interaction is 'mutual contact of what moves and what is moved'. Put another way, for any x and any y, if x is to cause y, then x must either directly or via a chain of intermediate causes come into contact with y. Since the body is in space and the mind is not, Gassendi argues, there can in principle be no contact between them, and so mind–body interaction becomes impossible. One way to reply to Gassendi's objection would be to show that this analysis of causality is mistaken, but no such line of reply has yet won general acceptance.

Descartes was never himself able to find a convincing line of reply to this point. His last words on the matter are found in the very detailed and exact record of an interview he gave towards the end of his life with a young man named Burman. Burman went to Descartes with a long list of prepared questions arising from the latter's ideas, and the replies to these questions Burman carefully noted and published. The issue of mind–body interaction – a much-discussed point at the time – naturally came up. Burman asked:

> [H]ow can the soul be affected by the body and vice versa, when their natures are completely different?

Descartes replied:

> This is very difficult to explain; but here our experience is sufficient, since it is so clear on this point that it just cannot be gainsaid. This is evident in the case of feelings and so on.
> (Cottingham 1976: 28)

In other words, Descartes simply asserts that since mind–body interaction manifestly occurs, it must be possible for the two types of substance to interact; but this goes no way at all to solving the logical problem of saying exactly how. Some years later, Leibniz noted with impatience that with regard to interaction,

> Descartes had given up the game on that point, so far as we can know from his writings.
>
> (Leibniz, *New System, etc.* in Weiner 1951: 113)

2 THE NEGATIVE CHARACTERIZATION OF MENTAL SUBSTANCE

There is a problem with the concept of immaterial or mental substance. All that Descartes has to say by way of describing it, beyond the claim that it is the substrate which unifies the mental experiences of a given person (and, by implication, that it exists in time) is by the way of negative description, e.g. that it does not exist in space. He offers no positive characterization of it whatsoever, and this is always a suspicious procedure in the construction of any theory. It is difficult to avoid the suspicion that this type of substance has just been invented to solve a logical problem – in this case, that of finding a way of making a given set of mental contents those of a single individual. This is related to the third problem we need to look at.

3 THE UNITY OF MIND AND BODY

We ordinarily think of the link between mind and body as very close indeed, and, as we saw in connection with the issue of interaction, Descartes was well aware of it: he is at pains to point out that the mind is not lodged in the body as the pilot in a ship, and so on. Except in very rare circumstances, our ordinary experience of being ourselves is not an experience we would describe as of two very different sorts of entity mysteriously and temporarily joined together, however closely. Ordinarily, if we think about it at all, we experience ourselves as unified beings. The question is, however, whether the conceptual framework of his dualism can do justice to this close link. The point is well developed by the Australian philosopher David Armstrong (1968: 25 seqq.). Armstrong argues that dualism inevitably breaks up the unity of the person. Recall that Descartes has denied that the mind is in space, so what other features of the mind and the body can he use in order to unify them? Only (a) temporal simultaneity and (b) causal relations. We have already seen that the substance dualist has no hope of using causal relations since, on any straightforward understanding of causality, mind and body cannot causally interact. All that remains, then, is to assert that mental events and physical events happen to run in parallel, independent but synchronized causal sequences. We shall look at a version of this view, called occasionalism, in the next section. One of the problems with such views is that they appear to entail the consequence that our intuition that persons are unities of minds and bodies is a mistake, and that persons are really composed of two separate parallel entities.

It might seem, in the light of these objections, that Cartesian dualism as a philosophy of mind is an impasse and that the right road to understanding the mind must lie elsewhere. Such a conclusion, however, would be premature. It is always necessary in philosophy to be very precise as to what has been proved, and all we have established so far is that Descartes' version of dualism, two-substance interactionist dualism, involves some very serious problems. The conviction that the mind is very different from the body, however, is not so easily dismissed, and it is possible to retain this basic premise of dualism, while not accepting all the premises of its Cartesian version. Various other forms of dualism have been advanced in response to the difficulties generated by its Cartesian form, and we will now look briefly at three of them.

THREE FURTHER FORMS OF DUALISM

OCCASIONALISM

It is the reverse of surprising that so powerful and innovative a philosophy as Cartesianism should have attracted many followers, and this is precisely what happened during the course of the seventeenth century. However, because of the difficulties, such as those we have looked at advanced by Hobbes, Gassendi, and Arnauld, it was necessary for those attracted by the main Cartesian doctrines to try to modify the details of the philosophy in order to meet the objections made to it: this is the typical procedure of philosophy which, as we shall see, goes on to this day.

The attempt to solve the problem over mind–body interaction gave rise to the philosophy of mind called occasionalism. This view was put forward by a number of Cartesians, but is most famously associated with Nicholas Malebranche (1638–1715), perhaps the most important of Descartes' followers.

Malebranche accepts Descartes' basic assumption that the correct fundamental concepts in terms of which mind and body are to be discussed are those of substance and quality. He also accepts the Cartesian view that what there is can be divided up into mental or non-extended substance and material or extended substance, and he accepts the major consequence of this view: namely, that each human individual has, as it were, two very dissimilar components, a mind and a body. Malebranche parts company with Descartes, however, over the question of interaction. Malebranche accepts the force of Gassendi's objection: there can be no causal interaction, he contends, between substances so dissimilar as those of mind and body as they are defined in the Cartesian philosophy. His solution to the interaction problem is to deny that interaction happens. What we mistakenly interpret in our daily experience as interaction is the result of constant interven-tion in the world by God. Whenever I decide to move my arm, for example, God moves it. Conversely, if I stub my toe on a stone, God causes a sensation of pain to register in my mind. My mind and my body are two separate entities, which appear to interact because God intervenes on each occasion – hence the term 'occasionalism' – on which such intervention is necessary. Malebranche describes the situation as follows:

> There is no necessary relation between the two substances of which we are composed. The modes of our body cannot by their own power change those of our mind ... There is no causal relationship between a body and a mind ... there is none between a mind and a body ... it is clear that a body, purely passive extended substance, cannot act by its own power

on a mind, on a being of a quite different and infinitely more excellent nature. Thus it is clear that with regard to the union of mind and body there is no other link than the power of the divine decrees, immutable and never deprived of their effect. God has therefore willed, and wills unceasingly, that the various changes in the brain are always followed by changes in the mind to which it is united; and it is this constant, effective will of the Creator which constitutes the real union between these two substances.

(Malebranche (1688), in Costilhes 1962: 12; my translation)

Malebranche sums up his position in one sentence in his most important work, *De la Recherche de la Verité* (The Search for Truth):

The whole link between mind and body which is known to us consists in a natural and mutual correspondence of the thoughts of the mind with the traces in the brain, and of the passions of the soul with the movements of the animal spirits.

(Malebranche (1674–5), in Costilhes (1962))

The key word here is 'correspondence': mind and body run parallel and, thanks to divine intervention, in perfect synchronization; but they never interact. Malebranche's account of the nature and relation of mind and body, then, we can characterize as two substance, *non*-interactionist dualism.

This version of dualism involves a number of important difficulties, notably what space Malebranche has left for freedom of choice on the part of individual human beings; if God is the only real causal agent in the universe (which is what this philosophy entails), in what sense can we be said to be *agents* at all? Again, occasionalism depends crucially on accepting that a god of the kind Malebranche needs (the Christian God) exists. Again, it is less than obvious that the appeal to God will help the dualist, for the orthodox Christian God is said to be an imma-terial substance existing outside both space and time, and accordingly it is necessary to show how it is possible for a being thus conceived to interact with material substance which is both spatial and temporal. On a less formal but non-ignorable level, it also seems to me profoundly counter-intuitive in that it does violence to our almost unnoticed bedrock experience of what it is like to be an embodied mind. It follows from Malebranche's premises that my deep conviction that I am in a profound sense a single integrated entity is false, and that all my beliefs as to the influence of my mind on my body, and vice versa, are false. It follows from Malebranche's assertions that all human beings are in fact composed of two radically different entities – a mind and a body which never interact and cannot do so – and the picture of the human condition which this involves is profoundly odd. All there is consists of two perfectly synchronized but never touching realms, the physical and the mental. Such informal considerations are not, as you will appreciate, in any sense *refutations* of Malebranche; but when a proposed account of the mind leads to conclusions which seem so odd, that is at least a *prima facie* reason for supposing that something has gone wrong some-where.

EPIPHENOMENALISM

This daunting-looking word is used to indicate a type of philosophy of mind whose central notion is much easier to grasp than this term suggests. In Greek, the prefix *epi* means 'which rests or depends on', so an epiphenomenon is something which rests or depends on something else, where the something else is not affected by it. We can get a rough idea of what is being driven at by considering the following example: while I am inputting these words into the computer, the depression of the keys makes a slight noise. If we define the phenomenon in question as the inputting of these words, the noise is an epiphenomenon of it: it has no effect on the production of the words, though it is an effect of that production. The same words would be produced if the keyboard were completely silent in operation, or if it made the same clatter as a rickety old typewriter. The central idea of epiphenomenalism as a philosophy of mind is that the mind is merely an epiphenomenon of events in the material world, generally in the brain. Mental events are epiphenomena – effects which themselves have no causal properties – of physical events, and no more than that.

In modern times, this view was most popular in the late nineteenth and early twentieth centuries. It can be found, for example, in the works of the mathematician and philosopher W.K. Clifford (1845–79) and in a more developed form in the philosophy of the Spanish-born philosopher George Santayana (1863–1952). As is not uncommon among philosophers who espouse epiphenomenalism, when he tries to describe what the mind is and how it is related to the body, Santayana turns to metaphor and analogy:

> The mind is itself ethereal and plays about the body as music about a violin, or rather as the sense of a page about the print and paper. To look for it *within* is not to understand what we are looking for.
>
> (Santayana 1906; Triton edition of Santayana's *Works* V: 118)

Again,

> consciousness is no substance, no concrete particular force, but only a new status and intensity of being which certain terms of animal life assume on occasion.
>
> (Santayana 1967: 286)

Other philosophers have used a different image, describing the mental as a phosphorescence emitted by material processes.

The core of epiphenomenalism, then, is the assertion that the mental is merely an epiphenomenon of the material. Though it counts as a form of dualism in the philosophy of mind, it is clearly very different from the substance dualisms advanced by Descartes and Malebranche. Epiphenomenalists deny that the mind is a substance, yet they remain dualists since they also hold that the mind is not reducible to material events.

As a view of the mind, it involves a number of difficulties, most notably that of finding an exact and literal way, as opposed to a metaphorical one, of saying precisely what an epiphenomenon is. Further, like occasionalism, it entails a consequence that is deeply counter-intuitive, which we can now try to work out.

EXERCISE 2.12

EPIPHENOMENALISM AND HUMAN CONSCIOUSNESS

Looking back at the preceding paragraphs, write an answer to this question: If epiphenomenalism is true, how would human behaviour – past, present and future – be different were all human conscious awareness (not life) extinguished? Or, put another way, what difference does consciousness make to the course of history?

SPECIMEN ANSWER

None at all. It is a consequence of epiphenomenalism that the mind makes no input whatever to the chain of causes and effects which unfolds through time. It is always an effect, never a cause. It follows that all my beliefs that my decisions to act (mental events) result in my actions are false, merely errors.

DISCUSSION

As is the case with the counter-intuitive consequence of occasionalism we looked at above, this is not a knock-down argument against or conclusive refutation of epiphenomenalism. It is logically possible that the epiphenomenalist is right, but the intuition that mental causation is a basic fact of mental life is *so* deeply embedded in our beliefs about the mind that it would certainly be preferable to try to find an acceptable account of the mind, if at all possible, which does not have this consequence.

ATTRIBUTE OR PROPERTY DUALISM

This form of dualism, designed to avoid the problems inherent in substance dualism but to do justice to the major features of mental life with which we are by now familiar, consists of the following basic assertions: (i) that a human being is a single material substance, but that (ii) this substance has *non-material properties*, i.e. properties which are irreducibly different from material ones and which cannot in principle be analysed in terms of any properties of matter; (iii) it is the possession of these properties which allows us to say that an entity has a mind; indeed (as Armstrong (1968: 37) puts it) these properties *are* the mind.

It has emerged in the course of discussion among philosophers that this style of view involves a number of problems (cf. Armstrong 1968: 47 seqq.; Churchland 1988: 12) as follows:

1 At what point in the development of an organism do these irreducibly

non-material properties arise? The attribute dualist has to be able to answer this question, to show at what point and for what reason when the organism reaches a certain level of complexity, these odd properties arise; but no one has yet identified a promising candidate for the right point in the growth of complexity, nor the ghost of an explanation of how these properties then emerge.

2 It is difficult to frame an attribute theory which can give an intuitively satisfying account of mind–body interaction. The attribute theory conceives of mental states as special non-material properties of matter – in effect, as properties of the brain. Once this is stated, however, it is hard to resist the view that the state of the mind is uniquely determined by the state of the brain, and not the other way round. If this is so, then the attribute theory, like occasionalism and epiphenomenalism, reduces the mind, counter-intuitively, to a condition of causal impotence.

3 Attribute dualism does not provide a clear account of how non-material properties are related to the brain. With a physical property – e.g. that of having electrochemical discharges or of being neuronally structured – it makes sense to ask certain questions: for example, Does the brain have this property all over or not? Yet it does not even seem to make sense to ask this of a non-material property. It looks very much, in fact, as if non-material properties are describable only in negative terms, and this procedure is unsatisfactory for reasons we have already come across in connection with non-extended substance.

Enough has now been said about dualism to show that the forms we have looked at each involve philosophical problems of some significance. This is not by any means all there is to be said about dualism – we will meet it again briefly later when we investigate artificial intelligence – but it is appropriate now to pause and summarize where we have got to in our investigation of the mind–body problem.

SUMMARY

In Chapter 1 we considered some basic features of the two terms of our problem, minds and bodies. We reviewed the various types of mental content (sensations, thoughts, emotions, and so on), and spent some time concentrating on two closely linked and important properties of mental life: subjectivity and privacy. We have a mode of awareness of our own experience which (it seems) no one else can have: each of us is a subject with a unique point of view not accessible by anyone else. This is in marked contrast to the material universe as revealed by science, a universe in which any entity can in principle be observed in the same way by all observers. Comparing our awareness of our own mental experience to our awareness of the material universe, a startling contrast emerges: it looks on the face of it as if the mind is an anomaly in nature, unique in respect of our mode of awareness of it and of its subjectivity.

This finding has profound and far-reaching implications for the way in which we conceive of ourselves and of the universe (i.e. all there is) as a whole. One reaction to it is to accept that the mind is radically different from all the rest of what there is; or, put another way, that the mind is irreducibly different in nature from the material or physical. Accepting this assertion is the common core of all the philosophies of mind which are called dualist, whether they are substance dualisms like Cartesianism or occasionalism, or regard mental phenomena as epiphenomena of material ones, or as special non-material properties of material phenomena.

Descartes, using the notion of substance as the central concept in his philosophy, puts forward arguments the goal of which is to show that mind and body are radically different types of substance, non-extended and extended, so different indeed that the mind can exist disembodied. His philosophy faces three very serious objections: (i) that it appears to make mind–body interaction impossible, since it is difficult to see how a non-spatial mind and a spatial body can causally interact, on any normal understanding of causality; (ii) mental substance is characterized only in negative terms; and (iii) Cartesian dualism does not give a convincing account of the basic fact of our experience that we do not ordinarily feel as if we are a compound of two very different sorts of thing, but rather a unified individual.

It was in response to the first of these difficulties that occasionalism was devised. Occasionalism is the view that, despite our constant intuitions to the contrary, mind and body never causally interact but run in two parallel, perfectly synchronized but (as it were) untouching, realms, the synchronism being brought about by divine intervention. This view relies entirely on the existence of a benevolent god, and is again unable to give a convincing account of our bedrock intuition of being a single unified being.

Epiphenomenalism and property dualism drop the claim that the mental is a different type of substance from the physical, but still count as dualist because they maintain the claim that minds are irreducibly different in nature from bodies. The epiphenomenalist claims that mental events are effects of physical events but have no causal properties of their own. This entails the view that consciousness has no causal role whatsoever: the whole history of the universe would be unchanged were consciousness absent from it. Property dualism is the thesis that the mind consists of non-spatial properties of a spatial thing (the brain). This view is open to the objection that it is difficult to say how these non-material properties are related to the material brain.

CONCLUSION

The conclusion we can draw from this survey of dualism is that all four of the versions we have looked at are open to serious objection. This does not entail that no form of dualism can be true; however, it is reasonable to suppose that if some form of dualism does turn out to be true, it is unlikely to resemble the four types we have looked at. In the light of arguments of this kind, many philosophers have quite reasonably taken the view that it is appropriate to explore another type of view of the mind in response to the mind–body problem. Such views are called monist views, and we will look at three of them in detail in the next chapter.

NOTES

1   The 'g' in *cogito* is hard, as in the English word 'cog'.
2   The Latin word *more* has two syllables: more-ray.
3   Descartes makes much the same point in his work *The Principles of Philosophy* (1644) I, 9, in Haldane and Ross (1931, I: 222).
4   The 'g' in *cogitans* is once again hard; the Latin word *res* is pronounced like the English word 'race'.
5   The point is also made by Kenny (1968: 92–3).
6   The sentence in quotation marks is a misquotation by Gassendi from *De rerum natura* (On the Nature of Things), Bk I, l. 305, by the Roman poet Lucretius (*c*.99–55 B C E).

FURTHER READING

Good introductory accounts of Cartesian dualism can be found in:

Nakhnikian, G. (1967) *An Introduction to Philosophy*, New York: Knopf.
Sprigge, T.L.S. (1985) *Theories of Existence*, Harmondsworth: Penguin.

See also the works by Anthony Kenny and Bernard Williams in the general bibliography: both are very detailed studies of Cartesianism, but more advanced in their treatment than the works listed above.

3 | Monism

In this chapter, we are going to look at accounts of the mind which begin from a different fundamental assertion, and these are called *monist* views. The term 'monist' derives from the Greek word *monas* which means 'one'. What all monist views have in common is the assertion that there is only one sort of stuff in the universe, not two as in dualism, and that therefore the mind must be a manifestation or form of this fundamental stuff. Monist views subdivide into two major classes, idealistic monism (or idealism) and materialistic monism (or materialism).

IDEALISTIC MONISM OR IDEALISM

This point of view generally strikes most newcomers to philosophy as the most counter-intuitive outlook they meet. The fundamental assertion of idealism is that everything that exists – the universe – is mental in nature and none of it is physical. It follows that what we call the material world is nothing of the kind, and is in fact mental in nature. The fundamental task for any philosopher accepting this view is to show that all the phenomena we ordinarily regard as physical in nature are in fact better understood on the assumption that they are ultimately mental. This view has had many powerful adherents in both the Western and oriental traditions of philosophy; indeed if one were just to count heads, as it were, across all these traditions, idealism would come out as one of the most popular philosophies of all time, though that is not a reason either for believing it or not believing it. Just as there are classic reasons for accepting dualism, there are a number of classic routes to the fundamental assertion of idealism, ranging from the analysis of perception to mystical encounters with divine presences. Regrettably, we do not have space here to look at this outlook further, though one of its attractions will be obvious: like all versions of monism, idealism solves the mind–body interaction problem at a stroke: since for the idealist there are no bodies, all causation takes place within one realm only, the realm of mind.

It is important to be clear that the usage of the term 'idealism' in the philosophy of mind is unrelated to its use in moral thought, where an idealist is a person whose conduct is directed by devotion to moral ideals, generally of an altruistic kind. An idealist in the philosophy of mind is simply someone who holds the view put forward above. This view does not as a matter of logic involve a commitment to moral idealism, nor vice versa.

MATERIALISTIC MONISM OR MATERIALISM

This is the view exactly contrary to idealism. Its fundamental assertion is that everything that exists is material (or physical) in nature and none of it is mental, i.e. in the sense of being irreducibly different in nature from the physical. It follows that the mind and all mental events, properties and acts are in fact material in nature. It follows further that a principal task for a materialist philosophy of mind is to show how all the properties of the mental with which we became familiar in our consideration of the nature of the mind–body problem and of Descartes' ideas – e.g. subjectivity and mental causation – can be convincingly accounted for in terms of concepts which do not involve any reference outside the realm of matter and its properties.

As with idealism, the use of the term 'materialism' in the philosophy of mind is unrelated to its use in moral thought. In the latter area, a materialist is someone who holds that the true good for humanity consists in the enjoyment of material things alone. There is no logical link whatever between this moral view and the materialist philosophies of mind we will be looking at, or indeed any others I know of. It is perfectly logically coherent to be a materialist with regard to the mind and at the same time to hold in the moral sphere, for example, that the highest human goal is some form of contemplation or the cultivation in some sense of the life of the mind.

Materialism has had adherents since ancient Greek times and not only in Western thought, though it has never been so widely advocated as in the latter half of the twentieth century. The reasons for this are not far to seek. The physical sciences have made very considerable advances in this period, and have succeeded in accounting for previously mysterious phenomena in purely physicalistic terms. Notable among these has the been the property of life itself. Prior to the great strides in biology made in the twentieth century, many philosophers believed that life was a special type of property different in nature from the purely material properties of biochemical organisms, and adherents of such a view are called *vitalists*. Vitalists contend that the properties of matter alone, however complex its organization, cannot give rise to the property of life, which they hold to be qualitatively different from the properties of biochemical compounds. At the present time, however, vitalism is more or less extinct as a view held by scientists and philosophers: as understanding of biology improved, it became possible to account for life without reference to any mysterious somewhat over and above the biological processes themselves. On grounds such as this, many philosophers have come to take the view that, like the property of life, the mind will one day be accountable for solely in the terms of physical science, and they have applied themselves, as we now shall, to an exploration of the conceptual problems which arise when the assumption is made that the universe consists only of matter and its properties, however complexly organised.

THREE FORMS OF MATERIALISM

In the present century, and especially since the 1940s, the majority of philosophers working in the area of the philosophy of mind have been attracted to one form or another of materialist or physicalist (these terms are interchangeable) theory of the mind. They have tended to do so not only, of course, because of problems with dualism, which were apparent almost from the time of its formulation (as we saw in the objections to Cartesianism made by Descartes' contemporaries) but also because of the very considerable advances that have been made in the twentieth century in many areas of the physical sciences, like those in the life sciences mentioned above. To more and more philosophers, as to many other people, it has come to seem probable that sooner or later empirical science will provide us with a complete physicalist account of the nature of things, and it would be untidy if the mind resisted this approach, since it would then end up as an irreducible oddity in an otherwise physical universe. This working hypothesis or outlook gains plausibility from a number of general arguments, e.g. evolutionist theory and biology have given a convincing account of the development of animal species and animal growth in entirely physicalist terms: it has not been found necessary to postulate any non-physical causes to account for how we get to be as we are: natural selection, DNA and environmental factors will do the job, or at least promise to do so, even if many of the details in this immensely complex picture remain to be filled in. It would be very odd if, in such an intellectual climate, philosophers of mind did not investigate the issues which arise when a serious attempt is made to understand the mind within a materialist framework: abstract discipline though it is, the philosophy of a given period never just comes out of the air, as it were, but is always related to other features of the intellectual climate of the time.

We will now proceed to examine some of the most influential materialist philosophies of mind put forward since the 1950s. The first of these, the subject of the next section, has a number of different names: you will find it referred to in books on the philosophy of mind as central state materialism or reductive materialism: here I will refer to it by the name by which it was first discussed: the mind–brain identity theory, or just the identity theory (for short). Before we get to it, however, we need to glance briefly at the view it succeeded and was meant in some ways to improve on, namely behaviourism. The philosophers we will be studying assume you know what behaviourism is, and so we need to pause to grasp the essentials of that theory.

Behaviourism exists in two major and related forms, psychological and philosophical. Psychological behaviourism, associated particularly with the work of the American psychologist B.F. Skinner (1904–90), rests on a principle which is both a rule of psychological method and an assertion about the mind, namely, that what we call the mind is no more than patterns of observable behaviour, not at all a ghostly something which causes the behaviour. As a rule of method, this entails that the psychologist deals only with observable, public phenomena, which can be measured in ways analogous to the ways in which scientists in other empirical sciences deal with their subject matter. This has the effect of freeing psychology from the objections of unscientificness often levelled against it, especially in its psychoanalytic forms. As an assertion about the nature of the mind, it solves the interaction problem at a stroke, since there are not two things to interact: there is only behaviour. What we call conscious states, in Skinner's view, are at the very best epiphenomenal and have no causal role whatever to play in the world.

Philosophical (or analytical) behaviourism is most thoroughly set out in *The Concept of Mind* (1949), the best known work of the Oxford philosopher Gilbert Ryle (1900–76). This work is a prolonged attack on Cartesian dualism, summed up by Ryle as the dogma of the ghost in the machine. Ryle's positive thesis is that Cartesianism arises from a systematic misunderstanding of the meaning of the expressions by means of which we talk about a non-physical (i.e. mental) object. Ryle's assertion is that talk about the mind is not talk about an *object* of any kind. His strategy in *The Concept of Mind* is to analyse the main types of expression we use in describing our mental life in an attempt to show that none of them, properly understood, involves any commitment to the existence of a ghostly something over and above our behaviour. For example, take statements about desires – i.e. expressions about things we want – according to Ryle, such statements are equivalent to a set of assertions about my actual or possible behaviour. Wanting a new radio is equivalent to buying magazines where they are advertised, seeking advice from experts about which is most reliable, working out what I can afford, and so on. Ryle's central assertion in all his analyses is that all mentalistic statements can be so analysed, and that none include an undeletable reference to a private something behind and additional to behaviour.

This view is not without its problems, notably with reference to utterances about pains: on the face of it, it is less than plausible to claim that my assertion that I have toothache means no more than that I am inclined to wince, hold my jaw, look sorry for myself and set off for the dentist as fast as I can go. It does seem in this case that I am referring to something else, additional to my public behaviour and in a real sense its cause, going on in me and private to me, namely a very unpleasant sensation in my jaw. (In discussions of the philosophy of mind, the actual qualities of our inner experiences – the way this pain or pleasure feels to me, the shade of colour I am aware of, and so on – are called 'qualia', a term we will meet again a little later in this chapter.) For reasons like this it came to be felt that analytical behaviourism could not be sustained in the form in which Ryle put it forward, and other varieties of materialist position have been explored. The first of these, which we will now examine in detail, is the identity theory. This was developed by a number of philosophers, including the Austro-Hungarian Herbert Feigl (1902–88). The version we will look at, however, is that of the British-Australian philosopher J.J.C. Smart (b. 1920), at one time a student of Ryle at Oxford. Smart's thesis is that mental events and brain events are one and the same set of events, to which we refer, however, by means of two different sorts of statement: (a) ordinary-language statements describing our mental life, and (b) neuroscientific statements describing brain processes.

SMART'S MIND–BRAIN IDENTITY THEORY

In this section we will examine in detail one of the most widely read papers in the philosophy of mind written since the Second World War, Smart's 'Sensations and Brain Processes' (first published in *The Philosophical Review* in 1959; we will study a revised version from 1962). We will use the same method as in our examination of Descartes, a slow and careful examination of each of the key assertions in the text. You will notice that, after some opening remarks outlining the view to be defended, the paper is cast in a traditional philosophical format: a series of objections to the theory (formulated by Smart himself as the result of discussion with other philosophers) with replies. As has been the case since the birth of Western thought in ancient Greek times, philosophy proceeds by means of the dialogue of thesis, objection and reply.

One major point first about the title of Smart's paper: it is important to be clear about what he means by the term 'sensation' – what he means by 'brain process' is not problematic. By 'sensation', Smart means what we would ordinarily think of as a mental experience: the way my sense experiences appear to me in my consciousness. As we have seen from our study of Descartes, philosophers have tended to regard such events as irreducibly different from physical ones, especially in respect of their privacy to me and my privileged access to them, i.e. my seeming inability to be wrong about what I am currently experiencing. It is precisely these properties of sensations and indeed of other types of mental phenomena which have led philosophers to regard them as irreducibly different from physical events, and one of the central problems for materialist philosophers of mind is to show how such properties can be accommodated in a physicalist view of the mind, and one of Smart's goals in his paper is to show just this.

PARAGRAPH 1

Reading
p. 181

Read the first paragraph of Smart's text.

EXERCISE 3.1

State in your own words what philosophical position Smart is going to try to avoid.

SPECIMEN ANSWER

Smart says he wants to avoid the view that statements such as 'I have a pain' or 'I am experiencing a yellowish-orange after-image' report the occurrence of events which are non-physical in nature. Smart uses the phrase 'irreducibly psychical': 'psychical' is an alternative for 'mental', where this latter term means 'something the nature of which cannot be analysed out into physicalist terms'. What Smart wants to avoid, in other words, is any form of dualism in the philosophy of mind.

DISCUSSION

You may have wondered why Smart should begin by talking, not directly about the mind, but about types of statement, i.e. relating to pains and after-images. He does so because of the background of philosophy against which he is writing, of which Ryle's views were a central and typical example. Different philosophies of mind entail different consequences with regard to how various types of statement in which we describe our mental life should be construed. For a Cartesian dualist, for example, statements about my inner life are regarded as logically similar in important ways to reports about objects in the material world. When a Cartesian reports having certain thoughts, this is construed as a report of changes occurring in a mental substance, much as talk about the water boiling reports changes to a material substance. Both types of statement, in Cartesian vocabulary, are reports of changes in the modes of substances, mental and physical respectively. When statements have, or are claimed to have, similar analyses in this way modern philosophers will describe them as having the same *logic* or *logical grammar*. (We will come across these phrases again.) For someone like Ryle, who denies that there are any mental substances or indeed anything beyond patterns of behaviour and dispositions to behaviour, it must follow that statements like 'I am in pain' cannot have a similar logic to statements describing physical objects, since there are no mental objects at all for them to refer to.

With this in mind, it should become a little easier to see why Smart begins where and as he does. Statements of the kind that he begins with – 'I am in pain' or 'I am experiencing an after-image' – are those which are most problematic for analytical behaviourists like Ryle to deal with, since they resist being analysed into reports of patterns of behaviour alone, and seem unavoidably to involve a reference to a private mental experience. Most of the first paragraph (from 'One answer to this question ...') is a summary by Smart of how an analytical behaviourist would analyse statements of this kind, e.g. by suggesting that 'I am in pain' does not refer to a private event at all but merely functions like a wince expressed in words. Smart is not going to accept the analytical behaviourist approach; but neither is he going to accept a Cartesian one, i.e. the view that statements of this kind are reports of goings on in a non-physical realm.

PARAGRAPH 2

Now read paragraph 2.

Reading
p. 182

Two expressions in this paragraph need explanation before we go any further: they are (a) Occam's razor and (b) nomological danglers.

(a) *Occam's razor*: William of Occam (or Ockham, both spellings are current), *c.*1285–*c.*1349, was an influential English philosopher of the late mediaeval period. Somewhat as did Descartes, Occam formulated some rules of philosophical method, and Occam's razor is the name given to the most famous of these, which is as follows: if you are faced with competing theories which are advanced as explanations of the same phenomena, the one to choose is the simplest theory. For example, faced with the choice between the heliocentric explanation of planetary motion and the geocentric explanation, Occam's razor determines that the heliocentric theory is to be preferred, since it allows us to explain planetary motion by means of fewer and simpler laws. Books on the history of thought usually give Occam's razor in the formulation: 'Entities must not be multiplied without necessity', and this is often quoted in its Latin form, *entia non sunt multiplicanda sine necessitate*. Occam scholars, however, have never found this form of words in Occam's writings. His preferred formulation was: 'Plurality is not to be posited without necessity' *(pluralitas non est ponenda sine necessitate)* but his meaning is clearest in a slightly less condensed form: 'What is explained by the assumption of fewer things is vainly explained by the assumption of more things' *(frustra fit per plura quod potest fieri per pauciora)*. Occam's razor remains to this day a guiding principle in the construction of theories in science and philosophy: the razor shaves off unnecessary complexity.

(b) *Nomological danglers*: This is a phrase coined by Herbert Feigl (in Feigl, Scriven and Maxwell, 1958: 428). 'Nomological' (derived from the Greek term *nomos* = law) means 'concerning the principles or concept of law'. The phrase 'nomological danglers' is used by Feigl in a passage discussing the relation of sensations (mental events) to scientific laws. He could make the same point (as could Smart) by saying 'nomological anomalies or oddities': Feigl's point is that a theory of the mind (like substance or property dualism) which includes the view that sensations are irreducibly non-physical must include laws which are anomalous or odd. Scientific laws (in Feigl's view) concern *public* events – that is, events which are in principle observable by any competent observer – and their relations. By contrast, a philosophy of mind which claims that there are non-physical items like sensations must involve the claim that there are laws which relate events that are in principle private (i.e. the sensations) to events that are in principle public (i.e. neural processes) and such laws must be very odd indeed. Feigl concludes that it is preferable, as a principle of method, to aim for a theory of the mind which does not generate such anomalies and which includes laws which are logically uniform. The easiest way to achieve that goal is to deny that there are any phenomena that are irreducibly mental.

EXERCISE 3.2

Summarize the reason Smart gives for wishing to avoid accepting a belief in the existence of anything non-physical.

SPECIMEN ANSWER

Science as it progresses is gradually furnishing us with an explanation of the nature of things which is entirely physicalist (or materialist) in nature. So far, it has proved difficult to accommodate the mind in this overall scheme, but it is reasonable to suppose that this is a temporary hold-up, and that when science does arrive at an accepted theory of the mind, that theory will be a materialist one. Not to accept this as a working hypothesis is to accept that there is a fundamental discontinuity in nature, and that one phenomenon in it, consciousness, lies outside the scope of physicalist explanation. Dualistic theories of the mind violate the principle of Occam's razor and include logically odd laws of nature.

PARAGRAPH 3

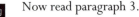 Reading p. 182

Now read paragraph 3.

EXERCISE 3.3

State the main philosophical claim put forward in this paragraph.

SPECIMEN ANSWER

Sensations are nothing over and above brain processes.

EXERCISE 3.4

Smart mentions two types of statement in this paragraph, sensation statements (which will from now on be abbreviated to s-statements) and
statements about brain processes (from now on bp-statements). How does he
relate them to one another in terms of meaning and logic (in the sense of this
term introduced above)?

SPECIMEN ANSWER

Smart says that s-statements and bp-statements do not have the same
meaning or logic, nor is it a requirement of the identity theory that they do.
However, he goes on, this does not show that s-statements and bp-statements
cannot both refer to the same events, namely brain events.

DISCUSSION

One of the many difficulties involved in understanding philosophical texts is to
see why it is that philosophers place the stress in their arguments as they do.
Here, for instance, Smart is manifestly very anxious to show that his version of
materialism does not entail that s-statements are equivalent to or can be
translated into bp-statements. This is for the good reason that the assertion
that these types of statement are inter-translatable is manifestly false, since
they do not have the same meanings: 'I have a toothache' (whatever it turns out
to mean) does not mean the same as 'My c-fibres are firing intensively at the
moment'. Accordingly, if any theory of the mind does entail the consequence
that s-statements and bp-statements are interchangeable without loss of
meaning, then that theory is false. (Remember the logical rule: if an argument
entails a consequence which is false, then the argument contains at least one
false premise.)

Again, you will notice from the stress given to the phrase by its italicization that
Smart is anxious to emphasize that the identity claimed between sensations (my
experiences of sensations as they are experienced by me in consciousness) and
my brain processes is *contingent*: it just happens to be the case that these items are
one and the same. Put another way, his view can be stated as the assertion that
the proposition 'Sensations and brain processes are identical' is a contingent and
not a necessary truth. It is this premise which allows him to avoid the consequence that s-statements and bp-statements are intertranslatable. This becomes
clearer if we examine a statement of identity which is a necessary truth. Smart
himself provides an example of such a statement in the next paragraph: '7 is identical with the smallest prime number greater than 5'. In such a case, either
component of the identity, in this case '7' and 'the smallest prime number greater
than 5' can be intersubstituted for the other in any proposition without affecting

the truth of the proposition concerned. This is precisely not true of an s-state-ment description of a mental event and the bp-description of the same event. What this point prompts us to do, however, is to ask what Smart means by 'iden-tical', and it is no accident that the next short section of his paper is intended to clarify this concept.

PARAGRAPHS 4–5

Reading
p. 183

Now read paragraphs 4 and 5.

EXERCISE 3.5

Sum up in your own words the two senses of 'identity' which Smart distin-guishes here, and say in which sense sensations and brain processes are claimed by him to be identical.

SPECIMEN ANSWER

The first sense of identity Smart calls 'strict' identity. In this sense, lightning is an electrical discharge: that is, the one is not a property of the other, nor a manifestation of the other. They are one and the same. The second sense of 'identity' is not given a name by Smart, but what his example of the small boy and the general indicates is that he has in mind the sense of identity in which we say that an object or life form, which exists through a reasonable length of time but may be subject to significant change in respect of some its properties, is yet the same individual. Thus human individuals will change significantly in the course of their lives in respect of many properties, not only physical ones such as height, weight and so on but also in respect of experience, memory, perhaps even traits of character, and yet will still be the same individuals. It is in the first and stricter sense that sensations and brain processes are asserted by Smart to be identical, i.e. in the same way as lightning and an electrical discharge.

DISCUSSION

This is a central point in the identity theory and it is necessary to dwell on it for a moment: clearly, if a theory asserts that 'x' and 'y' are *identical*, it is essential that we are told what this means, and the matter is less straightforward than it looks. As Smart himself has made clear in this paragraph, the term 'identity' has more than one sense, and this is a way of indicating that this concept is more complex than might appear at first blush.

In the last chapter, we met briefly the philosopher Leibniz, and some of the most important discussions of the concept of identity are to be found in his works. In particular, Leibniz formulated a principle which has come to be known as Leibniz's Law, which is as follows: for any 'x' and any 'y', if 'x' and 'y' are identical, then whatever is true of 'x' is true of 'y'. This looks like an innocuous spelling out of what we mean we say that things are identical, but it is a principle with stern consequences. If I want, like Smart, to assert that a sensation and a brain process are identical, i.e. are one and the same thing, then I must be able to show that whatever is true of the sensation in question is also true of the brain process with which it is asserted to be identical. If my sensations have certain properties, then my brain processes must have the same properties, and vice versa. We must bear this constantly in mind when dealing with versions of the identity theory: it will become clear that much of what Smart has to say is an attempt to make his theory satisfy the requirements of Leibniz's Law.

Having stated the theory he wishes to defend to his satisfaction, Smart now proceeds to state some objections to it, and to offer his replies.

OBJECTION 1: PARAGRAPHS 6–11

In order to understand what Smart is saying here, it is necessary to know something about an important thesis in the philosophy of language put forward by the German philosopher Gottlob Frege (1848–1925) in a much-quoted essay 'On Sense and Meaning' (*Über Sinn und Bedeutung*) (1892). Once again, this is an example of how closely linked the various branches of philosophy are. We have already noticed earlier in this chapter that philosophies of mind entail consequences in the philosophy of language. In the present case, as will become clear, a point in the philosophy of language is of direct relevance to the philosophy of mind: indeed, these two areas of philosophy are thoroughly intertwined.

Frege draws a distinction between the meaning or sense of an expression and whatever it is that the expression refers to, the item philosophers call the *referent* of the expression. The example he gives, used here also by Smart, is of the expressions 'the Morning Star' and 'the Evening Star'. These expressions have the same referent, in this case the same physical object, namely the planet Venus, but they do not have the same meaning. This point shows not only that the meaning or sense of an expression, whatever it is, is not what the expression refers to but also that expressions with different meanings can have the same, i.e. numerically identical, referent (see Geach and Black (1980) for Frege's essay; the Morning Star/Evening Star example is on page 57). We can call Frege's thesis the sense/reference distinction.

Now read paragraphs 6–11.

Reading p. 183

EXERCISE 3.6

State objection 1 and Smart's reply in your own words, showing how he makes use of the sense/reference distinction.

SPECIMEN ANSWER

The objection is that someone who has never heard of brain processes can describe their sensations perfectly well, and therefore sensations and brain processes cannot be identical. Smart's reply is that the objection would only be valid if sense and reference were the same. Since they are not, the objection is irrelevant. S-statements and bp-statements manifestly do not *mean* the same thing, but it is not a requirement of the identity theory that they do. The theory only requires that they have one and the same referent. One can talk perfectly well about the Evening Star without ever having heard of the Morning Star, even though these expressions have one and the same referent.

OBJECTION 2: PARAGRAPHS 12 AND 13

Towards the end of his reply to this objection, Smart refers to what he calls a 'Fido'-Fido theory of meaning. By this he means the view we have already come across that the meaning of a word is what it refers to, its referent. This is refuted by Frege's thesis considered above, but can also be rebutted by considering those nouns and noun phrases, like 'unicorn', 'elf' or 'the present king of France' which are perfectly meaningful but have no referents.

Now read paragraphs 12 and 13.

Reading
p. 184

EXERCISE 3.7

State objection 2 in your own words.

SPECIMEN ANSWER

The link between brain processes and the occurrence of sensations is contingent – it might have been otherwise. It is possible if unlikely that future physiological discoveries will show that some feature of the body other than the brain underlies or is the basis of sensation. Therefore, when we report a sensation we are not reporting a brain process.

EXERCISE 3.8

What is Smart's reply and on what principle does it rely?

SPECIMEN ANSWER

Smart argues that the objection rests on a false assumption about language, namely, that expressions which have the same referents must have the same meaning; he assumes the truth of Frege's assertion to the contrary, used already in the rebuttal of objection 1.

OBJECTION 3: PARAGRAPHS 14–20

In this section of his essay, Smart is dealing with a problem which is stated in terms of a venerable and much discussed distinction, that between primary and secondary qualities, and we will need to pause briefly to grasp the basics of this issue. Though versions of this distinction have been traced back to the ancient Greek philosopher Democritus (*c.*460–*c.*370 BC), its most authoritative form occurs in the philosophy of John Locke (1637–1704), in his *An Essay Concerning Human Understanding* (1690, Bk. II, ch. 8). Here Locke argues that material objects possess five primary qualities – extension (in the sense we have already encountered in Descartes); figure (= shape); motion or rest; number, and solidity – and many secondary qualities, including colour, taste, smell, sound and warmth or cold. Primary qualities, Locke asserts, are inseparable from material objects and are found even in their most minute parts; by contrast, secondary qualities are not true properties of objects but are merely powers in the objects to produce certain sensory effects in us. Thus the colour blue is the effect of the secondary quality blue, and this consists in the power possessed by the surface of the object to absorb some frequencies of light but to reflect others.

There is much to be said about this distinction and the presuppositions on which it rests, but for present purposes what matters is to grasp that secondary qualities are held to be dependent on the sensory constitution of the perceiver in a way that primary qualities are not. For example, because our ears are fully sensitive to sounds in a range from (on average) 30 Hz to 15 kHz or so, we do not hear sounds or overtones of sounds which fall outside this range, and so both musical and natural sounds have the timbre they do to us in perception because of the way our auditory system works; and the same is true for the other senses. By contrast, primary qualities are not dependent in that way on our sensory constitution: for example, whether an object is in motion or at rest does not depend on our sensory constitution.

The qualities of which we are often aware in sensation are secondary qualities – colours, sounds, smells, tastes and tactile sensations. Like pains, these experiences of secondary qualities have qualia, to use the term introduced above: qualities of which we are aware immediately in our own consciousness. Since Smart wants to identify sensations with brain processes, he is going to have to say something about secondary qualities.

Now read paragraphs 14–20

Reading
p. 185

EXERCISE 3.9

Can you see why, in the light of his remarks in paragraphs 14 and 15, Smart is so concerned about secondary qualities? (This is not easy, so don't worry if nothing leaps to mind at once.)

SPECIMEN ANSWER

Because it looks as if, on the face of it, secondary qualities cannot be fitted into a fully materialist or physicalist account of the mind. The experiences of secondary qualities have qualia, the qualities of which we are immediately aware: Smart also calls these 'phenomenal properties' (paragraph 18) following another accepted philosophical usage. My sensation of yellow has the phenomenal property of being yellow, whereas the identical brain process does not have the property of being yellow.

DISCUSSION

Behind Smart's worry is Leibniz's Law: for any 'x' and 'y' if 'x' is identical to y, then whatever is true of 'x' is true of 'y'. The force of objection 3 is that sensations have properties – phenomenal qualities or qualia – which brain processes do not have; therefore, it follows from Leibniz's Law that sensations cannot be identical to brain processes. This is an extremely powerful objection, and Smart must try to deal with it. If he cannot answer it, then what he will be left with is a theory which is almost but not quite entirely physicalist since qualia, properties of mental events, refuse to be identified with brain processes. To use his own phrase, he would be left with something irreducibly psychical.

EXERCISE 3.10

Can you see how Smart tries to answer this objection? (See paragraph 19: once again, this is a hard question; the key phrase is 'topic neutral'.)

SPECIMEN ANSWER

Smart addresses the objection by trying to show that it entails a consequence which is false. The consequence is a linguistic one. Those who hold that phenomenal qualities are irreducibly psychical are committed to the view that whenever we make an utterance reporting such a quality, e.g. 'I see a yellowish-orange after-image', these statements include a claim that my experience *is* distinctively psychical, i.e. this is what such statements *mean*. Smart proposes to show that they include no such claim, but are, as he puts it in a phrase borrowed from Ryle, neutral on this topic. Thus Smart claims that when I say 'I see a yellowish-orange after-image', I mean only that I am in a state similar to the state I am in when confronted by certain visual stimuli. Construed in this way, these statements make no claim at all about the nature of what is being experienced, i.e. they make no statement as to the psychical or material nature of what I am experiencing.

DISCUSSION

We will let this point rest here for the moment, and return to it in the concluding review of the identity theory below. Meantime, Smart has to deal with other objections which rest on Leibniz's Law.

OBJECTION 4, PARAGRAPHS 21–22

In his reply, Smart uses the Latin phrase *ignoratio elenchi*, which means 'irrelevant conclusion', and is the name of a common fallacy. As the name suggests, the premises advanced in an argument which exhibits this fallacy do not entail the conclusion they are supposed to entail, but a different and irrelevant one.

Now read paragraphs 21 and 22.

Reading
p. 187

EXERCISE 3.11

State objection 4 and Smart's reply in your own words, making it clear how the objector is relying on Leibniz's Law.

SPECIMEN ANSWER

As with objection 3, this objection claims that sensations and brain processes have different properties, and so, from Leibniz's Law, cannot be identical. In this case, the brain process has the property of being located in space, while the after-image does not. Smart's reply is that the objection is irrelevant: the claim of the identity theory is that sensations are identical with brain processes, and sensations are *experiences*. No one contends that the experience of seeing a yellow-orange after-image is itself yellow-orange, and so the objection miscarries.

DISCUSSION

The objector can reply once again to Smart, however, that experiences have a content, they are about something, and it isn't at all clear how a brain process can be about anything and so the asymmetry of properties reappears. Once again, we will return to this point at the conclusion of this selection.

OBJECTION 5, PARAGRAPHS 23–24

Now read paragraphs 23 and 24.

EXERCISE 3.12

Does this objection rest on Leibniz's Law, and how does Smart reply to it?

SPECIMEN ANSWER

The objection does rest on Leibniz's Law, in that it asserts an asymmetry of properties between sensations and brain processes. The latter could meaning-fully be said to be fast or slow, straight or circular, but such properties cannot meaningfully be ascribed to my experiences. Smart's reply makes use once again of the meaning/reference distinction: the fact that I can make different sorts of statements about brain processes and sensations does not entail that these types of statements may not have the same referents. Moreover, he asserts, the fact that at present we do not ascribe locations to our experiences should not be assumed to be beyond revision: it is perfectly coherent to suppose that when neuroscience has advanced to the point of being able to locate the brain processes that are my experiences, I may well then simply revise the way I conceive of my experiences, and come to regard them as having a spatial co-ordinate.

OBJECTION 6, PARAGRAPHS 25–26

Now read paragraphs 25 and 26.

EXERCISE 3.13

Summarize objection 6 in your own words, making sure that you relate it to Leibniz's Law; and summarize Smart's reply.

SPECIMEN ANSWER

The objection claims once again that there is an asymmetry of properties between sensations and brain processes. Sensations are private, whereas brain processes are public. Moreover, there is another epistemological asymmetry in respect of s-statements and bp-statements: a first person s-statement is incorrigible, whereas no bp-statement is incorrigible. Therefore, the identity theory infringes Leibniz's Law. Smart's reply is very similar to that he gave to objection 5. He contends that what the objector takes to be an unmodifiable difference in the way in which we talk about sensations and brain processes is in fact merely temporary, and is likely to change as neuroscience advances. It may very well come to be the case that we will be able to identify individual brain processes, and so will have a public test in an area where now we are forced to rely on introspective reports.

DISCUSSION

The property of privacy is one in respect of which the identity theory has attracted some searching criticism. It is appropriate here to consider an objection put forward by Professor Kurt Baier (Baier 1962 in Borst 1970). Baier contends that in respect of one subclass of sensations at least – namely, pains – the identity theory cannot be maintained. Baier's objection rests on a detailed analysis of the concept of privacy as it is used in the philosophy of mind, and since this is a key idea in these debates we need to pause to get a firm grip on it.

Recall that Smart has argued that s-statements are neutral with regard to the mental or physical nature of sensations, or, in other words, that they do not involve any claim which entails that sensations must fall into either of these classes. Baier argues that, in respect of pains at least, this claim is false. His counter-claim is that pain statements are necessarily about something private, and that being about something private is incompatible with being about something physical. Baier specifies what 'private' means as follows. That which is private is:

(i)   *necessarily owned*: i.e. there cannot be pain which is not someone's pain (or at least the pain of a sentient being). It is nonsensical to assert that there can be a pain which is not someone's pain;

(ii) *necessarily exclusive or unsharable*: two people cannot have numerically the same pain;

(iii) *necessarily imperceptible by the senses*: I cannot see, hear, touch, taste or smell my pains or anyone else's;

(iv) *necessarily asymmetrical in respect of mode of awareness*: I am aware of my own pains immediately, whereas I must interpret the behaviour of others to work out that they are in pain.

(v)   *such that whoever has the pain has ultimate authority regarding it*: I cannot be wrong about whether I am in pain; nor can someone else's

> statements override mine on such a matter. In respect of having a pain, the speaker has a way of coming to know about it which is not open to others.
>
> Accordingly, Baier claims, a pain-statement, which is about something private in this sense, cannot be about something which is also public, and so pain statements are not topic-neutral as Smart has claimed.

This seems to me a serious problem for the identity theory, notably in respect of properties (iii), (iv) and (v): these are properties which pains have because they are *conscious* phenomena. It has proved extremely difficult to make out a convincing case for the view that brain processes can have these properties, and if they do not then, by Leibniz's Law, it follows that whatever the relation between brain processes and sensations might be, it is not one of identity. The consequence of this is that the claim of strict identity for sensations and brain processes would have to be given up, and that then generates a further question as to whether the theory can be modified and yet remain an identity theory. We will return to this point in the conclusion of this section on the identity theory.

OBJECTION 7, PARAGRAPHS 27–30

Now read paragraphs 27–30.

Reading
p. 189

EXERCISE 3.14

How is the objection in paragraph 27 intended to show that the identity theory is false, and how does Smart reply?

SPECIMEN ANSWER

The objection is a way of making the assertion that our *concept* of consciousness does not include the concept of brain processes since, if it did, we would find it impossible even to imagine being turned to stone and yet having sensations. Smart's reply once again makes use of Frege's sense/reference distinction.

The line of reply is that the objection establishes only that s-statements and bp-statements do not mean the same thing, but this goes no way at all to establishing what the objector wants to establish, namely that these types of statements *refer* to different things.

OBJECTION 8, PARAGRAPHS 31–3

This final objection is of some complexity, and so rather than set an exercise on it I will try instead to show what philosophical difficulty concerns Smart here and how he tries to get around the problem. The logical structure of the objection is this: the objector is saying that the identity theory entails a consequence which is false and, therefore, that by elementary logic, it follows that the identity theory itself must be false.

Now read paragraphs 31–3.

Reading
p. 189

The first question then is: What is the allegedly false consequence the identity theory is claimed to entail? The consequence the objector has in mind is (once again) a linguistic one: it follows from the identity theory that s-statements are genuine reports. That is, s-statements report the occurrence of genuine events. Why should it be thought that this is false? The answer Smart has in mind is that this consequence is precisely what is denied by one of the most discussed arguments in the whole area of language and the mind – the so-called private language argument put forward by Ludwig Wittgenstein (1889–1951) in his *Philosophical Investigations* (1953). The passage to which Smart refers in paragraph 32 is as follows:

> If I say of myself that it is only from my own case that I know what the word 'pain' means – must I not say the same of other people too? And how can I generalize the *one* case so irresponsibly?
>
> Now someone tells me that he knows what pain is only from his own case! – Suppose everyone had a box with something in it: we call it a 'beetle'. No one can look into anyone else's box, and everyone says he knows what a beetle is by looking at his beetle. – Here it would be quite possible for everyone to have something different in his box. One might even imagine such a thing constantly changing – But suppose the word 'beetle' had a use in these people's language? – If so it would not be used as the name of a thing … That is to say: if we construe the grammar of the expression of sensation on the model of 'object and designation' the object drops out of consideration as irrelevant.
>
> (Wittgenstein 1949, Part I: 293)

Wittgenstein's argument can be summed up as follows:

P1   Languages are rule-governed structures.
P2   If a language were wholly private, i.e. such that its rules were known only to one person, there could not be a distinction between following the rules and failing to follow them, since there could be no way of checking whether the rules had been followed.
P3   A language without testable rules is not a language.
C1   Therefore, there cannot be a private language.

This argument is certainly valid, but its soundness has been extensively debated, the debate being focussed on the truth, or otherwise, of P2. For present purposes, we do not need to pursue the issue further here. All we need do is grasp the implications of this argument, assuming it to be sound, for the philosophy of mind. We have noted several times already that theories of language and of the mind are intimately linked, and there is no more striking example of this than the private language issue. It has been widely assumed in philosophy that s-statements are logically similar, or have a comparable logical grammar, to physical object statements. That is, it has generally been assumed that s-statements are statements which refer to events, just as do physical object statements, with the difference that the events referred to happen to be private. The private language argument entails that this must be false since such utterances would constitute a private language. It follows that whatever first-person s-statements might look like – i.e. however similar in terms of grammatical construction they may look to statements concerning physical events – they cannot be genuine reports of private mental goings-on at all.

Smart's reply is to assume for the purposes of argument that the private language argument is sound, but to deny that he is committed to the view that s-statements are genuine reports of private events. He repeats his assertion, made in reply to objection 3 above, to the effect that these statements are topic neutral, i.e. they do not contain any assertion as to the nature of what they are about.

CONCLUDING PARAGRAPHS 34 AND 35

Reading
p. 190

Now read paragraphs 34 and 35.

Here, Smart addresses the so far unraised question of what he terms the 'logical status' of the identity theory. By this he means whether the identity theory is a wholly empirical theory or whether it is in part a conceptual theory. In the present context, a wholly empirical theory is one whose acceptability will depend solely on the evidence of neuroscience as it advances to ever more precise knowledge of brain functions. If a theory is partly conceptual, then among the reasons for its acceptance or rejection will be features such as its 'parsimony and simplicity', as he puts it; this is another way of asking whether the theory satisfies rules for theory construction such as Occam's razor. He concludes that the identity theory is partly conceptual: the philosopher faced with a choice between dualism and monism, provided each theory is equally consistent with the facts, will choose monism on the grounds of its greater simplicity.

CONCLUDING REMARKS ON THE IDENTITY THEORY

One of the difficulties involved in close reading of philosophical texts is that one can become so taken up with the fine detail of the logic of individual arguments and objections that one loses sight of the overall picture, and it is always useful, every so often, to take a step back and see what general direction, if any, the argument overall has taken. Let me try to sum up what our detailed investigation of Smart's arguments has shown about the identity theory.

Smart's thesis is that certain mental events (sensations) are identical with certain physical events (brain processes). His way of advocating this theory is to summarize it, and then to state the objections made against it and to reply to them. His ultimate reason for advocating a materialist theory of the mind is that it would avoid an anomaly in the otherwise entirely materialistic view of nature furnished by science: dualistic views, he argues, violate Occam's razor.

A number of the objections he considers turn on the assertion that sensations and brain processes cannot be identical because s-statements and bp-statements do not *mean* the same thing. I would argue that Smart, by using Frege's distinction between the meaning of a statement and what it refers to, shows that these objections are without force. He is less successful, in my view, in dealing with objections which rely on Leibniz's Law and assert an asymmetry of *properties* between brain processes and sensations. He does not seem to me to have shown how a brain process can have the quality of pain, for example, of which I am aware as a sensation.

There remains a further problem for the identity theory which has not come up in any form in our discussion of Smart's paper. The problem I have in mind has the daunting name of the multiple realizability of mental states, but it is much less complex than this form of words suggests. This objection to the identity theory begins with a thought experiment: imagine an alien with a biology based not on carbon (as is human biology) but on another element, say, silicon (a plentiful element in the universe). It is highly likely that such a being would have evolved the capacity to feel pain, one of the functions of which is to warn us of bodily damage. It follows from the hypothesis that this being is silicon-based that whatever its neural or brain process equivalent of pain is must be different from the human brain process, since it is a state of a silicon-based brain not of a carbon-based brain. It follows further that the sensation of pain can therefore be realized in more than one kind of neurological system. Now the version of the identity theory we have been considering involves a presupposition which has not so far been made explicit, and which is made explicit by a consideration of this objection. This presupposition is that any given type of sensation (say, pain) is identical with a given type of brain process (say, the firing of c-fibres). What the objection from multiple realizability shows is that this cannot be sustained. The point the objection makes is that it is logically possible that the same sensation could be identical with different types of brain process, carbon- or silicon-based as the case may be, and so it is necessary to modify the identity theory so that it embodies a weaker form of identity claim. The weaker claim is that individual sensations (called in a technical sense of the word *tokens*) are identical with individual brain processes which may be of different types. Smart's version of the identity theory is accordingly called a type/type identity theory; the modified version is called a token/token identity theory.

Despite the resourcefulness, inventiveness and ingenuity of identity theorists like Smart, the objections we have considered above have caused many philosophers to seek a different account of the mind, though still within the framework of materialism. Broadly speaking, there have been two major alternatives to the identity theory in recent decades. One of the major sources of difficulty for the identity theory is the problem of the multiple realizability of mental states, and this notion of multiple realizability is one of the central factors motivating the next philosophy of mind we will examine, called functionalism. There are many variants of the view, but common to them all is the assertion that the mind is best understood in terms of its functional role in the economy of the individual. Put another way, functionalists hold that what is distinctive about the mind is its function.

A second serious type of objection to the identity theory, as we have seen, arises from apparent asymmetries of properties between mental events and brain processes, e.g. over the privacy and subjectivity of pains as opposed to the public nature of brain processes. Privacy and subjectivity are features of the way in which we ordinarily talk about our mental lives: they are embedded in what we may call our *folk psychology*. One response to this problem is to say that this way of speaking about the mind is not at all the fixed point it is taken to be and that the progress of neuroscience will inexorably lead to its complete elimination. It is held to be radically misleading as a description of our mental life, and destined for the lumber-room of discredited scientific explanations, along with the geocentric conception of the universe and the phlogiston theory of combustion. This is the central contention of the philosophy of mind called eliminativism or eliminative materialism. We will now examine each of these views in turn.

FUNCTIONALISM

At the time of writing, functionalism is the most widely held view in the philosophy of mind. To be absolutely accurate, functionalism is a view of the mind which is designed to be *compatible* with materialism: it is logically possible to be a functionalist and to be an idealist or a dualist, but it is certainly the case that the modern functionalism we are going to discuss is advanced in the context of a general adherence to materialism. Functionalism exists in a variety of different versions and can trace its philosophical pedigree back to Aristotle (cf. Smith and Jones 1986: 177 seqq.), though we will be concerned here with only one very central version of it. However, we will also look at some objections relevant not only to this version but to many others as well.

However complicated it may become in its technically advanced versions, the basic assertion of functionalism is not difficult to understand and it is easiest to grasp it if we compare functionalism to Cartesian dualism in one particular respect. Though the point has not been made explicitly so far, you will notice that when Descartes thinks about the mind, the fundamental assumption he makes is that it is a sort of *thing* and the fundamental question he is asks himself is: What sort of thing is it? Is it an extended thing or a non-extended thing? In functionalism, the emphasis is different and it is not assumed that when we speak of the mind, despite the fact that we use the noun 'mind', we are speaking of a thing – an individual entity of some kind – at all: rather, the focus of interest are the questions: What does the mind *do*? What is its function in the complex whole we call an individual? In considering these questions, functionalists have concluded that what is *distinctive* about the mind and its states – or, put another way, what it is that makes a mental state *mental* rather than physical – is its *function*. One must be careful not to overstress the contrast with Cartesianism: Descartes does have things to say about the function of various mental states, and indeed it would be very odd if he did not, but he is not inclined to identify the *nature* of the mind with its *function*.

Before we approach our example of a functionalist text, we need to dwell for a moment on the concept of function, and try to make it a bit more concrete. Functionalists generally prefer to talk about mental states rather than the mind, and in this we can follow them for the moment. Their central claim, put in this vocabulary, is that a mental state is a functional state, i.e. that what is distinctive about a *mental* state is that it has a characteristic function. A functional state, they claim, is a state consisting in a disposition to act in certain ways, and to have certain other mental states, granted that I have certain inputs from my senses, and certain other mental states, notably my beliefs and memories of what the world is like (cf. Block 1978: 268; Churchland 1988: 36 seqq.). We can see better what this means with an example. Suppose that in the course of a country walk I have come to a stream that I have to get across, and I have to work out whether and how I can do so: this process of reflection is a mental process. When I reflect, I am in a mental state. A functionalist would analyse the situation as follows: my reflection on the situation is triggered by sensory stimuli: I see the stream; see the stepping stones across it; see how fast the water is running after the recent rain (which I remember, having been in it); see how deep it is; look to see if the stones are slippery or whether their surface looks as if it will give a good purchase; and finally decide, on the basis of my past experience of comparable situations, that it is safe to use the stones to cross. The mental state of reflection or making up my mind is brought about, first, by information supplied by my senses. Second, it involves quite a number of other mental states, which we can sum up as remembering past experience, and, third, making a judgement. Finally, it tends to result in behaviour, in this case crossing the stream by using the stepping stones. One can put this point also as the claim that what makes a mental state *mental* is that it has a particular *causal role* in bringing about behaviour in the context of a given set of sensory information and standing beliefs about the way the world is. What makes the mental mental, the functionalist claims, is not what it is made of, but what it *does*.

This way of conceiving mental states does have a number of undeniable advantages. Notably, it is coherent with a number of important scientific claims, especially those arising from the perspective on the human individual furnished by evolutionism. From the point of view of evolutionism, the mind and the brain with which it is associated came about first as the result of a process of random mutation, and they continued in existence because they have a survival value; creatures that have a mind–brain survive better than those that don't. The mind–brain has a survival value because it helps us deal more successfully with the environment in which we find ourselves and on which we depend. The mind–brain, in this perspective, has as its primary *raison d'être* the bringing about of behaviour appropriate to the circumstances in which we happen to find ourselves. For the evolutionist, appropriate modification of behaviour is precisely what the mind–brain is for.

Further, many scientists, especially those involved in work on artificial intelligence (as we will see later in this book), are unhappy with any view of what constitutes a mind which would restrict possession of it to only one type of biochemical entity, namely the type that has our sort of grey matter. If there are aliens out there somewhere, or if we manage to make a machine we are all agreed has a mind, it is highly unlikely that the hardware with which that mind is associated (to put the relationship no more precisely than that) will be biochemically identical to or even like ours — an oxygen-fuelled, neuronally-organized, multi-layered brain.

EXERCISE 3.15

FUNCTIONALISM AND EVOLUTION

Can you see why functionalism appeals to thinkers with these concerns?

SPECIMEN ANSWER

The central claim of functionalism is that the nature of mental states is to be identified with the function they have in affecting behaviour. Any state which affects behaviour in the appropriate way is a mental state: functionalism makes no stipulations at all about the biochemical or other hardware needed for the realization of these states.

DISCUSSION

Functionalists standardly phrase this point using the terms we came across above in dealing with objections to the identity theory, namely: functional states are *multiply realizable*, i.e. mental states can be realized in many different sorts of hardware. I have italicized this phrase only because it comes up regularly in discussions of functionalism.

We will now go on to examine a functionalist text in more detail, a piece written by the American philosopher Sydney Shoemaker (b. 1931). Shoemaker's procedure is analogous to that of Descartes and Smart: he states his position, and then, much as Descartes does in his *Objections and Replies* and Smart in the paper you have just read, considers the main objections which other philosophers have made to it. One last general point before we examine the text: many of the objections to functionalism take the form of what are termed thought experiments. Some of these may seem at first sight to be well into the realm of the fanciful. The point to bear in mind when evaluating thought experiments is this: a large part of the business of philosophers is the making of assertions about the meaning and logical relations of the very general concepts which are the framework of our thought. The intention behind a thought experiment is to show that a given claim about some important concept cannot be sustained: the apparent far-fetchedness, even whimsicality, of some of the scenarios advanced in these experiments should not deflect us from the seriousness of the logical point they are seeking to make.

 Reading p. 193

Now read the first paragraph of Shoemaker's essay 'The mind–body problem' (Reading 6).

EXERCISE 3.16

FUNCTIONALISM AND THE MIND–BODY PROBLEM

1 How does Shoemaker understand the mind–body problem?
2 Into what two sub-problems does he divide it?

SPECIMEN ANSWER

1 The mind–body problem is the problem of how the mind is to be understood on the assumption that reality is 'fundamentally physical'.
2 The first sub-problem is how to deal with 'Cartesian intuitions' about the mind, and the second how to deal with key features of the mental – intentionality (a term we will discuss shortly), consciousness, subjectivity, etc. – making the same basic assumption that reality is 'fundamentally physical'.

DISCUSSION

We need to pause for a moment to weigh these assertions. When introducing the concept of materialistic monism at the start of this section, I said that a major task for the materialist in the philosophy of mind is to show how the central features of the mental can be accounted for on the assumption that all there is in the universe is material in nature, and Shoemaker is here saying much the same thing. (You will see that Shoemaker takes care to reiterate this point in his final summary of his point in paragraph 9.) Just why this is a major task and why it is so difficult is something that will only become clear as we go along and see the materialist story unfold.

Now read paragraph 2 of Shoemaker's essay 'The mind–body problem' (Reading 6).

Reading
p. 193

EXERCISE 3.17

COMPATIBILITY OF FUNCTIONALISM

In paragraph 2, Shoemaker says that functionalism is compatible with two other philosophical assertions or positions. Can you say which they are?

SPECIMEN ANSWER

Shoemaker asserts that functionalism is compatible with (a) materialism and

(b) the Cartesian intuition that any given mental state cannot be *identical* with any physical state.

DISCUSSION

The term 'compatible' is a key one in philosophy: to say that two views or the statements in which they are expressed are compatible is to assert that both can be true at the same time. For example, the statement 'I am a married man' is compatible with the assertion 'I am constantly in debt' but incompatible with the assertion 'I am a bachelor', where this last refers to the same period of time as the first. Assertions that major positions are compatible are usually of the first importance in philosophical arguments and should be examined with the greatest care. The first such assertion that Shoemaker makes in this paragraph – that functionalism is compatible with materialism in the philosophy of mind – is a very large claim indeed and is one which has not gone unchallenged, but we are not yet, at the outset of our examination of materialism, in a position to evaluate it. Let us concentrate for the moment on his second compatibility claim: namely, that functionalism is compatible with the Cartesian intuition that a mental state cannot be identical with any specific physical (or 'material' – remember these terms are interchangeable) state.

EXERCISE 3.18

FUNCTIONALISM AND CARTESIAN INTUITION

Bearing in mind Descartes' views on the nature of mental and physical substance, can you see why the claim that a mental state cannot be identical with any physical state should be described as a 'Cartesian intuition'?

SPECIMEN ANSWER

Because this claim is a logical consequence of Descartes' views. Mental and material substances, Descartes argues, have different natures or essences, and therefore no mental state can be identical to a physical state, or vice versa.

DISCUSSION

We need to pause to try to see why, right at the start of his exposition, Shoemaker should want to point out that functionalism and this assertion are compatible, and, just as importantly, why it is philosophically desirable that they should be compatible. To answer these questions, we need a bit of philosophical analysis and a bit of recent philosophical history.

The philosophical analysis concerns the concept of identity, a key term in the assertion we are considering. In order to appreciate the force and magnitude of the claim Shoemaker is making here, we need to remind ourselves of what it means to say of two things that they are identical with each other. As we saw in our investigation of the identity theory, most philosophers accept that the standard analysis of the concept of identity is to be found in the work of Leibniz, and it is summed up in a principle referred to as Leibniz's Law: for any A and any B, if they are identical, then whatever is true of A is also true of B, and vice versa. We have already seen how this law can be used to frame powerful objections to the identity theory.

Shoemaker also has in mind here, in this second paragraph, the further very powerful objection urged against the identity theory, called the objection from multiple realizability. You will recall that the basic version of the identity theory asserts that every individual sensation is identical with an individual brain state. This has the consequence that only beings constituted with our sort grey matter can have sensations, i.e. since sensations and brain states are identical, it follows that only creatures with our sort of brain can have them. As we noted above at the start of this section, this has seemed to many philosophers an unduly restrictive consequence. To repeat: suppose there are aliens out there whom we might wish to describe as being intelligent and as having minds, or suppose we do one day manage to make a machine we are willing to describe in the same way, in either case it is very improbable indeed that the hardware – the 'brain', if you like – with which this mind is associated will be a carbon-based, oxygen-fuelled system such as ours. In the face of considerations such as this, philosophers have generally adopted it as a requirement of philosophies of mind that they are conceptually accommodating enough to allow us to say that beings physiologically very different from ourselves can also be said to have minds. Put another way, philosophies of mind have to allow that mental states can be realized in more than one sort of physical hardware, not just our sort of grey gook. This is what is meant by the claim that mental states are multiply realizable: more than one sort of physical basis for mental states is possible.

With this in mind we can now see why Shoemaker should be keen to make these compatibility claims for functionalism right at the start of his essay. Functionalism was evolved in part to improve on the identity theory (and dualism), and so has to be able to avoid the difficulties to which these other views are liable. Because functionalism identifies the nature of the mental not with any kind of substance, non-extended or extended, but with the *function* of mental states, it is on the face of it compatible with materialism because (as we noted above) it is neutral on the issue of what kind of stuff the mind is made of. Further, and for the same reason, it can happily allow for multiple realizability: it can accommodate whatever hardware allows the same *functions* to be performed, from grey gook to microchips.

Now read paragraph 3 of Shoemaker's essay 'The mind–body problem' (Reading 6).

Reading
p. 194

In this paragraph, Shoemaker asserts that his version of functionalism is a 'radically "nonreductive" version of materialism'. He is making use of a key concept here used in many branches of philosophy, namely, that of *reduction*, and we need to be clear as to what this means before we can proceed. (It will come up again in the next section, when we look at the eliminativist theory of mind.) This is a technical use of the term, and its sense in philosophy bears only a tangential relation to its ordinary use, i.e. 'to diminish'.

In the present context, and in the philosophy of science, reduction or its reverse is a relation between two theories or two types of discourse (e.g. the ordinary everyday discourse we use to describe our mental life and the discourse of neurophysiology). A theory or type of discourse *x* can be reduced to another *y* if every event and entity in *x* can be *completely* redescribed in terms of the concepts of *y*. The paradigm instance of the *reduction* in this sense of one theory to another is that of the reduction of thermodynamics to mechanics. Thermodynamics described the phenomenon of heat. Heat was regarded as a substance whose tendency was to move from hot bodies to cold ones, the rate of transference depending on the constitution of the bodies concerned. Classical or Newtonian mechanics was concerned with the effect of bodies on one another, whether in motion or at rest. However, when it was discovered that bodies are composed of atoms, it became possible to redescribe heat completely in terms of the agitation of atoms, and every phenomenon previously regarded as the province of thermodynamics became completely describable in terms of the atomic theory of matter. In this case, thermodynamics is said, in this technical sense of the term, to have been reduced to the latter branch of science.

This same concept of reduction is also used in the philosophy of mind, and you will regularly find such philosophies classified into those which are reductive and those which are non-reductive, together with a great deal of argument about whether the claims of some given theory to be reductive or not can be sustained. Typically, the debate concerns the issue of whether a given theory reduces (in this sense) the mind to matter or not. Remember that, in this technical sense of the term, what this means is that, if a given theory of mind is reductive, it includes the view that all mental phenomena can be completely redescribed in terms of material phenomena, and that in this redescription, no aspect of the mental (mental causation and subjectivity included) is left out, but can be completely redescribed in materialistic terms. The logical pressure to design a reductionist theory of the mind has been intensely felt. To repeat an important point made earlier: it has seemed to many that, unless such a reduction can be carried out, the realm of the mental is in danger of staying stubbornly outside the realm of matter, and so of preventing the construction of a unified theory of all there is in materialistic terms. Had the mind–brain identity theory been sustainable, it would have gone a long way towards satisfying this need. All this makes it clear why Shoemaker should feel the need to state unequivocally his own position on the question of reduction.

EXERCISE 3.19

FUNCTIONALISM AND REDUCTION

What is Shoemaker's position on the issue of reduction?

SPECIMEN ANSWER

Shoemaker states that his version of functionalism is *non*-reductive. He holds a materialist view of the world, but he does not accept that mental phenomena as conceived in our ordinary common-sense way can be made to correspond to physical phenomena in the way required for there to be a reduction of the former to the latter.

DISCUSSION

1   You will note that Shoemaker concludes this paragraph by saying that, although mental phenomena cannot be reduced to physical phenomena (in particular he has in mind brain states), there is a relationship between them, which he describes as 'compositional'. By this he means much the same as by saying that mental events are realized or implemented in physical systems (cf. paragraph 2): this is a way of saying that the mental requires the physical in order to exist – which is a consequence of materialism – but in a way which commits him neither to any form of dualism nor to reductive materialism.

2   This paragraph, in effect, completes Shoemaker's outline of the functionalist theory he regards as the best currently available in the philosophy of mind: a mental state is to be defined in terms of its causal relations to inputs (sensory stimuli), outputs (behaviour) and to other mental states. This view is claimed to be compatible with materialism, but is not reductive, i.e. it does not include the claim that mental phenomena can be reduced to physical ones.

For the rest of his paper, he is concerned to fill out this short exposition by considering and replying to the chief objections which are brought forward against his view.

Now read paragraph 4 of Shoemaker's essay 'The mind–body problem' (Reading 6).

Reading
p. 194

In paragraph 4, Shoemaker introduces a term we have not so far come across, but which is of central importance in the philosophy of mind, the concept of *intentionality*. Before we can see how crucial an objection to his own view Shoemaker has raised here, we need to spend some time on working out just what this term means.

Philosophers, especially in recent decades, have tended to use a synonym for the term 'intentionality' which gives a hint as to what both these terms mean: that synonym is *aboutness*. The idea behind both terms owes its current prominence to the German philosopher and psychologist Franz Brentano (1838–1917). Brentano was trying to find a single property which is common to all mental phenomena – and only mental, as opposed to physical – and the property he fastened on is this: all mental phenomena, in his view, have an object, i.e. they are always *about* something. Take any type of mental content you like, and they all display this property. For example, I never just want, I always want *something*; I never just fear, I always fear somebody or something; I never merely believe, I always believe that something is or is not so; I never just love or hate, I always love or hate somebody; I never just see (hear, taste, smell, touch), I always see (etc.) something. Any mental state whatever, Brentano contends, has this property of having an object, and it is this property which, following a usage from mediaeval logic, he calls intentionality. (In its mediaeval usage, this term just means 'directedness to an object or content'.) Some philosophers argue that in fact some mental contents do not have this feature, notably pains, which they contend have no object. There is not space here to pursue this line of thought. For the moment we can note that, even if it is true, a great many mental contents, which the materialist has to account for, *do* have this property.

We need to grasp two more points about intentionality or aboutness before going on to see why it is so serious a problem for materialist theories of the mind. The first of these is that, in this technical sense, intentionality has nothing particularly to do with the class of mental contents we call intentions – our intention to do this or abstain from doing that. Intentions, like all other mental contents, have the property of intentionality: I never just intend, I always intend to do or not do something. Intentions always have a content or object. But they are not in any way special among mental contents; in a way the word 'intentionality', so similar to 'intention', is unfortunate, making it look as if Brentano must mean that intentions are in some way a specially important type of mental content, but this is not so. The more recent term 'aboutness' avoids this misunderstanding, and it is this term which I will generally use for the rest of this book to refer to this property of mental contents.

The second important point concerns the objects which the mental contents are about. As Brentano points out, there need be nothing in the real world that corresponds to these mental objects: I can wish to be in a situation which never comes about or which perhaps could never come about, e.g. I might wish not to age; or I can believe that certain things are so when they are not; I can be mistaken in what I perceive (i.e. have a hallucination), and so on. It follows that these mental objects which are the contents or objects of my thoughts, beliefs, sensations, emotions, wishes (and so on) need to be described in a special way which does not imply that there need be anything in the real world which corresponds to them. Brentano makes this point by saying that these mental objects have what he calls inexistence. By this he does not mean that they are *non*-existent: what he is driving at is that these mental objects exist *within* my thoughts: hence *in*existence (cf. Brentano (1995) [1874]: 88–9).

The next point to master is why aboutness is such a serious problem for those wishing to put forward a materialist theory of the mind or, like Shoemaker, those putting forward a theory meant to be compatible with it. What these philosophers have to do is to give an account of intentionality or aboutness wholly in materialist terms. Put another way: How do you give an account of aboutness in terms which make no reference outside the realm of the purely material? As we have seen, it is a property of mental states that they have a content, that they are about something. All materialists agree that these mental states are realized in some sort of hardware, in the human case the brain: the problem is that it does not look likely that states of the brain – sets of neuronal firings – can meaningfully be said to be about anything. The same objection can be made to the states of any other sort of hardware, say a set of microprocessors. How can a set of on and off states of an electrical circuit be about anything? Note that this is a conceptual problem not an empirical one; it doesn't matter how complex the states or arrangements of matter might be: the issue is that states of matter just do not look as if they are even candidates for being about anything else. Take an example: from my window I can see four elm trees. Looked at from one point of view, they are each very complicated atomic structures; but it seems hardly even to make sense to assert that their complex atomic arrangements are *about* anything, and it is the fact that this idea doesn't make sense which indicates that we have a conceptual problem here. It is not that arrangements of matter, however complex, have a content we just don't understand yet – it is that they are not the right type of things to have a content at all, just as (to take another example) it makes no sense to ask what colour the number three has because numbers are not the right sort of things to have colours.

Now to adopt a materialist view of the world entails accepting the idea that everything there is – including the mind and all its properties – can ultimately be accounted for in terms of matter and its properties, and I hope it is now becoming clear why aboutness is, on the face of it, so serious an issue for those wishing to adopt a materialist view. If states of matter, brain states included, do not have content because they are not the right sort of things to have a content, and if having a content is a central property of the realm of the mental, then it follows that the realm of the mental has at least one type of property which cannot be accounted for in materialist terms, and from this it will follow that materialism, insofar as it claims to be an account of *everything* there is, is false. Aboutness, therefore, is as serious a problem for materialists, it seems, as is interaction for a two-substance dualist, and so Shoemaker has to say something about it.

Shoemaker goes on in paragraph 4 to refer to some attempts which have been made to solve this problem, by trying to show that intentionality can be fully redescribed in terms of causal relations: causal relations are a leading feature of the material world, and so if such a line of analysis could be made to work it would show that aboutness could be a property of matter. (This is what he means by the attempt to 'naturalize' intentionality, i.e. to make it part of the scientifically describable order of nature.) Shoemaker has to admit, however, that none of these attempts at the naturalization of aboutness has won general acceptance: intentionality remains a problem for materialism.

As you might expect, granted how important a feature of the mental it is, there is more to be said concerning aboutness, and about the closely related concept of having meaning (or as philosophers often say, having semantic properties): both these ideas are going to come up quite regularly from this point on.

Rather than deal with paragraph 5 now, I suggest we come back to it in conjunction with paragraphs 8 seqq., with which it forms a neater sequence. I want to turn next instead to paragraphs 6 and 7 where Shoemaker addresses one of the most testing sets of objections made against functionalism. They all make use of a notion we have met briefly in the context of the identity theory, that of *qualia*: this is a plural noun, the singular being *quale* (two syllables: qua-lay). It is now appropriate to dwell more closely on this concept.

Now read paragraphs 6 and 7 of Shoemaker's essay 'The mind–body problem' (Reading 6).

Reading
p. 195

EXERCISE 3.20

QUALIA

On the basis of the opening of paragraph 6, up to 'a certain causal role' at the end of the second sentence, say in your own words what you understand by the term 'qualia'.

SPECIMEN ANSWER

Qualia are what I am directly and immediately aware of in my conscious experience. For example, when I see a colour, I have a quale of precisely that colour then; and the same is true of sounds, smells, tastes and sensations of touch. Analogously, bodily sensations – pains, itches, tickles, and so on – have a quality each their own and this quality is their quale. What makes my sensation a sensation of redness of shade x is the quale I experience of redness of shade x.

DISCUSSION

Shoemaker goes on in paragraph 6 to mention two objections to functionalism which make central use of the concept of qualia. They are called the knowledge argument and the spectrum inversion argument, the latter also being referred to sometimes as the inverted qualia argument. We will begin our investigation of qualia by looking at these in turn, and then look at some other problems which turn on this concept.

THE KNOWLEDGE ARGUMENT

As Shoemaker notes, this argument is associated chiefly with the philosopher Frank Jackson (in his essays 'Epiphenomenal Qualia' (1982) and 'What Mary didn't know' (1986) (also discussed in Braddon-Mitchell and Jackson 1996: 127 sqq.)) and to some degree with Thomas Nagel's essay 'What is it like to be a bat?' (1974).

The knowledge argument, which begins with a thought experiment, goes as follows. We are to imagine Mary, a brilliant neuroscientist. Mary spends her life in a world in which the only colours are black and white. She has a black and white TV and a library of books all with illustrations and covers in black and white. From these sources Mary learns everything there is to know about physics and neuroscience, and consequently knows all there is to know about the functions of our mental states. She knows that the colour of some roses and of blood is red and knows when she and others will appropriately use the English sentence 'That is red', and so on, for all the colours other than black and white. From the functionalist point of view, Mary acts precisely as does anyone else when required to make colour discriminations and knows the complete functional characterizations of colour-seeing states. However, it is clear that in one respect (the objection goes) her experience is importantly different from that of anyone brought up in a normally coloured environment: she does not know what it is like to see red, or indeed any colour other than black or white. If Mary is allowed to go into a normally coloured environment, there is something she will learn, namely, what it is like to see red (and all the other colours).

EXERCISE 3.21

FUNCTIONALISM AND QUALIA

Can you see why this argument presents a problem for the functionalist?

SPECIMEN ANSWER

The central assertion of functionalism is that what is distinctive about any mental state is its functional role; the aim of the knowledge argument is to show that this assertion must be false, because mental states can be identical with respect to their function but different with respect to their qualia. Mary's mental states while in her monochrome world are functionally identical to the mental states of anyone in the normal polychrome world – for example, the experiences of both would result in correct behavioural responses (e.g. use of sentences such as 'That is red'). Yet Mary's mental states lack the quale of redness which is a feature of the visual experience of redness of normally sighted people in the normal polychrome world. Therefore, the functionalist account of what is distinctive of mental states leaves out something about them of great importance, namely that they are characterized by their qualia.

DISCUSSION

You will note that at the end of paragraph 7, Shoemaker states that he believes the functionalist can produce a reply to this objection, though he does not produce it here. Without wishing to attribute it to Shoemaker, I will now set out a reply which has been made to the knowledge argument (*cf.*, for example, Lewis 1990). This turns on a distinction often used in epistemology and the philosophy of mind, the distinction between knowing how and knowing that: we will return to this distinction at more length at the start of Chapter 4 in the context of our investigation of artificial intelligence. 'Knowledge that' is knowledge which is statable in the form of propositions and tells us something about the world. 'Knowledge how' is an ability, which we manifest in being able to do certain things. For example, I can know all there is to know propositionally about the contents of manuals on how to drive a car without knowing how to drive a car and conversely, like most people, I know how to drive a car while being in considerable ignorance of a great deal of the possible propositional knowledge concerning driving. Using this distinction, the reply states that what Mary learns when she emerges into the normally coloured environment is knowledge how, not knowledge that: for instance, she gains the ability to *imagine* redness, which she couldn't do in her black and white environment.

I myself am not convinced by this reply: when she sees real red for the first time, there is something she learns which is propositional in nature: she learns what things actually look like. Mary can only imagine redness (or any colour other than black or white) because she now has a memory of what it is like to see redness, a memory she could not have before she had actually seen the colour red.

There is more to be said about the knowledge argument (see Braddon-Mitchell and Jackson 1996), but we do not have the space here to go into all the details which are necessary for an exhaustive investigation. Even if a reply can be found, the functionalist has a further difficulty to deal with, which is the next argument we will consider.

THE SPECTRUM INVERSION OR INVERTED QUALIA ARGUMENT

Once again, this argument begins from a thought experiment. Suppose there are twins, James and John, identical in every respect but one: when James sees a ripe tomato he has a visual experience of red exactly as does any normally sighted person. However, when John sees a ripe tomato, he has the visual experience a normally sighted person would call the experience of green, and this difference repeats itself systematically throughout his experience of colours. When James sees a given colour, John sees its complementary. This systematic difference (the argument goes) would not manifest itself in any behavioural differences between the twins, including verbal behaviour. John uses all colour words exactly as does James and makes all the same moves as his brother when colour is the main cue for behaviour, e.g. at traffic lights. It follows from the premises of functionalism that, since their mental states have exactly the same causal relations to their behaviour, these mental experiences are functionally equivalent. However, the objection concludes, they are importantly different in respect of their qualia, and so functionalism is incomplete as an account of the nature of mental experiences.

In paragraph 7, you will note that Shoemaker gives a very brief outline of a reply to this argument, attempting to establish that the notion of a quale is itself a functional one. Even if he can prove this, however, there is a further and more radical objection to functionalism, not mentioned here by Shoemaker, but since it too involves the notion of qualia, it is best considered at this point in our investigation.

THE ABSENT QUALIA OR CHINA BRAIN ARGUMENT

This is an argument developed by the American philosopher Ned Block (see, in particular, his 1978). Once again we begin with a thought experiment.

Suppose the government of China is converted to functionalism, and they are persuaded that it will add enormously to their international prestige if they use their entire population – let us say of one billion people – to act for one hour as does a human brain. Each person performs the function of one neurone, communicating with other individuals/neurones via radio to an artificial body which will manifest human behaviour when the network of individuals, the China brain, makes the right set of interconnections among themselves. No doubt this system will operate at a speed vastly slower than the normal human brain, but remember that functionalism includes no stipulations about speed of operation. Nor is it absurd to suppose that the artificial body is connected to the China brain by radio – perhaps in the future human brains could be removed for restoration while being connected in this way.

The objection goes on as follows. The China brain functions exactly as does a normal human brain, its constituent individuals acting as do individual neurones in a normal brain. Therefore, the system of the China brain is functionally equivalent to a normal brain, but there is absolutely no reason to suppose that the China brain (as opposed to the individuals who compose it) experiences qualia at all. It follows from the premises of functionalism that the China brain must have mental states, since it is functionally indistinguishable from a normal brain. Therefore, functionalism attributes mental states to systems to which intuitively we would wish to deny them, since we are intuitively unhappy about attributing mental states to systems which do not have qualia at all as an aspect of their experience.

Philosophers of mind often put this last point by saying that functionalism is guilty of what is called, in a technical sense of the term, *liberalism*: this means that the theory of the mind in question allows too many entities into the class of those that have minds. The contrary defect is called, again in a technical sense of the term, *chauvinism*: a philosophy of mind is chauvinistic if it unduly restricts the types of entity which may be allowed to have minds. The basic version of the mind–brain identity theory we considered in the preceding section above was regarded as chauvinistic in this sense, since it restricted the possession of minds to entities with our sort of brain. These two complementary faults are the poles, as it were, between which philosophies of mind have to steer.

We have spent long enough for the present on the notion of qualia, and it is clear that the advocates of functionalism will need to provide convincing replies to these and similar objections using this concept. Qualia are an unignorable aspect of mental life, and no philosophy of mind is going to be satisfactory which does not give them due consideration.

It is appropriate now to return to Shoemaker's essay, looking at paragraph 5 in conjunction with paragraph 8. In these two paragraphs, he considers some further difficulties for functionalism.

 Reading pp. 195,196

Now read paragraphs 5 and 8 of Shoemaker's essay 'The mind–body problem' (Reading 6).

EXERCISE 3.22

DIFFICULTIES FOR FUNCTIONALISM

In paragraph 5, Shoemaker lists three distinct issues which appear to be difficulties for functionalists. Can you say which these are?

SPECIMEN ANSWER

1   The question of privileged access to their own mental states. I am aware of my own mental states in a way which is non-inferential: I do not need to observe my own behaviour in order to know what I am experiencing.

2   When I introspect, what I am aware of is a combination of sensory experience about the world, internal bodily sensations, and whatever my thoughts and feelings happen to be at the time. None of these mental contents presents itself to my consciousness as a state of my brain.

3   Equally, when I introspect, the contents of my consciousness do not present themselves to me as functional states, i.e. when for example I experience a sensation or feel an emotion or reflect on a belief, these mental contents do not present themselves to the mind as items whose central function is a causal one.

DISCUSSION

You will notice that Shoemaker labels the first of these issues in particular as a 'Cartesian intuition' and it is worth pausing to see why. Descartes believed that we have a mode of access to the contents of our own consciousness which has no parallel with regard to our awareness of the external world. It is clear from what Descartes says about the *cogito* that he believes that we are aware of the contents of our own consciousness with certainty: he believed that we cannot be wrong about what is going on in our own minds.

It is also worthwhile to pause here to ask why the topics Shoemaker raises here are indeed problems for functionalism. The first two are problems for any materialist philosophy of mind, not just functionalism, for the following reason.

As became clear as a result of our discussion of aboutness, to be philo-sophically satisfactory, a materialist theory of the mind must show that all types of mental content and their properties can be completely described in terms of the concepts with which we describe the material world. This task has proved to be much less straightforward than one might expect, and the chief sources of the difficulty are exactly those properties of the mental we have already met several times already. For example, events in the material world are, in an important sense, public: that is, that they can in principle be observed by any suitably placed observer. Events in any brain, including my own, are public in this sense. By contrast, it looks very much as if the access I have to my own mental contents is not public in this way. It hardly seems even to make sense to suppose that you could be aware of my experiences in the same way that I am, or vice versa. Again, as we have seen there are analogous difficulties over other mental properties such as intentionality or aboutness, as we saw in paragraph 4 of Shoemaker's essay. How can arrangements of matter, even of the fantastic complexity of the brain, be *about* anything, i.e. have a content?

The third difficulty Shoemaker raises in paragraph 5 is specific to function-alist accounts of the mind: if the essential nature of mental states lies in their function, why do they not present themselves to consciousness in a way which indicates this? Before reading this section on functionalism, would it have occurred to you to think of the contents of your mind as primarily functional? I suspect that for most people the answer would be 'no', but it is important to note that this is not by any means a knock-down argument against function-alism. It may turn out to be perfectly possible to give an explanation of why mental states present themselves to consciousness as they do in functionalist terms. What the objection shows is that it is necessary for the functionalist to provide such an explanation.

In paragraph 8 Shoemaker gives the outline of a functionalist account of one of the Cartesian intuitions which have to be dealt with by any materialist philosophy of mind.

EXERCISE 3.23

FUNCTIONALISM AND 'SPECIAL ACCESS'

Say in your own words what view Shoemaker is summarizing in the phrase 'Cartesian intuitions about our special access to our own mental states' in the first sentence of paragraph 8.

SPECIMEN ANSWER

He has in mind the view which Descartes appears to hold that a peculiarity of mental states is that there is no distinction to be drawn in their regard between being in them and being aware that one is in them: there is something logically odd about supposing that, for example, I can have a thought and only later discover in some way that I am having it.

DISCUSSION

Shoemaker's attempt to account for special or privileged access in function-alist terms is rather compressed, so I will try to paraphrase what he is saying here. Bear in mind that what he has to do is to show that this special access to our own mental states can be described in terms which are wholly materialist, and so do not involve postulating events or properties which are non-material.

He begins by borrowing an idea from the Australian materialist philosopher David Armstrong, whom we have already come across in our investigation of some problems with dualist views (cf. Armstrong 1968: 92–100 and Ch. 15). Armstrong asserts that to be introspectively aware that I have a given mental content is just to have the belief that I am having it. That is all that being aware of my own mental contents is: it is not a question of a ghostly 'I' reviewing goings on in my non-extended soul, like a spectator in a non-spatial cinema. Rather, being aware that I see a chess board consists in (a) my seeing one and (b) my believing that I am seeing one. These beliefs about my mental contents are produced by a basic and reliable mechanism in the mind–brain.

To this assertion Shoemaker adds a second, functionalist claim. The essence of mental states, according to functionalism, is their function, notably in bringing about behaviour appropriate to our circumstances. Awareness of mental states is clearly of great importance if this overriding function is to be fulfilled efficiently. For example, the function of sense perception is to inform us about the environment, and this function would be greatly impaired were we generally unaware of the sensations we have. The same is manifestly true of bodily sensations: one of the functions of pains is to inform us that something is amiss, and to do this effectively we must be aware of them. Therefore, Shoemaker argues, not only is awareness of one's mental states compatible with functionalism, it is a consequence of it.

The addition Shoemaker makes to Armstrong's argument is one to which the latter would be sympathetic, making good sense in the context of an evolu-tionist outlook. The big step in this argument is the first one, i.e. the assertion that all there is to awareness is the having of beliefs about one's own mental contents. That, however, is a large question we will just have to bear in mind for the moment. We will be in a better position to take a view on it when we have done some more work on materialism.

Let us pause briefly once again to review what is by now becoming a quite lengthy argument. By this point in the book I hope you have begun to see why the philosophy of mind is both so intriguing and so tricky. We have seen that trying to give an account of the mind in dualist terms, either substance dualism of the classic Cartesian kind or the other forms of dualism we looked at briefly, leads to very serious philosophical problems, principally in the area of mental causation and in its failure to do justice to the bedrock datum of our experience that we are unified beings, rather than two very different sorts of thing somehow hooked up together. Equally, it should be becoming clear that trying to give a materialist account of the mind is by no means straightforward either. Materialist views do not have a problem with mental causation: since on the materialist view there is only one sort of basic stuff, namely, matter, there is no special problem over mental and physical events causing one another, because all causation takes place within the one realm of matter. On the other hand, the materialists we have looked at so far do have a problem framing a satisfactory account of some other aspects of mental experience. As we have discovered in our consideration of the essays by Smart and Shoemaker, it is necessary for materialists to provide convincing accounts of such features or properties of mental experience as qualia, aboutness and privacy or subjectivity, and doing this has not proved easy.

This is a classic instance of a centrally philosophical sort of predicament. As Ludwig Wittgenstein (1889–1951) once put it in conversation with the American philosopher Norman Malcolm (1911–90):

> A person caught in a philosophical confusion is like a man in a room who wants to get out but doesn't know how. He tries the window but it is too high. He tries the chimney but it is too narrow.
>
> (Malcolm 1958: 51)

Very often, investigation of a philosophical problem can make it seem as if one is trapped, like a fly in a bottle, hitting obstacles in every direction (cf. Wittgenstein 1953, I, paragraph 309).

One of the standard responses which has been made throughout the history of philosophy in all its branches when an apparent impasse of this sort is reached is to try to articulate, unveil or make explicit the presuppositions or unquestioned assumptions made by all the theories in question. It has often proved to be the case that the cause of coming to a seeming dead halt in a promising line of argument lies in one or more assumptions which have gone unnoticed and/or unquestioned: modify or reject one or more of these, and the problem often disappears. Now all the philosophies of mind we have looked at so far, dualist and monist, have an assumption in common which we have noticed briefly but not so far questioned. This assumption is that the way in which we ordinarily conceive of our mental life – in terms of the having of sense experiences, beliefs, emotions, thoughts, attitudes, of being able to introspect these in a unique way and without the possibility of error more or less at will, and so on – has logical coherence and will not be overturned by future developments in science. Put another way, we have assumed so far that our ordinary conception of our minds is a fixed point, and that both science and philosophy have to accommodate themselves to it, and not the other way round. Functionalism, for example, takes this for granted, and indeed the root source of the logical problems faced by this view, as we have seen, is that this ordinary picture of the mind includes concepts, e.g. aboutness, whose logic appears to be irreducibly different from the logic of concepts describing brains or other hardware. The central assertion of the next materialist view of the mind we are to look at – eliminativism – is that this assumption of the unquestionability of our common-sense view of the mind is false.

ELIMINATIVE MATERIALISM (ELIMINATIVISM)

We will now investigate eliminativism by means of a detailed reading of part of one of the most influential philosophical papers in which it has been advocated, 'Eliminative materialism and the propositional attitudes' by the Canadian-born philosopher Paul Churchland (1981).[1] Before we approach the text, however, we need to take an introductory look at the key concepts which are used in this theory, which are as follows: folk psychology, ontology, propositional attitudes, empiricism and reduction.

FOLK PSYCHOLOGY

Folk psychology (nearly always abbreviated to FP) is the name given by eliminativists to the common-sense shared understanding of the mind described in the first chapter of this book, and which we have not so far questioned. In an essay written later than the one we are about to read, Churchland sums it up as follows:

> 'Folk psychology' denotes the prescientific, common-sense conceptual framework that all normally socialized humans deploy in order to comprehend, predict, explain, and manipulate the behaviour of humans and the higher animals. This framework includes such concepts as *belief, desire, pain, pleasure, love, hate, joy, fear, suspicion, memory, recognition, anger, sympathy, intention*, and so forth. It embodies our baseline understanding of the cognitive, affective, and purposive nature of persons. Considered as a whole, it constitutes our conception of what a person is.
>
> (Churchland in Guttenplan 1994: 308)

In other words, FP is the set of concepts we all use all the time to characterize both our own mental life, that of other persons and, with some modifications, to describe the mental life of higher animals. To attribute a motive to myself or someone else; to say I am having sensations or memories or imaginative mental images; to say I or someone else is feeling a certain emotion and to account for behaviour in terms of emotion; all this and more is cast in the concepts of FP. As Churchland stresses, it is fundamental to our understanding of what a person is: to see how basic a part of our outlook it is, try to imagine describing either your mental life or anyone else's without using *any* of the concepts italicized in Churchland's remarks just quoted. I stress this here and will return to it as we go along because it is important not to underestimate the radicality and profundity of the central claims which eliminativism makes.

ONTOLOGY

This is a key term in the technical vocabulary of philosophers, and it is important to have an idea of what it means. It is derived from the Greek term *ontos* which means being or existence. In one of its two central uses, the term ontology is the name of the branch of metaphysics which deals with what sorts of things can be said to exist. As we have seen, the philosophy of mind is one of the areas of philosophy in which sharp disagreements on this matter come to the fore: dualists assert that there are two radically different sorts of existent, the mental and the physical, while monists assert that there is only one sort. This leads us to the second common usage of the term 'ontology', the sense in which it is used in discussions of eliminativism: any philosophy of mind (and indeed almost any philosophical point of view) involves assertions or assumptions about what sorts of things exist, and these assertions or assumptions are said to constitute the ontology of the point of view in question. According to the eliminativists, FP includes an ontology which in their view is a fiction, i.e. it asserts falsely that mental contents as ordinarily conceived exist. We will return to this point presently.

PROPOSITIONAL ATTITUDES

Propositional attitudes are a major subset of the concepts which make up FP. This term, coined by Bertrand Russell (1872–1970), is meant to draw attention to a crucial feature of these central components of FP. As we have seen, we make sense of both our own mental life and that of others in terms of concepts such as *belief, desire, hope, fear, intention, wish*, and so on. These terms express distinct attitudes: I can believe *x* with or without desiring *x*, hoping for *x*, fearing *x*, and so on. Further, we *identify* a given wish or hope or fear (etc.) by stating a *proposition* which gives its content: I wish that I could do well in my exam; I hope that the weather will not be too foul when I have to drive a long way; and so on. Hence it is convenient to refer to this sort of element of FP as the class of propositional attitudes: they are attitudes articulated in and identified by means of propositions.

The propositional attitudes share the property common to the elements of FP of being absolutely fundamental to our understanding of ourselves and so of a wide range of social practices. More or less every explanation or prediction of behaviour we give is couched in terms of propositional attitudes. The propositional attitudes also have the property of being very hard to account for in the terms of a materialist theory of the mind: they have the property of intentionality or aboutness, and as we have seen in the previous section, it is not obvious how a state of any material thing, including the brain, can be *about* anything. Indeed, it is not too much to say that the propositional attitudes have, for this reason, constituted the major stumbling block for such materialist views. Churchland is well aware of this, and argues that eliminativism provides a radical solution to this difficulty.

EMPIRICAL THEORY

Eliminativism makes central use of the concept of *theory*, and we need to pause to see what exactly is being asserted by the use of this term. By 'theory' is meant a set of concepts and a set of general laws which allow us to characterize, explain and predict a certain area of experience or phenomena. For present purposes, we can understand the term empirical to mean concerning occurrences in the realm of public fact, and testable by reference to such facts. There are also non-empirical theories: indeed most philosophical views, which are views about *concepts* rather than empirical facts, constitute non-empirical theories. Scientific theories, such as those of relativity or evolution, are the paradigm instances of empirical theories: they are meant to give us a framework of concepts by means of which to explain and predict natural phenomena. If too many phenomena fail to fit the explanations offered, then the theory will be regarded as having been falsified by events and a new theory will be needed; conversely, if more and more phenomena become explicable as a result of a new theory, or if experiments continue to confirm it, then the theory is said to have been verified or confirmed by the facts. The important point to fasten on for present purposes is that an empirical theory is open to verification or falsification by facts: if another theory comes along which explains the same phenomena more accurately or which includes some phenomena the first theory could not explain, then the first theory will be abandoned in favour of its more powerful replacement.

REDUCTION

We have met this term already in the discussion of functionalism: please read again now the comments made above in connection with paragraph 3 of Shoemaker's essay.

CENTRAL ASSERTIONS OF ELIMINATIVISM

With these five concepts in mind (FP, ontology, propositional attitudes, empiricism and reduction), we can now give a preliminary summary of the central assertions of eliminativism, which are as follows: FP is an empirical theory; it does not promise to reduce at all well to emerging neuroscience, and it fails to explain many mental phenomena. Since FP is an empirical theory, it has no special immunity to being replaced by a better theory of mental life when such a theory emerges in the future, as neuroscience advances. It is likely that the ontology of FP – asserting the existence of mental phenomena of the kind epitomized in the propositional attitudes: beliefs, wishes, fears, hopes, and so on – will prove to be a fiction. FP will be replaced by a completed neuroscience, and from that time on humanity will cease to think of itself in the terms of FP: we will no longer characterize ourselves as having wishes, desires, beliefs, and so on. What the new scientific mental vocabulary will look like, no one knows, but it is clear that the shift in outlook implied here is huge and radical. We will now examine the arguments Churchland advances in support of these views.

EXAMINATION OF CHURCHLAND'S ARGUMENTS

Now read paragraphs 1–3 of Churchland's paper 'Eliminative materialism and the propositional attitudes' (Reading 7).

Reading p. 199

In view of what we have read in the previous chapter and this one, these paragraphs should not contain any surprises. The first paragraph defines eliminativism, while the second refers to the difficulties over qualia we encountered earlier, especially in connection with functionalism: the term 'raw feels' is merely an alternative for 'qualia'. (Churchland is rather sanguine in his claim that the barrier to materialist theories formed by the objections based on qualia is dissolving, but we can let that pass for the moment.) Paragraph 3 announces the theme for the major set of arguments in the essay.

EXERCISE 3.24

CHURCHLAND'S THEME

What will these arguments attempt to show?

SPECIMEN ANSWER

The arguments will attempt to show that FP, to which Churchland here refers as the 'relevant network of common-sense concepts', does constitute an empirical theory.

Reading p. 200

Now read paragraph 4 of Churchland's paper 'Eliminative materialism and the propositional attitudes' (Reading 7).

EXERCISE 3.25

FP AS A THEORY

What benefit is here claimed by Churchland to follow from adopting the view that FP is a theory?

SPECIMEN ANSWER

The view that FP is a theory is here claimed to simplify and unify a large area of the philosophy of mind.

DISCUSSION

Some of the questions to which Churchland refers here, e.g. intentionality, we have already met under that name. The question of the semantics or meaning of mental terms is one we have come across in a number of places: what he has in mind are issues such as those which exercised philosophers who held the mind–brain identity theory. You will recall that it was pointed out that mental-event descriptions do not *mean* the same as brain-event descriptions, and this was held to be a *prima facie* objection against the central claim of the identity theory, namely, that mental events and brain events are the same events merely referred to in two ways. For example, the statement: 'There is currently intense neurochemical excitation in area *x* of my brain' manifestly does not *mean* the same as a statement recording an experience of mine, such as 'I can see a yellow disc on a blue ground'. (As we have seen, this objection can easily be rebutted using Frege's sense-reference distinction.)

The other issue Churchland mentions, the question of other minds, we will come to briefly in paragraph 7. The main point to hang onto here is that Churchland is claiming that the view he is about to argue for, like any successful theory, makes it possible to answer a lot of questions which competitor theories cannot deal with satisfactorily. This is a bold and large claim, and one to bear in mind as we go along.

Now read paragraph 5 of Churchland's paper 'Eliminative materialism and the propositional attitudes' (Reading 7). The unusual adjective 'quotidian' (four syllables: quo-ti-de-an) simply means 'everyday', with the same connotation of ordinariness.

Reading
p. 200

EXERCISE 3.26

FP AS A THEORY

How do the assertions Churchland makes here support his conclusion that FP is a theory? Set out your answer in the form of premises and conclusion. (Note: The argument is not stated completely here. You will need to supply an unstated or suppressed premise in order to exhibit the formal structure of the argument.)

SPECIMEN ANSWER

Premise 1	The function of a theory is to allow us to characterize, explain and predict a given set of phenomena. (This is the unstated premise.)
Premise 2	FP allows us to characterize, explain and predict human behaviour.
Conclusion 1	Therefore, FP is a theory.

It is appropriate to pause here and expand on some of Churchland's remarks. In particular, it will be useful to develop what he means by 'common-sense laws' and to set out explicitly how behaviour is explained by means of FP.

By 'common-sense law' he has in mind statements of the following type: if A desires that *p*, and believes that doing *x* will bring it about that *p*, then, other things being equal, A will do *x*. Put more concretely, if I want to do well in my examination, and I believe that following the revision plan my tutor has suggested will bring this about then, other things being equal (i.e. provided I am not prevented from doing so by unforeseen circumstances), I will revise on the plan suggested. All the central concepts of FP – hope, fear, desire, intention, and so on – can figure in laws of this kind, on the basis of which behaviour can be explained. Churchland is not maintaining that we mentally rehearse deductions of this kind every time we observe someone's behaviour. As he notes, the awareness we have of these laws is generally tacit; but we can refer to them when we have to, notably in cases where the behaviour in question is puzzling.

It is important to the eliminativist case that FP should include laws and that its explanations should be formulable if necessary – as in the example of revising – as deductions from such laws. It is important because this makes FP very similar in logical structure to the theories of empirical science.

Now read paragraphs 6 and 7 of Churchland's paper 'Eliminative materialism and the propositional attitudes' (Reading 7).

Reading
p. 200

In paragraph 6 Churchland begins to set out what he asserts to be some of the philosophical benefits of adopting the view that FP is a theory like any other, rather than a set of truths in some way standing outside the range of possible theories and constituting an unquestionable set of data which all theories of the mind must attempt to accommodate.

The first benefit Churchland claims for his approach concerns what he calls the semantics (i.e. the meanings) of the terms in 'our familiar mentalistic vocabulary', i.e. FP. In paragraph 6 Churchland claims that eliminativism entails a logically straightforward position on this issue: if FP is a theory, then the terms it uses (hope, desire, wish, fear, intention, experience, and so on) are, like the key concepts of other empirical theories, given their meaning by the context in which they occur. Just as the terms 'natural selection', 'survival of the fittest', 'mutation', and so on have a special sense in the context of the theory of evolution and stand or fall with it, the same is true (Churchland argues) of all the familiar terms of FP. The point to fasten on for present purposes is that for the eliminativist the terms of FP are *not* logically special or privileged: they stand or fall with the theory which uses them, and are not an immutable fixed point.

Another philosophical benefit of viewing FP as a theory, Churchland argues in paragraph 7, is that it allows a straightforward and convincing solution to a problem in the philosophy of mind which we have not so far come across, namely, the problem of other minds. The traditional account of this problem is as follows: as we have seen, my experiences are, in a strong sense of the term, private to me. In a strong sense of 'cannot', I cannot have your experiences, nor can you have mine. Therefore, I can in principle have no direct evidence that any other person or animal is the subject of mental states. How then can I logically justify my conviction that anyone else does have mental experiences? In other words, how can I justify my belief that there are *any* other minds whatsoever? Note that the fact that the conviction that there are other minds is psychologically irresistible is no answer, since there is no reason to assume that whatever is thus irresistible is true. The *philosophical* question at the basis of the other minds problem remains to be addressed: What logical foundation can be given for the belief in other minds?

As Churchland notes, a number of solutions to this question have been offered, some asserting that we deduce the existence of other minds from the behaviour of other individuals and others claiming that a belief in other minds can be justified as an inductive generalization from my own case, and both these approaches involve serious problems of their own: for example, induction provides no logical justification for belief in other minds, since one case (my own experience of mental states) offers no safe ground on which to base the generalization that others are also the subjects of mental states. The thesis that FP is a theory offers another and much simpler way of dealing with this problem: the proposition that there are other minds is simply an explanatory hypothesis generated by the theory, comparable (for example) to the hypothesis that change in the characteristics of a species requires the occurrence of mutation. Such a hypothesis is acceptable to the degree that it is successful in allowing the explanation and prediction of the phenomena in question – in the case of other minds, that of human and animal behaviour. No special sort of logical justification is needed for this sort of belief.

 Reading
p. 201

Now read paragraphs 8–11 inclusive of Churchland's paper 'Eliminative materialism and the propositional attitudes' (Reading 7).

Churchland next draws attention to the way in which accepting the thesis that FP is a theory affects the way in which the mind–body problem is conceived. Since for the eliminativist, the true description of the mind, when it is finally worked out, will be a materialistic theory cast in the terms of completed neuroscience, then the central issue on the relation of mind and body is not one (by contrast with dualism, for example) of how one sort of substance is related to another (since the eliminativist holds that there is only material substance), but rather a question merely of how two theories are conceptually related. The two theories are FP and completed neuroscience, and the eliminativist expects that the former will simply not prove to be reducible to the latter and will instead just be junked by future generations.

Churchland makes clear in paragraph 9 how this position on the relation of FP to neuroscience differs from that entailed by the other philosophies of mind we have encountered: dualism, the identity theory and functionalism. For the dualist, FP will be irreducible to neuroscience.

EXERCISE 3.27

FP AND DUALISM

Can you say why FP will be irreducible to neuroscience for the dualist?

For the substance dualist, for example, the mind is a non-physical realm, and therefore is beyond the explanatory scope of any materialistic theory, including completed neuroscience. Therefore the true description of the mind is irreducible to any materialistic concepts.

DISCUSSION

Functionalists would agree with dualists that FP will prove irreducible to neuroscience, but for a quite different reason. For the functionalist, the mind is a set of functional states which can be realized in a number of different physical bases, and so cannot be reduced to a theory which simply describes one particular sort of material base, namely the human brain. Finally, the identity theorist, by contrast, expects a smooth reduction of FP to neuroscience. Since for the identity theorist, mental and physical events are identical, then a complete neuroscience must describe mental events, since these brain events are the same events as are described by FP.

This tracing of consequences might at first seem like an abstract game, but a little reflection will show that it is of some philosophical importance: every philosophy of mind must include a view on how that philosophy is related to neuroscience, and it is always worth pausing to work it out.

Now read paragraphs 12 and 13 of Churchland's paper 'Eliminative materialism and the propositional attitudes' (Reading 7). (Note: The unusual term 'aetiology' ('etiology' in American spelling), which is used in paragraph 13, means 'the study of causes': the aetiology of any phenomenon is the search for what causes it, and so what explains it.)

Reading
p. 201

Having argued for his first premise, that FP is a theory, Churchland now moves on to present his arguments for his second major premise, namely that FP may well be false and its ontology an illusion. He notes in paragraph 12 that FP might be thought to enjoy considerable explanatory success, but goes on in paragraph 13 to claim that this is a superficial impression which is undermined by a more searching examination of the situation.

EXERCISE 3.28

FP

Churchland suggests in paragraph 13 that it is necessary to examine FP in detail in three respects. What are they?

SPECIMEN ANSWER

1 We need to examine those areas in which FP *fails* to explain important facts about mental life.

2 We need to consider whether FP has the potential to improve, i.e. to come to include more phenomena within its sphere of explanation.

3 We need to examine to what extent FP promises to cohere with other relevant domains of knowledge, e.g. the theory of evolution, neuroscience and so on.

Reading
p. 202

Now read paragraphs 14–16 of Churchland's paper 'Eliminative materialism and the propositional attitudes' (Reading 7). These paragraphs contain Churchland's argument concerning the first of the respects identified in my specimen answer to the preceding exercise.

EXERCISE 3.29

FP'S SHORTCOMINGS

Summarize Churchland's argument in paragraphs 14–16.

SPECIMEN ANSWER

Large areas of mental life and some important mental phenomena are not only not explained by FP but are not even addressed by it. Chief among these are: mental illness; creative imagination; intelligence differences between individuals; the nature and function of sleep; complex motor co-ordination; perceptual illusions and memory. Again, FP has nothing of interest to say about how learning is accomplished, both in the form which involves conceptual change and in its non-linguistic form, which is by far the commonest in nature. In particular, FP does not explain how we learn to manipulate and store the propositional attitudes which are central to its own conception of the mental. Churchland notes that these arguments do not *entail* of themselves that FP is false, but claims that they do show that FP is superficial and that it is not foolish to entertain the belief that FP is deeply misleading.

DISCUSSION

This argument has not gone unchallenged, and it is appropriate here to look at some objections brought against it by two American philosophers, Terence Horgan and James Woodward (1985). They argue that Churchland's assertions are misleading in two important respects. The first is that, while FP itself may have little to say about the subjects Churchland lists as outside its explanatory scope, theories based on concepts deriving from FP have a good deal to say about them. For example, cognitive psychologists have developed extensive and detailed theories about visual perception, memory, and learning that employ concepts recognizably like the folk-psychological concepts of belief, desire, judgement, etc. ... That all such theories are unexplanatory is most implausible, and in any case requires detailed empirical argument of a sort Churchland does not provide.

(Horgan and Woodward 1985: 200)

This objection makes clear, amongst other things, one of the dramatic consequences of Churchland's position, namely that if eliminativism is true, then all types of psychology which use concepts from or are derived from FP (usually termed 'intentional psychologies', in the sense of 'intentional' we have used in this block) are false and that includes by far the greater percentage of all current psychology. That eliminativism has this consequence does not show either that it is true or that it is false: but it does show how radical a theory it is.

EXERCISE 3.30

FP DEFENDED

As you know, arguments may be criticized chiefly in one of two ways:

1 by claiming that one or more of the premises, explicit or unstated, is false;
2 by claiming that the premises do not entail the conclusion.

Into which of these classes does Horgan and Woodward's objection to Churchland's first argument fall?

SPECIMEN ANSWER

Into the first class: Horgan and Woodward are arguing that Churchland's assertion concerning the explanatory failures of FP is simply false.

Horgan and Woodward go on to make a second objection to Churchland's first argument, as follows:

Churchland's argument seems to impose the *a priori* demand that any successful psychological theory account for a certain pre-established range of phenomena, and do so in a unified way. Arguments of this general type deserve to be treated with scepticism and caution ... The general point is that reasonable judgements about which phenomena a theory of some general type should be expected to account for require considerable theoretical knowledge; when our theoretical knowledge is relatively primitive, as it is with regard to many psychological phenomena, such judgements can go seriously astray. There is no good reason, *a priori*, to expect that a theory like FP, designed primarily to explain common human actions in terms of beliefs, desires and the like, should also account for phenomena having to do with visual perception, sleep, or complicated muscular co-ordination. The truth about the latter phenomena may simply be very different from the truth about the former.

(Horgan and Woodward 1985: 200–1)

EXERCISE 3.31

OBJECTION TO CHURCHLAND'S ARGUMENT

What type of objection is this to Churchland's first argument?

SPECIMEN ANSWER

This is again a claim that one of Churchland's premises is false, though in this case the premise is an unstated one. Churchland assumes without argument that, if FP is to be a successful theory, it must offer explanations for all the phenomena he lists; Horgan and Woodward point out that there is no reason to accept that this assumption is true. In advance of there being an explanation of the functions of sleep or of how complicated motor co-ordination works, there is just no reason to assume that such theories and explanations will be within the legitimate province of FP at all. For example, they might turn out to be largely physiological rather than psychological matters.

Let us now turn back to Churchland's text and consider his second argument concerning the inadequacies of FP.

Reading
p. 203

Now read paragraphs 17 and 18 of Churchland's paper 'Eliminative materialism and the propositional attitudes' (Reading 7). (Note: Imre Lakatos (1922–74), referred to in paragraph 18, was a Hungarian philosopher specializing in the philosophy of mathematics and science. We can think of Lakatos's concept of a 'research program', which Churchland mentions here, as meaning much the same as what Churchland means by the term 'theory'.)

EXERCISE 3.32

FP CRITICIZED

Summarize the argument of paragraphs 17 and 18 in your own words.

SPECIMEN ANSWER

This argument concerns the history of FP and its potential for future development. The general pattern of the history of FP is one of a diminution in its area of application. In primitive times, FP in the form of animism was widely used to explain many natural phenomena, but it has in this area had to retreat in the face of better theories from the area of empirical science. In its remaining area of application, human and animal behaviour, it has become stagnant. We use the same conceptual apparatus for the explanation of behaviour as was current in classical Greek times. Granted the range of its explanatory failures, the stagnation of FP is a further major cause for concern.

DISCUSSION

Once again, Horgan and Woodward have counter-arguments to advance against this view. Their first point is that there is reason to believe that FP *has* changed over the centuries, enriching its conceptual apparatus:

> For example, it is a plausible conjecture that Europeans in the 18th or 19th centuries were much more likely to explain human behaviour in terms of character types with enduring personality traits than 20th century Europeans, who often appeal instead to 'situational' factors. (Certainly this difference is dramatically evident in 18th and 20th century literature; contrast, say, Jane Austen and John Barth.) Another example of empirically progressive change, perhaps, is the greater willingness, in contemporary culture, to appeal to unconscious beliefs and motivations.
>
> (Horgan and Woodward 1985: 201)

Second, intentional psychological theories (i.e. those using concepts derived from FP) have 'led to a number of novel and surprising predictions, which have been borne out by experiment' (p. 202).

EXERCISE 3.33

OBJECTION TO CHURCHLAND'S ARGUMENT

What sort of criticism are Horgan and Woodward making of Churchland's second argument in this last quotation?

SPECIMEN ANSWER

It is a claim that a major premise in the argument – that FP is a stagnant theory, incapable of advance – is false.

Reading
p. 203
Now read paragraphs 19–23 of Churchland's paper 'Eliminative materialism and the propositional attitudes' (Reading 7). These paragraphs contain Churchland's third and potentially most serious argument for the rejection of FP, together with (in paragraphs 22 and 23) a brief summary of all three of his major arguments. (Note: The German term *lebenswelt*, in paragraph 22, means 'lifeworld', our ordinary, common-sense experience and the conceptual framework around which it is organized.)

EXERCISE 3.34

FP AND SCIENCE

Summarize the argument of paragraphs 19–21 in your own words.

SPECIMEN ANSWER

The advance of the physical sciences has furnished us with an increasingly inclusive understanding of the universe and its contents, an understanding based on a set of monistic materialist assumptions. Even at its present stage of development, this scientific-materialist approach is furnishing us with powerful insights into areas such as sensation, neural activity and motor control. In no case does this scientific approach use concepts with the property of intentionality, and does not couch its explanations in terms of propositional attitudes. It is therefore very different from FP; therefore, it is unlikely that FP will prove to be reducible (in the technical sense of that term in which we are using it in this book) to neuroscience; therefore, like alchemy and Aristotelian cosmology, FP is a candidate for outright elimination from our world-picture.

DISCUSSION

This is an extremely interesting argument, stating as it does with great clarity and concision some of the most powerful general reasons regularly put forward for supposing that some version of materialist theory of the mind is very likely to turn out to be the true one. There can be no doubt that many philosophers would agree with Churchland that the explanations of phenomena offered by the physical sciences so far have no place for intentionality in their framework of concepts, and it therefore seems unlikely (and untidy) that one area of phenomena, the mental, should be radically different in kind from everything else science has managed to explain to date. However, one can accept all that and yet not be fully persuaded by what Churchland has to say here. Horgan and Woodward comment as follows on this argument:

> We certainly agree that an ideal, or approximately ideal, reduction of FP to

natural science would be *one* way of salvaging FP. And we also agree that such a reduction … is an unlikely prospect, given that FP is at least twenty-five centuries old and hence obviously not formulated with an eye toward smooth term-by-term absorption into 20th century science … But even if FP cannot be reduced to lower-level theories, [i.e. theories couched in terms of the ultimate physical components of the brain as opposed to persons and their intentional states, for example] and even if lower-level theories can themselves provide a marvellous account of the nature and behaviour of *homo sapiens*, it simply does not follow that FP is radically false, or that humans do not undergo the intentional events it posits … [Churchland] is just mistaken to assume that FP must be reducible to neuroscience in order to be compatible with it.

(Horgan and Woodward 1985: 203–4)

EXERCISE 3.35

OBJECTION TO CHURCHLAND'S ARGUMENT

What sort of objection are Horgan and Woodward making here to Churchland's third argument? Is it an attack on the truth of one or more premises or an attack on the way the premises are said to support the conclusion?

SPECIMEN ANSWER

Unlike the previous arguments advanced by Horgan and Woodward, their objection in this case is that Churchland's argument is not valid. The objection is that the premise:

FP is probably not reducible to neuroscience;

does not entail the desired conclusion:

FP is probably false.

DISCUSSION

This seems to me a fair point. It remains logically possible for there to be a materialist view of the mind which is (a) non-reductive and also (b) non-eliminative, though there is not at present a version which has received general acclaim. The most powerful version of this type of theory has been put forward by the American philosopher Donald Davidson (b. 1917) which he calls anomalous monism. (See especially, Davidson 1970.) Davidson argues that there

> are no such things as minds but that people have mental properties. These change constantly and the changes are mental events, yet Davidson contends that all this can be true within a materialist framework. If this is so, then Churchland has not made his case, at least on the grounds presented here.

We do not have the space here to go into Davidson's views; for the moment, we must content ourselves with the conclusion that the three major arguments Churchland has put forward in this essay are in various ways unsatisfactory. As we have seen before, however, this does not show that eliminativism is untenable, only that it has not been established by argument. I want next to look at some objections designed to show that this view of the mind *is* untenable.

SOME FURTHER ARGUMENTS AGAINST ELIMINATIVISM

The arguments we have looked at from Horgan and Woodward by no means exhaust those which have been brought against eliminativism, and in this section we will look at a few of the more significant ones from other sources. The first is based on the work of the American philosopher Daniel Dennett (b. 1942; see especially, Dennett 1981).

Dennett argues that the eliminativists fail to notice that FP is not merely a descriptive and explanatory theory. FP, Dennett contends, is not merely descriptive: it is also *normative*. By this he means that FP not only allows us to say what our wishes, desires, hopes, and so on, are; it also embodies an *ideal* or recommendation of how we should deal with them if we are rational, i.e. FP includes *values*. A related objection points out that the concepts of FP also allow us to carry out many social practices: the concepts of FP allow us to do things such as promise, greet, reassure, question, demand, offer, advise, and so on, for all the activities which are carried on by means of these concepts. (See Wilkes 1981, 1984.) Another way of putting this, using an accepted philosophical term, is that FP includes what are termed *performative utterances*, i.e. forms of words such that when we utter them this use *constitutes* the activity concerned as opposed to merely describing or reporting it. I can only promise to do *x* by saying (or writing, of course) 'I promise to do *x*'. In saying those words, I *do* it; I do not describe doing it; and the same is true for advising, demanding, offering, and so forth.

EXERCISE 3.36

ELIMINATIVISM AND THE NORMATIVE

Can you see how these objections conflict with eliminativism?

SPECIMEN ANSWER

Eliminativists state that FP is an empirical theory. Such theories, like quantum physics or evolution, are composed only of declarative statements, i.e. statements which simply state how things are and do not embody values or norms or statements the very use of which constitutes a certain sort of social practice. Therefore, neuroscience, which is an empirical theory, cannot be a complete replacement for FP, which contains ideals and practices as well as descriptions.

DISCUSSION

This may seem to be a clinching argument against eliminativism, but as so often in philosophy – and as you will have noticed by now – matters are rarely that simple.

Though it would take us too far into the philosophy of science to pursue the reply in detail, it is open to the eliminativist to counter-object that this objection rests on a simplistic and false view of what scientific theories are like. It can be argued that accepting a scientific theory involves entering a community with shared values and expectations, and therefore that empirical theories also involve normative aspects. However that may be, the objections do make it clear that FP is not just a set of laws and deductions from laws cast as declarative statements. It includes non-declarative elements, and the eliminativist has got to find a way of dealing with them.

A second line of objection attacks the fundamental premise of eliminativism that FP is a theory (see Gordon 1986 and Goldman 1992). The argument is as follows: if FP is a theory, then anyone who has mastered FP (which is any sane adult, in fact) must be in command of a huge set of FP laws, which they can recall at will, on which to base the explanations and predictions of behaviour which we constantly make. It is argued that only if this is true can FP be held to be a theory in a way analogous to other physical theories which, it is argued, function in this way. If I want to understand how my car engine converts fuel into kinetic energy, I need to understand a reasonable amount about chemistry and mechanics. Only if I know the appropriate physics and chemistry can I explain and predict what will happen under certain conditions. The problem is, the objection continues, that we do not have possession of the vast number of psychological laws we would need in order to explain behaviour, and nor do we go through the mental gymnastics needed to apply them. When we explain the behaviour of others, this simply isn't the way we go about it: we just don't, except in very rare cases, work out explanations of behaviour in the way which we should do if FP is indeed an empirical theory. Therefore, we do not behave as if FP were a theory like other physical theories.

Once again, there is a long and complicated line of possible reply, to the effect that the objection rests on a falsely simple model of what theoretical explanations are like. The only point I would like to make here is that both this objection and the previous one do show at the very least that the eliminativist case is not by any means as simple to make as might at first appear. The three arguments put forward by Churchland are not alone sufficient to carry the day, and a great deal of extra argument is needed to deal with the non-declarative elements of FP: it is quite wrong to assume that FP is made up of components all of which are (to put the matter technically) logically homogeneous – that is, that all the statements which can be made using the concepts of FP are logically of one kind, i.e. declarative utterances.

Our investigation of Churchland's three major arguments in favour of elimination of FP tends to show that his case is not made by them and that, if his view is to be defended, it will need much more by way of sophisticated argumentation than he here provides. What we have not proved conclusively is that eliminativism cannot be so defended, and one should avoid underestimating the force of some of the considerations Churchland advances. There is no reason to suppose *a priori* that FP is sacrosanct: as Bertrand Russell once remarked, ordinary language embodies the metaphysics of our remote ancestors, and it is quite possible for it to change.

The real problem with this philosophy, in my view, is that in the absence of conclusive arguments either for it or against it, what we are left with is in effect just a sort of prophecy, namely, that our way of conceiving ourselves will alter profoundly at some indefinite point in the future when neuroscience is complete, and there is no way of testing a prophecy except to wait and see what happens. One major point, though, is worth stressing again, and that is just how radical this view is: if eliminativism is true, then it follows that every time you or I attribute to ourselves or anyone else a desire, a wish, an intention (and so on), we are entertaining a belief which is just *false*, because the ontology of FP is an illusion. Now that is quite an assertion.

SUMMARY

In this chapter we have been investigating accounts of the mind which are examples of the type of view to which philosophers refer as monism. Monism is the view that everything that exists in the universe is the same basic sort of stuff. Materialistic monism or materialism is the view that this basic stuff is matter, from which it follows that the mind must also be material in nature.

We glanced first at the view called philosophical behaviourism, as exemplified in the work of Gilbert Ryle. Ryle contends that all the propositions we use about the mind and its contents, properly understood, involve no undeletable reference to any phenomena other than behaviour, certainly not to private or ghostly events in a non-spatial substance. However, it was found difficult to sustain this claim in certain cases, notably in respect of utterances about pains. The mind–brain identity theory was in part designed to improve on this point of view. Its central contention is that mental events and brain events are identical, are one and the same thing, but referred to in two different vocabularies. These two vocabularies do not need to have the same meaning, since utterances with different meanings can have the same referents. However, while the identity theory can accommodate the difference in meaning between s-statements and bp-statements, it is liable to objections concerning the asymmetry of properties between mental events and brain events, objections derived from the application of Leibniz's Law. In its basic version, it is also open to serious objection on the grounds of chauvinism, since it cannot allow for the multiple realizability of mental events.

It was partly in response to this difficulty that the functionalist account of the mind was proposed, a view designed to be compatible with a materialist account of what there is. The central claim of functionalism is that what makes a mental state mental is not what it is made of but what it does, i.e. what its role or function is in bringing about our behaviour. This has the merit of fitting in well with an evolutionist outlook, i.e. because the mind does have a manifest survival value. However, functionalism is open to a number of powerful objections, chiefly centred on the concept of qualia. The thrust of the objections is that there can be states identical in respect of their function but different in respect of their qualia, or indeed lacking them completely. Since qualia are a key feature of experience, if functionalism cannot account for them, then functionalism is importantly incomplete as an account of the mind.

None of the theories mentioned so far questions the acceptability of the vocabulary in which we ordinarily describe our mental life and on the basis of which we explain and predict the behaviour of others. The central assertion of eliminativism is precisely that this assumption is unjustified. Eliminativists argue that (a) this everyday vocabulary, folk psychology or FP, is an empirical theory; (b) accordingly it is subject, like all empirical theories, to modification or outright rejection if it fails to fit the facts; and (c) that the concepts of FP are not logically coherent with the concepts of neuroscience, failing to explain many areas of mental life; and so (d) FP will be rejected as a false theory when neuroscience is completed.

There are difficulties, however, both with the arguments by which these assertions are supported and with the claim that FP is a theory in the same sense as relativity or evolution.

CONCLUSION

In general terms, what emerges from our investigation of these materialist theories is not only that each involves difficulties of its own but that certain features of the mental emerge as serious problems for all materialist views, notably aboutness and subjectivity. A materialist theory has to be able to give an account of these in terms which make no reference to any features of the world other than those of matter, and no materialist theory has yet succeeded in doing this to the general satisfaction. In the case of aboutness, the nub of the problem is that it seems not even to make sense to suppose that an arrangement of matter, however complex, can sensibly be said to be about anything, any more than a number can be said to have a colour. With regard to subjectivity, it has not proved possible to show how the special mode of access I have to my own mental life can be fitted into a scientific world picture geared to the investigation of inherently public phenomena, i.e. phenomena observable in principle by any observer. Just as Cartesian dualism runs into very serious trouble with mental causation, so materialist theories have equally serious difficulties with these properties of the mental. So, we seem now to have grounds for an interim conclusion that neither the dualist nor the materialist monist approach is free of problems. How then is it appropriate to proceed in our investigation of the mind–body problem? Perhaps what is needed is a fresh approach, to come at the problem from a different point of view. At present, there is an area of investigation which claims to be able to shed light on this question and it is to that area that we turn next.

NOTE

1   Churchland, as he himself would agree, was not the first philosopher to argue for this approach. So far as I know, it was first advanced by two other philosophers: Paul Feyerabend (1963: 49–66) and Richard Rorty (1965: 24–54).

SUGGESTIONS FOR FURTHER READING

(a) On the identity theory
Borst, C.V. (ed.) (1970) *The Mind/Brain Identity Theory*, London: Macmillan. (This book also contains a useful bibliography of further pieces on this view of the mind.)

(b) On functionalism
Braddon-Mitchell, D. and Jackson, F. (1996) *Philosophy of Mind and Cognition*, Oxford: Blackwell.
Churchland, P.M. (1988) *Matter and Consciousness: A Contemporary Introduction to the Philosophy of Mind*, Cambridge (Mass): MIT Press, rev. edn.

(c) On eliminativism
The two books listed above under functionalism also give excellent accounts and criticisms of eliminativism. There are also excellent essays in the relevant entries in:

Guttenplan, S. (ed.) (1994) *A Companion to the Philosophy of Mind,* Oxford: Blackwell.

4 Artificial Intelligence

OBJECTIVES

The overall aim of this chapter is to introduce you to some important claims made by those who assert that the human mind is in certain ways relevantly like a digital computer, a view with important implications for the mind–body problem. By the end of this chapter you should:

- be able to discriminate between different strengths of claim about artificial intelligence;
- understand what a process must be like in order to be computable, including the concept of an algorithm;
- understand the important Chinese Room argument, and some of the principal objections to it;
- understand some further objections made to AI claims, notably those arising from the nature of human skills and abilities, and from the difficulties involved in programming a computer to select relevant data;
- have further consolidated your grasp of the techniques involved in philosophical reading.

It may seem rather disappointing, after so much hard work, not to have arrived at any conclusions more positive than those we have come to. So far in this book, we have examined a number of the most respected accounts of the nature of the mind and its relation to the body and have found that they all – both dualist and monistic materialist – involve logical problems of a distinctly non-trivial kind. Part of the reason for the position in which we find ourselves – indeed a large part of it – lies in the fact that the issue we are trying to grapple with is of great complexity. One of the commonest results of any philosophical investigation into the nature of some important feature of the universe is that the initial question (in our case: What is the mind and how is it related to the body?) turns out very rapidly to involve unsuspected and baffling extra questions. So not to have come up with an answer so far is no disgrace and not a surprise.

However, it might well be that we can make some progress if we come at the question from a new angle. Many advances in human thought have come from applying findings from one branch of inquiry to another, and there is an area of thought at present which claims to shed light on our understanding of the mind – and that is the study of Artificial Intelligence, standardly abbreviated to AI. AI is a vast field and the term is used to refer to a wide variety of research programmes, some of which have no real relevance to the questions we are concerned with in this book (e.g. the development of so-called 'expert' computer programs which allow rapid fault diagnosis in complex systems, both human and artificial). We have the space here to look at just a few central claims made by AI researchers, and the criterion for selection is that they involve assertions about the nature of the mind or its properties or processes which are of philosophical interest. The ultimate goal of much AI research is the construction of machines which can be said to think, in a sense of 'think' comparable to that in which it is applied to human beings and perhaps higher mammals of other species. Many AI enthusiasts would admit that the practical realization of this goal is some distance away; but they are unshaken in their conviction that the enterprise is in principle possible. They hold that there are no problems at the philosophical or conceptual level in what they are trying to achieve, and it is precisely at this level that philosophy has something to contribute to the exercise. Investigating the fundamental assumptions made in AI has the effect of bringing out very forcefully certain features of the mental, and that is a considerable philosophical benefit. (For those seeking more detail and a wider coverage of issues than there is space for here, this is an area well supplied with readable introductory surveys: see the books by Boden 1990, Copeland 1993, Crane 1995, Garnham 1998 and Haugeland 1985 in the bibliography. I would like here to record my debt to these works.)

One of the difficulties which needs to be faced straight away is the need to make the claims of AI researchers and their critics sharp enough to be testable. I doubt if there is any area of research which has produced so much hype and euphoria, or which has generated so much ill-informed nonsense in the press. Only recently I read in a newspaper the opinion of a scientist who claimed that humans would blend with computers within a few decades (the appeal of this future, of course, is that it would give us immortality of a certain kind), apparently innocent of the serious objections there are to the very possibility of so doing, some of which we will come to presently. Again, on a much lower level, the manufacturers of all manner of gismos are now very ready to label their products 'intelligent' when in fact the very simple logic circuits in these products exhibit far less by way of intelligence than the average amoeba.

SOME DEFINITIONS, DISTINCTIONS AND ASSUMPTIONS

In order not to fall into the hype and nonsense trap we need some definitions and distinctions, and to spell out some key assumptions made in AI.

AI comes in a number of different versions, and we can distinguish the principal versions as follows:

AI1   Computers are capable of thought.

AI2   Only computers are capable of thought.

AI3   A machine can think simply as a result of instantiating the appropriate sort of computer program.

AI4   Computer models are useful in the study of the mind.

(Versions 3 and 4 are what John Searle calls strong AI and weak AI respectively: we will be studying one of Searle's papers in detail shortly.) Version 4 is not especially controversial, and we will not consider it further here: just as computer simulations are useful in all sorts of applications, from weather forecasting to economics, there is no reason to doubt that they have their uses in modelling some aspects of mental life. The philosophically interesting claims we shall have to deal with arise from versions 1, 2 and 3, which can be accepted in different combinations. Version 2 is one of the strongest claims: if it is true, and since human beings are capable of thought, it follows from it that human beings are computers. The combination of 1 and 3 is less dramatic, but it does make the production of thinking machines possible: all we need do is write the appropriate program and run it, and we have a thinking machine.

Though this sounds dramatic and interesting, we need to master some more basic concepts before we have a proper focus on precisely what the advocates of AI are claiming, and these concepts are those which lie behind all computing. Don't worry if you are not a computer buff, never use one and know nothing about either computer software or hardware. You don't need to be or do any of these things in order to understand the general concepts we are about to meet. The concepts concerned come up when we try to answer these questions:

What must something be like in order to be *computable*?
What is it that computers actually do?

The answer to the first question involves one of the most important concepts in the theory of computing: in order to be computable, a phenomenon or process must be formulable as an *algorithm*. (The term is derived from the last syllables in the name of a ninth-century Persian mathematician, Abu Ja'far Mohammed ibn Musa *al-Khowarizm*.) A procedure is algorithmic when:

1   every step is specifiable entirely without ambiguity;
2   at every step, there is no ambiguity about what the next step must be: no insight, inspiration or creativity is needed;
3   provided each step is correctly executed, the procedure will produce the desired result in a *finite* number of steps.

All sorts of activities in life, many of them very homely, can be algorithmically specified. As the philosopher Jack Copeland points out:

if you've mixed up your keys and can't tell by sight which one fits your front door, the well-known expedient of trying them in succession is an algorithm for finding the right key: the procedure is sure to work eventually (assuming you haven't lost the key) ... Algorithms are handy things and they crop up in such diverse forms as knitting patterns, the recipes in cookery books for the culinarily inept and the mechanical procedures we learn at school for long multiplication and division.

(Copeland 1993: 1)

For present purposes, it is important to note further that all computers operate algorithmically: a computer program in effect is a specification of the algorithms that the machine will follow. If any phenomenon cannot be specified as an algorithm, because it breaks one or more of the defining conditions for algorithmicity specified above, then it cannot be computed: no program could in principle be written which could model it.

Now we can turn to our second basic question: What do computers do? I am going to ignore analogue computers and deal solely with digital ones, since this is the type of machine with which AI is concerned and with which we are familiar. What a digital computer does – from the basic laptop on which I am writing this to the fastest supercomputer – is to manipulate symbols in accordance with the algorithms specified in the program. So, whereas Copeland's key-finding algorithm involves manipulating pieces of metal, computers manipulate symbols. Typically, such manipulation involves storing and retrieving symbols, testing whether two symbols are the same or not, carrying out simple arithmetical operations such as addition and subtraction and storing the result, and so on. From such a fairly basic repertoire of manipulations, the much more complex operations that we associate with computers – for example, word processing or complex calculations – are constructed.

The silicon-based electronic machines we all know use binary mathematics as their basic symbol system because an electronic circuit has two basic conditions, on or off. All other symbol systems, like natural languages, are encoded in binary form in order to be usable by the machine: e.g. each letter of the Roman alphabet is given a binary value, and so on. There are conventions for the way in which this is done. For example, you may well have come across the acronym ASCII, short for American Standard Code for Information Interchange: in ASCII, typing the letter A on a computer keyboard produces the digit-string 100001 in the circuitry, and analogously all letters (and other characters) have a unique digit string assigned to them. There are other systems for doing this, but they need not concern us here; all that matters is to grasp that what goes on inside a digital computer is the lightning fast manipulation of strings of binary digits according to algorithms. (The phrase 'lightning fast' is not an exaggeration: the transistors on a microchip switch on or off in a billionth of a second; a neurone in the brain fires in a few milliseconds. The neurone is therefore about one million times slower than the transistor. We will see later how the brain makes up for this relative slowness.) To sum up, a digital computer is an algorithmic symbol manipulator.

We need to master one further basic idea and then we can get to grips with AI. This idea is associated with two thinkers, who appear to have arrived at it independently, the American logician Alonzo Church (b. 1903) and the English mathematician Alan Turing (1912–54). What Church and Turing argue comes down to this: once the capacity of a computing machine has reached a certain degree of complexity, it can be made equivalent to *any* other such computing machine. Put another way, machine A can by means of suitable software be made to act exactly as does machine B, and vice versa, except in respect of the time taken to run the program. Any machine of this kind is called a universal Turing machine. I should stress that this claim by Church and Turing is a *hypothesis*, not a proposition which has been formally proved, but it is universally accepted and there are no counter-examples to it. We can take it for granted in what follows.

With these ideas under our belts, we can now focus much more clearly on what advocates of strong versions of AI are claiming with regard to the mind. The strongest version – that *only* computers can think – involves the following claims:

1   All human mental attributes, consciousness and all its modes, are algorithmically specifiable forms of symbol manipulation.
2   The hardware (or rather wetware, as it is often referred to) on which the computation is carried out happens to be the brain, but this is not an essential feature of thought. Thought can be realized in any form of computer hardware with sufficient capacity – this follows from the conjunction of claim number 1 with the Church–Turing hypothesis. There is in principle no reason (AI advocates claim) why thought cannot be realized in a silicon-based machine rather than the neuronally organized electrochemical brain.

There is a further consequence which is involved here which it is important to make explicit: that is, that no specific features of the physical architecture of the brain are being relied on when we think. This simply follows from claim 2. In other words, for strong versions of AI, what is sufficient for (in the sense of a sufficient condition for) thought is the program, not the hardware.

These claims and others like them – all of which make major claims about the nature of mental processes and their relations to physical ones – have attracted strong criticism from some philosophers, and we will consider some of these objections and some replies to them now. Throughout, our aim will be to see what these arguments tell us about the nature of the mind. The first objection has been developed over a number of years by John Searle: if Searle's objection is sound, then the whole enterprise of the type of strong AI he is attacking is doomed, in principle, to failure.

THE CHINESE ROOM: FOR AND AGAINST

Now read paragraphs 1–4 of Searle's essay 'Is the brain's mind a computer program?' (Reading 8).

Reading
p. 205

These opening paragraphs cover some ground which should be familiar after the introductory material you have just read, with one exception. In paragraph 3, Searle refers to another idea put forward in an essay by Alan Turing (Turing 1950). Turing here puts forward a test which he claims will enable us to settle the question: Is a given machine manifesting *intelligence*? The test involves two humans and a computer. One of the humans is the assessor. The assessor sees only a terminal on which appear the answers to questions which are put to either of the other two participants in the test, the second human or the computer. The assessor can direct questions at participant A or participant B, but has no idea at the outset of the test which is the machine and which the human participant. The goal for the assessor is to try to identify whether A or B is the machine by asking any question he chooses to put. Turing's assertion is that, if the assessor cannot decide on the basis of the answers which is the machine and which the human, then we must conclude that the machine in question is manifesting intelligence.

This test, generally referred to as the Turing test, has always been controversial and we will return to it when we consider paragraph 40 of Searle's piece, below.

Reading
p. 206

Now read paragraphs 5–9 of Searle's essay 'Is the brain's mind a computer program?' (Reading 8). These contain the kernel of the Chinese room argument.

EXERCISE 4.1

SEARLE'S CHINESE ROOM

Summarize the argument of paragraphs 5–9 in your own words.

SPECIMEN ANSWER

The system described in the Chinese room thought experiment is meant to be operating exactly as does a digital computer running a program: as standardly defined, the Chinese Room *is* a digital computer. First, there is an input – the persons outside the room handing in slips on which there are Chinese characters. Second, there is a processor running a program – the person in the room with a rule book written in English stating what slips to pass out when given slips are passed in (the person in the room does not understand Chinese). Finally, there is an output – the slips, again with Chinese characters written on them, which are passed out by the person in the room in accordance with the instructions in the rule book. The point is that, though the output is exactly what a person who understands Chinese would expect, the person in the room understands nothing of Chinese. The person in the room, like the computer, merely processes symbols in accordance with rules, i.e. operates algorithmically. In order to *understand* Chinese, I have to know what the characters *mean*, and the person in the room – or the computer – has no idea what the characters mean.

Reading
p. 207

Now read paragraphs 10–16 of Searle's essay 'Is the brain's mind a computer program?' (Reading 8). Searle now states his argument more formally, using some technical terms.

EXERCISE 4.2

SYNTAX AND SEMANTICS

What do you understand by the distinction between syntax and semantics?

SPECIMEN ANSWER

If a symbol system has *meaning*, if it is *about* something, then it is said to have semantics. No one can be said to understand a system which has semantic properties unless they understand the meaning of its symbols. By contrast, if a symbol system can be manipulated successfully solely by the application of formal rules, then it has a syntax – a set of formal rules – but no semantics.

DISCUSSION

We can now restate the central claim of the Chinese room argument in terms of Searle's distinction between syntax and semantics. A computer program is a purely syntactical symbol system, and entirely lacks semantic properties. By contrast, human mental states have a content (i.e. have intentionality or about-ness) and because they have a content they are about something. Put in other words, they have semantics. Therefore human thought is strongly disanalogous to a computer program. Since a program is purely syntactic, running a program cannot be a sufficient condition for having thoughts. Another way of para-phrasing the Chinese room argument is simply to assemble Searle's Axioms 1, 2 and 3 (which are his key premises) and his Conclusion 1. (I should point out that the distinction between syntax and semantics as presented here is intended to be a summary of Searle's view. Other philosophers take a different view of this distinction: notably some would contend that the distinction is not so clear cut as Searle here presents it as being, and if that is so then there are serious consequences for the Chinese Room argument.)

Now read paragraphs 17–22 of Searle's essay 'Is the brain's mind a computer program?' (Reading 8). Searle pauses here in order to make clear what he takes to be established and not established by the Chinese room argument.

Reading
p. 209

EXERCISE 4.3

SEARLE'S ASSERTIONS

Paraphrase the key assertions of this section in your own words.

SPECIMEN ANSWER

(a) The Chinese room argument does not establish that no computer can think (nor is it designed to establish this conclusion).

(b) The same argument does not show that only biological systems are capable of thought – this is an empirical question to which as yet we don't know the answer.

(c) Strong AI, in Searle's sense, involves the thesis that running a program is equivalent to thinking, and the Chinese room argument is designed to refute this view. All a program does is to manipulate symbols in accordance with syntactic rules, and this is not sufficient for understanding.

DISCUSSION

It should now be clear why it is so necessary in philosophy to state the position which is being defended or objected to as precisely as possible, and, in the present case, why it is necessary to be very careful to discriminate the many different positions which can be and are taken up by advocates of AI. The Chinese room argument is intended to refute only one possible position in AI: many others are unaffected by it.

Reading p. 209

Now read paragraphs 23–7 of Searle's essay 'Is the brain's mind a computer program?' (Reading 8) in conjunction with the following account of two technical terms he uses here that we have not so far come across: 'parallel distributed processing' and 'von Neumann computer'. It is easier to begin with the latter.

All the computers with which we are familiar are built on principles first set out in the 1940s and associated with the mathematician John von Neumann (1903–57): these machines are said to have 'von Neumann architecture'. Among the principles are the following (see Burks *et al.* 1946):

1   A von Neumann computer operates in a step by step fashion, i.e. it carries out the instructions in its program one after the other.

2   Any string of symbols is stored in one memory location only.

3   Each memory location has a unique 'address' (i.e. a binary number which uniquely individuates it).

4   Access to any string of symbols is possible only by using the address of the string.

5   The process is controlled from a central element in the system, the central processing unit (CPU).

It is interesting to note that in almost every important respect, the human brain does not operate on these principles. Though the story is far from complete at the moment, it first appears that the brain operates on a principle called parallel processing, i.e. many operations are carried out simultaneously, rather than one after another as in a von Neumann computer. This is how the brain compensates for the relative slowness of the firing of neurones (you will recall that we noticed above that the transistors on a microchip operate about a million times faster than do neurones). Second, the brain uses what is termed *distributed storage* for any items in its memory: that is, the same item is stored in many places and a given neurone can participate in the storage of more than one memory item, again entirely different from the unique-address von Neumann principle. Third – and very important for the nature of human thought processes – human memory has the property of being *content addressable*: we are able to recall items from our memory on the basis of fragments of their content, i.e. what they are about, or on the basis of analogies to some aspects of the content of the memory, or at the prompting of an indefinitely large number of linguistic descriptions. To state the obvious, when we try to recall something, we do not do so by trying to recall where in our head it is stored: we try to recall a specific content – Where did I leave the car keys? What was the name of the person I met at so-and-so's last month? What did Descartes say about interaction? What do functionalists believe? And so on. It is the fact that our memory is content-addressable that makes the very basic process of the association of ideas possible. It is what lies behind the common experience of being reminded of one thing by some aspect of another to which the first bears only a partial resemblance or analogy – indeed it is hard to imagine what our mental experience would be like if our memory did not operate in this way, and I would argue that it is a necessary condition for creative thought in all areas. The basic literary devices of metaphor and simile, for instance, rely on our capacity to see illuminating analogies between things which are superficially dissimilar. There is no analogue to content addressability in the operation of a von Neumann computer: its program will tell it, for example, to go to memory location 001000110 and it will do so and then do with the contents of that location whatever the next instruction tells it to. I am not aware that anyone has managed to incorporate anything like viable content address-ability in a von Neumann computer.

One of the most interesting and exciting lines of research currently being pursued in the area of AI is the development of machines which do not use von Neumann architecture but instead are wired up somewhat as are the neurones in the brain, albeit (at present) in a vastly simplified fashion. Combining the terms we have just met, these machines are said to incorporate *parallel distributed processing* or PDP. The same principle, because of the multiple interconnections of the units in the system, is also referred to as *connectionism* (see Rumelhart and McClelland 1986, Vol. 1, especially essays 1–4). The neurones in the brain are interconnected in an extremely complex way – (see Figure 4.1 below). The wiring of a PDP machine mimics this in a basic fashion (see Figure 4.2). Though this area of research is still in its infancy, its results are promising.

With all this in mind, we can now return to Searle's text. He states his main thesis about connectionism in paragraphs 24–7, where he claims that the type of architecture employed by a computer is irrelevant to the force of the Chinese room argument. A computer simply runs a program; a program is merely a set of syntactic instructions, and so a connectionist computer can no more be said to understand than can a von Neumann machine.

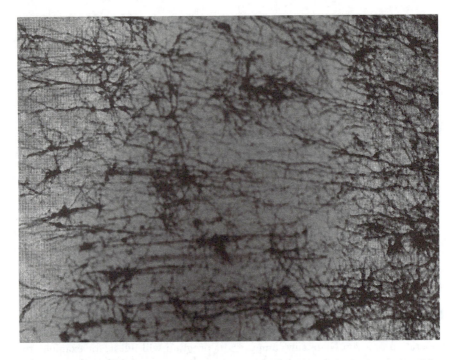

Figure 4.1   The arborizations of about 1% of the neurons near a vertical slice through the visual cortex of a rabbit

Source: Photomicrograph by Hendrik Van der Loos. Reproduced from Blakemore (1977: 84) by permission of the publisher.

Note: The full height of the figure corresponds to the thickness of the cortex, which is in this instance about 2mm.

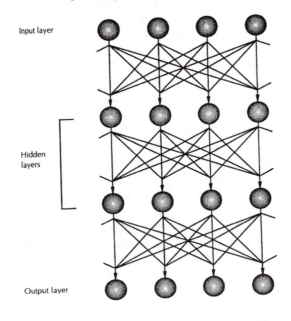

Input layer

Hidden layers

Output layer

Figure 4.2   Connections between the layers of artificial neurons in a PDP network

Source: Reproduced from Copeland (1993: 211) by permission of the publisher.

EXERCISE 4.4

CHINESE GYM ARGUMENT

In paragraph 25, Searle also modifies the Chinese room argument in a way intended to make it fully applicable to connectionist computers, and this new version he calls the Chinese gym argument. State the Chinese gym argument in your own words, being careful to highlight which conclusions are being drawn from which premises.

SPECIMEN ANSWER

The Chinese gym is intended operate as does a computer with connectionist architecture. The people in the gym operate as individual elements in a connectionist computer. Given a detailed instruction manual (i.e. program) the system composed by the Chinese gym will give correct answers in Chinese to questions posed in Chinese. The key premise and conclusions are:

Premise 1	No individual in the gym understands Chinese.
Conclusion 1	Therefore, the information in the gym is processed without regard to its semantic properties.
Conclusion 2	Therefore, the system as a whole cannot come to understand Chinese.

DISCUSSION

We can leave the Chinese gym argument at that for the moment. We will return to it presently when considering objections to Searle's views.

Now read paragraphs 28–36 of Searle's essay 'Is the brain's mind a computer program' (Reading 8).

Reading
p. 210

Searle here goes on to argue that there is a further important disanalogy between the activity of the brain and the execution of a program by a computer.

EXERCISE 4.5

MIND AND BRAIN ACCORDING TO SEARLE

What view of the relation of mental events to brain events is Searle advocating here?

SPECIMEN ANSWER

That mental events are caused by physical events, specifically by neurophysiological events in the brain. He sums this up in his Axiom 4: brains cause minds.

DISCUSSION

We can now set out Searle's complex argument, incorporating Axiom 4, designed to prove his Conclusion 4 in paragraph 36. The argument can be stated as follows:

Premise 1	The basic processes of computation (in our terms, the execution of the algorithms specified in the program) can be realized in more than one type of hardware.
Premise 2	Brains *cause* mental events in virtue of specific neurophysiological processes which occur in them.
Premise 3	Mental events are always effects of brain events, never vice versa.
Premise 4	A simulation of a given type of event is not the same as an instance or duplicate of that type of event (e.g. a simulation of the workings of the economy does not generate wealth or bring about poverty: only the actual workings of the economy do that).
Premise 5	In particular, simulations of events do not have the causal powers of the actual events they simulate.
Premise 6	Computer programs which model brain processes are simulations of these processes.
Premise 7	Like effects can only be produced by causes having at least equivalent causal powers.
Conclusion 1	Therefore, any cause capable of causing a mind must have causal powers at least equivalent to those of the brain (Searle's Conclusion 2; this follows from Premise 2 and Premise 7).
Conclusion 2	Computer simulations of brain processes lack the causal powers of brain processes; (this follows from Premise 5 and Premise 6).
Conclusion 3	(Searle's Conclusion 3) Therefore, any artefact that produced mental phenomena, any artificial brain, would have to be able to duplicate the specific causal powers of brains, and it could not do that just by running a formal program; (this follows from Premise 7 and Conclusion 2).
Conclusion 4	(Searle's Conclusion 4) Therefore, the way that human brains actually cause mental phenomena cannot be solely by virtue of running a computer program.

The key assertion in this argument is that brains cause minds. Another way of putting this is to say that, for Searle, minds are hardware-dependent for their existence. There cannot be a mind which does not need some form of material basis for its realization. The reason he gives here for this view is an empirical one: namely, that so far as is known at present, every mental event is dependent for its existence on a particular organization or structure of neurones – neuronal architectures, as he puts it. He is, therefore, contending that disembodied mental existence is not possible. Notice, however, that Searle does not say that mental events are *numerically identical to* neuronal events, or (to put the same thing another way) are the same thing as brain events. Equally, he does not say exactly how he thinks mental events and brain events are related. We will come back to the issue of the relation of the brain and the mind in the conclusion to this book as a whole.

Now read paragraphs 37–46 of Searle's essay 'Is the brain's mind a computer program' (Reading 8).

Reading
p. 212

We can now turn to consider objections to the Chinese room argument and its Chinese gym variant. Searle lists five objections which have been made to it in paragraph 38. Of these, the most commonly made and discussed is what Searle calls the systems reply, to which he devotes paragraph 40, and we will restrict our attention here to this point. (This has always been and continues to be the most discussed reply to the Chinese room: cf. Copeland 1993, ch. 6 *passim* and p. 226, where he uses the same objection against the Chinese gym variant; and Braddon-Mitchell and Jackson 1996: 107 seqq.)

EXERCISE 4.6

SYSTEMS OBJECTION TO SEARLE

State the systems reply – objection (c) in paragraph 38 – in your own words, showing how it is meant to refute the Chinese room argument.

SPECIMEN ANSWER

The reply concedes that the person in the room does not understand Chinese, but denies that this entails that the system as a whole of which the person is a part does not understand Chinese. Put more formally, the premise:

Premise   The operator in the room does not understand Chinese
                 does not entail the conclusion Searle wants, i.e. that:

Conclusion   The whole system of which the operator is a part does not
                 understand Chinese.

DISCUSSION

Searle's reply is straightforward: the systems objection in no way establishes that the system is aware of the semantics, i.e. the meaning, of the Chinese symbols, and only if the system is aware of the semantics can the Chinese room argument be refuted by this objection. Therefore, the objection fails. He emphasizes this by his revision of the argument: there is no need to imagine the operator locked in a room. Given a good enough memory, the rule book for symbol manipulation can be memorized by the operator, who can do all the manipulations mentally. The operator will then behave like someone who understands Chinese, but manifestly does not understand Chinese so long as he is unaware of the meanings of the symbols he is manipulating.

That is not the end of the story, however. Other philosophers have argued that here Searle is making his thought experiment so simple that it bears no relation to the degree of complexity that would be needed, in respect of both hardware and software, in any system that could produce the sort of answers that the Chinese room would have to produce in order to be fully intelligible to a Chinese speaker; and further, that this complexity matters in the argument. One version of this objection is developed by the American philosopher Daniel Dennett (b. 1942) in his *Consciousness Explained* (1991: 435–40). Dennett puts his point as follows:

> any program that could actually hold up its end in the conversation ... would have to be an extraordinarily supple, sophisticated, and multilayered system, brimming with 'world knowledge' and meta-knowledge and meta-meta-knowledge about its own responses, the likely responses of its interlocutor, and much, much, more. Searle does not deny that programs can have all this structure, of course. He simply discourages us from attending to it. But if we are to do a good job imagining the case, we are not only entitled but obliged to imagine that the program Searle is hand-simulating has all this structure – and more, if only we can imagine it. But then it is no longer *obvious*, I trust, that there is no genuine understanding ... going on. *Maybe* the billions of actions of all those highly structured parts produce genuine understanding in the system after all. If your response to this hypothesis is that you haven't the faintest idea whether there would be genuine understanding in such a complex system, that is already enough to show that Searle's thought experiment depends, illicitly, on your imagining too simple a case, an irrelevant case, and drawing the 'obvious' conclusion from it.
>
> (Dennett 1991: 438)

One can put the criticism more formally (as Dennett goes on to do): Searle's Chinese room argument is an enthymeme and turns on a suppressed premise whose truth is not obvious. We can show the bare bones of his argument as follows:

Premise 1   Any section of program small enough for us to imagine manifestly doesn't understand anything (i.e. because it is only a statement of an algorithm for transforming strings of symbols according to a rule).

Premise 2	More of the same (i.e. running ever more complex programs), no matter how much more, will not produce understanding.
Conclusion 1	Therefore, just running a program, however complicated, cannot produce understanding.

It is Premise 2 which is the unstated premise in the Chinese room argument, and it is Dennett's contention that it is by no means obviously true.

The next question is: Who believes that sheer complexity makes a difference and why? The answer to that is: quite a lot of scientists, and on good observational grounds. We need to dwell for a moment on this idea of complexity in order to appreciate the force of Dennett's reasoning. (There is an excellent, straightforward account of complexity by a physicist in Trefil 1997, ch. 13.) In the language of science, a *complex system* is one which is composed of many elements or agents, which mutually interact. A simple example (given by Trefil ibid.) of a complex system is a pile of grains of sand. Up to a certain size, such a pile is static: the web of forces generated by the mutual interaction of the constituent grains is such that the forces cancel one another out. But at a certain point, if you go on adding grains, the result is an avalanche somewhere on the pile. That is, when the pile reaches a certain degree of complexity, its behaviour changes radically and it exhibits an entirely new sort of property, in this case the avalanche. Such a new sort of property, generated by increasing complexity, is called an *emergent property*, because it only emerges when the system is sufficiently complex. These sorts of sudden changes in the behaviour or properties of complex systems are fairly common in the natural world.

Dennett is relying on this idea in making his objection to Searle. His point is this: it genuinely isn't *obvious* that a program which is as complicated as it would have to be to give out correct sentences in Chinese (or any other natural language, of course) does not manifest understanding. Understanding, it is suggested, may well be an emergent property of such systems. I want to leave this point at that for the moment: I will come back to the idea of complexity in the conclusion to the book as a whole.

Paragraphs 41–6 inclusive need not detain us here. They deal with a variant of the systems reply put forward by Paul and Patricia Churchland. You will see that the reply takes the form of an argument from analogy. Searle's reply is that the objection fails because the alleged analogy breaks down. There is no relevant similarity between the formal symbols which make up a computer program on the one hand, and electromagnetic radiation on the other. The latter consists of energy waves, and stands in a causal relation to observable physical effects, and to other forms of energy; the former by contrast have no relevantly similar causal properties. Accordingly, the two items alleged to be analogous are not analogous at all in any relevant respect.

Now read paragraphs 47–50 of Searle's essay 'Is the brain's mind a computer program' (Reading 8).

Reading
p. 215

In these concluding remarks there are two points of serious philosophical interest which take up some issues we have met earlier in this book. The first concerns the Turing test for intelligent behaviour that we came across earlier in this chapter.

EXERCISE 4.7

CHINESE ROOM AND THE TURING TEST

Observed from the point of view of its output, would the Chinese room system as described in paragraphs 5–7 satisfy the Turing test?

SPECIMEN ANSWER

In my view, the answer to this question must be 'yes': the system gives out linguistic output indistinguishable from that of a native Chinese speaker, and so on the Turing test it would have to be counted as intelligent. What this shows, as Searle (among others) indicates, is that the test is too lenient – it allows too many things to count as intelligent.

Another point I want to highlight concerns dualism. Searle makes the interesting claim that the Strong AI he has been arguing against in this essay is committed to a form of dualism in the philosophy of mind, not the two-substance dualism of Descartes but a form of dualism nonetheless. What he is driving at is this: he makes the point repeatedly in his essay that for Strong AI, what matters about thought is the program not the hardware (or wetware). This presupposes that the mind is in some way *radically* different in nature from whatever physical basis – silicon or neurones – it happens to be realized in. Only if this is true can the other assertions of Strong AI be made consistent. On this view, minds are not dependent for their realization on the existence of any one specific form of physical basis. Now that may not entail that they are substances in the Cartesian sense, but it does make them remarkably different in nature from bodies, and to believe that is to all intents to accept some form of dualism, albeit one which is not fully specified. Thus, Searle argues, we find a paradox at the heart of AI: a branch of research at the cutting edge of technological advance, firmly rooted in materialistic science, finds itself committed to a form of dualist ontology.

SOME FURTHER CONSIDERATIONS ABOUT AI

Let us suppose that a watertight rebuttal of the Chinese room argument, in all its versions, could be found: would it follow that the most serious philosophical problems arising from the claims of AI had been solved? I want now to look at some arguments put forward by philosophers who believe the answer to this question is a resounding 'no', and once again we will focus on views which include philosophically interesting assumptions about the mind and its operations.

We can begin by fleshing out the central claims of the advocates of the stronger versions of AI, the versions we have called AI 1, 2 and 3. In 1958, one of the staunchest advocates of this sort of view, Herbert Simon, wrote the following:

It is not my aim to shock you … But the simplest way I can summarize is to say that there are now in the world machines that think, that learn and create. Moreover, their ability to do these things is going to increase rapidly until – in a visible future – the range of problems they can handle will be coextensive with the range to which the human mind has been applied.

(Newell and Simon 1958: 6)

With his fellow researcher Allen Newell he went on to claim:

Intuition, insight, and learning are no longer the exclusive possessions of humans: any large high-speed computer can be programmed to exhibit them also.

(ibid.)

Three years later Newell and Simon published a paper in which they make explicit the key assumptions about the nature of human thought processes on which these claims rest:

It can be seen that this approach makes no assumption that the 'hardware' of computers and brains are similar, beyond the assumptions that both are general-purpose symbol-manipulating devices and that the computer can be programmed to execute elementary information processes functionally quite like those executed by the brain.

(Newell and Simon 1961: 9)

As the American philosopher Hubert Dreyfus goes on to explain, this passage has the virtue of spelling out what assumptions have to be true for this sort of strong AI programme to be possible. As he also explains, however, these assumptions are not small ones: rather, they make very large claims about the human mind and its workings which are by no means immune to criticism. The four key assumptions either explicit or presupposed in the passages by Newell and Simon are as follows (cf. Dreyfus 1992: 156):

1   A biological assumption that at some level of operation the brain processes information in separate operations which are the biological equivalent of on/off switches: remember that a microchip is in effect a device consisting of a very large number of switches, each of which has only two possible states, on or off.

2   A psychological assumption that the mind can be viewed as a device operating on bits of information according to formal rules. Remember that, as we saw in the opening section of this chapter, this is precisely what a digital computer does: all the information in it is encoded as binary digits, which it manipulates according to algorithms, themselves also encoded as binary digits. If it turns out, therefore, that the mind does not operate, or does not operate all the time, algorithmically, then the mind is not a computer. A computer is a device which manipulates symbols according to rules.

3   An assumption about the nature of human knowledge, namely that all human knowledge can be formalized, or, put another way, that anything that can be understood can be stated in terms of logical relations. (Only if knowledge

has this property can it be manipulated in accordance with rules. A digital computer can only operate in a strictly rule-governed fashion, and if any elements of human knowledge are not rule-governed, a computer could not emulate them.)

4   An assumption so basic in what it asserts about the way the world is structured that it belongs to the branch of philosophy called ontology, a term we met when we considered eliminativism in Chapter 3. This most fundamental assumption made by classical AI is this: What exists — what there is — is a set of facts each of which is logically independent of all the others. (This assumption is needed because only if it is true can any item of information that can be the object of (human) thought can be fed into a computer. A computer can handle information only in the form of independent bits, and therefore, if it turned out that any elements of human thought are not like this, then in principle they could not be fed into a computer and accordingly a computer could not copy that aspect of human thought. This is a very abstract assumption indeed, but I will try to show that it is not as hard to grasp what Dreyfus is driving at than it might seem at first blush.)

In the next section, we are going to look at some of the objections Dreyfus and others make to the last three of these assumptions. Before doing so, however, I want to stress a basic point: what Dreyfus is doing is a centrally *philosophical* activity. He is articulating or unveiling the basic assumptions which are being made in a given field of enquiry, in this case of course AI, and then subjecting these assumptions to close logical scrutiny. If it turns out that these assumptions are logically untenable, then it will follow that *this* sort of AI is doomed. This is one of the ways, unsuspected by those who have never done philosophy, in which philosophy genuinely contributes to the advance of knowledge. There is no area of human intellectual activity which does not rest on some basic general assumptions, and it is with the identification and scrutiny of these assumptions that philosophers are centrally concerned.

SOME PROBLEMS WITH THE FOUNDATIONS OF AI

As just noted, Dreyfus (among others) takes issue with three of the closely related presuppositions of AI set out above: that the mind processes bits of information according to formal rules; that whatever can be understood can be stated in terms of logical relations, and that the world consists of a set of logically independent facts. The arguments we are about to consider have as their goal to show that each of these assumptions is not true of human experience. If these arguments are successful, it will follow that human experience is in important respects non-computable. From that in turn it will follow that a digital computer cannot in principle think in the same sense of the term 'think' in which it is applied to human beings.

We can begin from a distinction widely used in philosophy and which we have noticed briefly before, the distinction between *knowing that* and *knowing how*. 'Knowledge that' is any sort of knowledge which can be stated in a propositional form. A great deal of what we learn in life is of this kind, and ranges from the sort of academic knowledge summed up in encyclopaedias and learned works of all kinds, to the much more homely but essential set of items we need to know to get about our daily business, e.g. what to feed the cat with; what time your favourite programme comes on; where you keep the car keys, and so on. On the other hand, a great deal of what we all know, and some of the things you have learned from working through this book, does not consist of knowledge that but consists of abilities or skills, and this sort of knowledge philosophers call knowledge how.

Knowing how to drive a car; how to play a musical instrument; how to behave appropriately in a situation you have never met before; how to spot the logical order of premises in an argument are all examples of knowledge how. Dreyfus, in company with many other philosophers, argues – and this is a key assertion in their strategy – that knowing how cannot wholly be reduced to (remember that term from our study of eliminativism) knowing that. Put another way, they claim that the possession of a certain skill, knowing how to do something, cannot be summed up in a set of propositions, however exhaustive the set of propositions might be. We can take driving a car as our example. Certainly when you learn to drive, part of what you do is to absorb some propositional knowledge: in a manual-gearbox car, the pedal to the left of the brake is the clutch; to bring the car to an imperceptible, smooth stop, it is best to release the pressure on the brake just before stopping; in snow and ice, it is often better to start in second gear, as this diminishes the chance of wheel spin, and so forth. Yet, the argument goes, there is much more to being able to drive a car than knowing these propositions and many more like them: as we all know, there is more to it than that. You do not possess the skill of driving until you have learned to handle a real vehicle in the varied conditions of the real world. Moreover, what you do when you do gain this ability (the argument goes) is not just to learn more propositions: you gain the open-ended property we call a skill. One of the most important features of skills is that they allow us to respond appropriately to situations we have not met before: skills allow us to adapt fairly readily to the demands of a reality so complex as to appear to us most of the time as unpredictable. As has often been pointed out, human problem-solving skills are (as has been indicated) open-ended and creative in their application: fortunately for us, there is no point at which we can know definitively in advance that these skills will be exhausted. The most complex situations we meet characteristically involve getting on with other people, and this is a crucial area in which we rely on our ever-evolving skills. To point out the obvious, no two individuals are the same, and so (as the Japanese proverb has it) every meeting is unique. We have some rules in the form of laws, morals, manners and etiquette, but appropriate responses involve rather more than using rules. Real skill begins where the benchmark rules end.

Finally – and this is another key premise in the argument – we should note that having abilities of this kind does not involve being able to state in the form of propositions what one is doing. Those who can do these things just do them: they do not need to rehearse principles in their heads and make deductions before doing the skilful thing. Indeed the speed of execution needed in the execution of many skills just will not allow you time to do any reasoning: if you reason what to do while your car is skidding you will crash before you arrive at a decision as to what to do. The same is true of other complex skills such as being able to play a musical instrument: skilful players do not ratiocinate about finger pressures or embouchure, and so on: they just play, and it is highly unlikely that they could verbalize what they are doing if asked, especially in those rare and special performances we call 'inspired'. What follows from this (the argument goes) is that having a skill or knowing how to do something is at least in part a non-propositional aspect of human knowledge. That we recognize this is shown in the way we teach people these skills: you do not learn to drive, or to use any instrument or tool in a skilful way, just by learning propositions: you have to practise – often for years – and when you have practised enough, you are not master of more propositions: you just do it.

Now knowledge of this kind, knowledge how, is a central component of human intelligence, and if a machine is to be intelligent in the sense in which a person is intelligent, then it must be able to show this sort of intelligence.

EXERCISE 4.8

COMPUTABILITY AND HUMAN EXPERIENCE

Granted what you have read in this chapter so far, you should now be able to sum up the main premises of the argument designed to establish the conclusion that a major element of human experience is not computable. Set out the main steps of this argument, beginning from the definition of a computer.

SPECIMEN ANSWER

Premise 1	Computers are devices which manipulate symbols according to rules (or algorithms).
Premise 2	Having skills or 'knowledge how' is a major aspect of human intelligence.
Premise 3	Skills or 'knowledge how' are not wholly reducible to obeying rules and acquiring 'knowledge that' (or propositional knowledge).
Conclusion 1	Therefore, knowledge how is not wholly computable.
Conclusion 2	Therefore, a major aspect of human intelligence is not wholly computable.

DISCUSSION

As you know, there are two major ways in which an argument can be defective: either it can be invalid (i.e. its conclusion does not logically follow from its premises) or it can be unsound (i.e. one or more of its premises may be false). The argument in my answer to the preceding Exercise is valid, and so advocates of the sort of AI we are considering, when arguing against it, have to argue that it is unsound. What they typically do is to argue that Premise 3 is false: they claim that it *is* possible to state every aspect of human knowledge as propositions or rules. If this turned out to be true, then a major obstacle of principle in the way of producing a machine that can think would have been cleared away. The most thoroughgoing attempt to date to demonstrate that Premise 3 is false is the CYC project. We will take a brief look at this project next, and we will see once again how important philosophical considerations can be when applied to a project which looks on the face of it to be a purely empirical blend of science and technology.

THE CYC PROJECT

The CYC project – the term is derived from the word 'encyclopaedia' – was established in 1984 by the Microelectronics and Computer Technology Corporation of Texas. The goal of the project, and it is a key element in the programme of the sort of AI we are considering, is no less than to state human common-sense knowledge entirely in propositional form, and to enter it into a digital computer as a database. The computer would then have a knowledge base comparable to that of an average adult human. The initial estimate was that one hundred million propositions would be needed and this huge figure, if you reflect on the matter, is not likely to be an overestimate. Let us think for a moment about what you would need to tell the computer for it to have a store of knowledge comparable to that of an average adult human. Putting in the specialized knowledge, largely propositional, that one learns in educational establishments or is summed up in encyclopaedias is the easy part. It is much more difficult to spot and programme in the much more basic elements of common-sense knowledge which guide one's behaviour but which would hardly ever be explicitly noticed in the course of an entire adult life. For example, as Dreyfus points out (1992: 235 seqq.), a huge amount of our common-sense knowledge is derived from the fact that we have bodies of a certain size and strength: our estimates of size, weight, strength and position; our sense of inside and outside, accessibility and inaccessibility all derive ultimately from the fact that we are embodied in a certain way. A computer has no body in this sense, and so every aspect of human experience which reflects this condition of being embodied in a particular way has to be converted into propositions and input into the machine. Again, we gain most of our knowledge of the world from sense perception, and so a way has to be found to tell the computer what it is like to perceive. Again, we have purposes which we endeavour to accomplish through action, often with emotions among their motives: a computer must therefore be told in some way what it is like to have emotions and purposes.

To see what the CYC programmers are up against, we need take only a very humdrum example: What would you have to tell a computer in order for it to respond as would an adult human walking into a room and seeing a chair? The programmers need to tell the computer what it is like to have a body of a certain size which sometimes needs to rest. Our embodied condition governs our beliefs about whether the room is large or small; well-lit or dark; whether the windows are too high or too low or just right; whether the room is the right temperature or not, and so on. And then there is the issue of what is involved in recognizing the chair. Here there is a deeper problem, which Dreyfus describes as follows:

> To recognize an object as a chair ... means to understand its relation to other objects and to human beings. This involves a whole context of human activity of which the shape of our body, the institution of furniture, the inevitability of fatigue, constitute only a small part, and these factors in turn are no more isolable than the chair. They all get *their* meaning in the context of human activity of which they form a part.
>
> (Dreyfus 1992: 210; author's italics)

Dreyfus is here suggesting that the fourth of the assumptions we noticed above – that the world is a set of independently statable facts – is false. He is suggesting that human experiences cannot be described as can states of the physical universe, because human experiences have meanings. We do not generally have to work out these meanings: we experience the world as having meanings, and these meanings are derived from the very complicated context of beliefs, practices and institutions we call a culture. The difficulty for the CYC programmers is that it is not clear how experience thus structured can be split up into facts which are logically independent of one another. For example, how do you formulate a proposition that states what a chair is which does not presuppose and imply a host of other propositions, let alone a proposition which specifies when it is impolite to use a chair? To sum up this point: human experience is the experience of an embodied, mortal animal of a certain size and strength moulded within the complex set of institutions called a culture. Our experiences have the meanings they have for us because of these standing conditions, and these meanings are not logically independent. For the sort of AI we are considering to succeed, a way would have to be found to articulate these features of experience in a propositional fashion, and it is not at all clear that this can be done. Let us call this *the meaning problem*.

A second problem facing the CYC enterprise is one we can call *the ontology problem*. The common-sense knowledge possessed by every adult human rests – even if most adults are unaware of the fact – on a framework of concepts of great generality which taken together classify everything there is into some broad, basic classes. Put another way, to use a term we have come across before in this book, common-sense knowledge includes an ontology, a set of assumptions about what sorts of things exist and what sorts of fundamentally different things there are. If a computer is to stand any chance of thinking in the way that a human being does, then its database must include an ontology which reflects ours. The CYC programmers have adopted provisionally a division of what there is into five fundamental types of thing. This amounts to the claim that everything in the universe falls into one of the following five classes: tangible objects; intangible objects; composites (by which is meant items which have both a tangible and an intangible component – people are said to fall into this class); events; and finally mathematical objects. The problem, as the philosopher Jack Copeland points out, is that this list is both untidy and much too simple:

CYC's category of 'intangible object' is nothing more than a ragbag. It contains such disparate things as the world recession, people's pains (you can touch 'where it hurts' but you cannot touch the pain itself), northerly gales, CYC's own internal representations, and the meaning of the sentence 'Curry is hot'. Nor is it at all clear that the category of events belongs in this list: events may not be a type of object at all. Two different objects cannot be in the same place at the same time, yet it seems that two different events can: Fred may simultaneously jump into the river and escape the charging bull ... Turning to meanings, is the meaning of 'Curry is hot' really an object at all?

(Copeland 1993: 104–5)

Copeland's general point is that our common-sense ontology is much richer in its distinctions than this fivefold proposal from the CYC team recognizes. Only when all our common-sense distinctions have been properly identified will a computer have a chance of emulating human intelligence.

Third, as if the two problems mentioned so far were not enough, another major difficulty faces the CYC team, a difficulty referred to as *the frame problem* (cf. Copeland 1993, ch. 5; Dreyfus 1992: 43 seqq.; Dennett: 'Cognitive wheels: the frame problem of AI' in Boden 1990). We have established that human experience involves a vast apparatus of both knowledge how and knowledge that; it involves a subtle ontology and is an experience of meanings derived from the rich set of institutions we call a culture. Now even if – and this is a big 'if' for the reasons we have just encountered – some way could be found of codifying all this in a form a digital computer can handle, this would not be a sufficient condition for intelligence in the sense in which that term is applied to humans. It is a necessary condition for human intelligence that we should be able to select from this vast and subtle array of knowledge that and knowledge how those items which are *relevant* or *appropriate* to the situation with which we happen to be faced. We do this selection constantly and almost always without conscious deliberation, but a computer does nothing its program does not tell it to do, and so a way must be found to enable a computer to select from its colossal database precisely and only the relevant items. A simple example given by Copeland (ibid.: 115) shows just how difficult this is.

EXERCISE 4.9

RELEVANCE

Are the following two statements relevant to one another?

1   For the last eight years the rains in Malawi have not started until the end of November.
2   Timber production in Zambia has increased 500 per cent in the period 1972–92.

SPECIMEN ANSWER

It all depends on the context. If you are trying to work out reasons for climate change in sub-Saharan Africa, then possibly yes; but in many other cases no.

DISCUSSION

The problem, obvious once it is pointed out, is that there is no way of specifying in advance all the possible contexts or frames of reference there are, and what cannot be specified by means of rules cannot be computed. The CYC team's response to this problem has been to formulate what they call relevance axioms, e.g. items are mutually relevant if they are close together in time. But, first, this is much too vague to be useful (how close exactly?) and, second, just false on any reasonable understanding of the phrase 'close together in time'. For example, in order to understand why Western culture embodies the values and assumptions it does, it is necessary to know something of the culture of Greece in classical times, two and a half millennia ago. Is that close in time? Again two and half millennia are less than a blink, as it were, in cosmic timescales, and yet events in cosmic time are relevant to our present existence. One of the conditions for the existence of life on this planet is the existence of certain heavy elements. These were formed in stellar supernovae of a remoteness in time and space we can only grasp mathematically; but the supernovae have a direct causal bearing on our being here at all.

By implication, what the frame problem shows is the fantastic agility of human thought processes in selecting relevant data from a huge store at the prompting of a vast and unspecifiable range of different stimuli: bear in mind that many of our reactions are reactions to language, and that the number of well-formed sentences in natural languages alone is to all intents infinite. As the point is often put, human thought is massively adaptable in the face of the complicated, untidy variousness of reality, and unless a machine can match that there is no real reason to suppose it is intelligent in the way that we are. Further, only a theory of the mind–brain which can explain how this massive adaptability is possible will be worth considering.

EXERCISE 4.10

REVISION

Summarize briefly the three objections to AI we have considered in the preceding section.

SPECIMEN ANSWER

1   The meaning problem: human experience is experienced as meaningful, and it derives its meanings from a complex culture. It is not easy to see how such experience could be stated in such a way as to be computable.

2   The ontology problem: common-sense knowledge involves a compli-

cated set of assumptions about the basic classification of what there is. No one has yet produced a computable version of this.

3   The frame problem: intelligent thought requires that we select from our knowledge base only those items which are relevant to the context in question. Since it is impossible to specify all contexts in advance, it is hard to see how a computable version of this selection process can be devised.

SUMMARY

In this chapter we have considered some of the fundamental claims advanced by advocates of AI, and investigated some of the philosophical difficulties associated with them. If the claims made by advocates of AI were true, they would have major implications for our understanding of the mind.

We began with an analysis of what precisely is being claimed in the stronger versions of AI, notably that all our mental operations consist of the manipulation of symbols in accordance with algorithms, and then moved on to consider one of the most discussed of all arguments against AI, Searle's Chinese Room. Searle's aim is to show that the mind does not stand to the brain as the program does to the computer. He argues that a computer program has a syntax but no semantics, i.e. it is a set of rules without a meaning. Since our mental experience is an experience of meanings, i.e. it has a semantics, our mind cannot simply be a computer programme.

A number of objections have been urged against this argument, of which the most powerful is the systems objection. This is the claim that just because the operator in the room doesn't understand Chinese, it doesn't follow that the system as a whole doesn't understand Chinese. An important feature of the thought experiment at the heart of the Chinese Room argument is that it is very simple. It can be argued persuasively that it is much too simple: any system capable of producing convincing sentences in Chinese (or any other natural language of course) would need to be so complex that it is not obvious that one could confidently say in principle that it does not understand Chinese.

We then considered three further problems of a philosophical nature raised by the claims of AI: the meaning problem, the ontology problem and the frame problem.

CONCLUSION

It may seem that our study of the claims of the sort of AI we have been looking at, the sort which claims that there is a great similarity of principle obtaining between digital computers on the one hand and the mind–brain on the other, has been purely negative. In one sense this is so: the arguments we have looked at do tend to show that the claims of this sort of AI – which the philosopher John Haugeland has christened Good Old Fashioned AI, or GOFAI – are decidedly optimistic. Yet, on the positive side, we have found out a good deal about what philosophy can do when applied to a discipline at the sharp end of science and technology. We have found that GOFAI is suspicious because it rests on assumptions about human experience which are unacceptable for *philosophical* reasons: it makes claims about the mind which involve conceptual confusions, and these need to be exposed. Some of these reasons involve important concepts we have come across before – notably, aboutness – which come up repeatedly in discussions of the mind, whether under this name or as the closely related notions of semantics and the meaningfulness of human experience.

Let us be clear, though, about how much and how little is established by the arguments we have looked at. They show that it is highly unlikely that a digital computer can be programmed to exhibit anything like human intelligence; they do not show that no artificial device whatsoever – it is a moot point whether we would want to call such a device just a *machine* – could be constructed which might do this, only that such a device would not be a digital computer as we now understand that phrase. The study of AI will certainly continue, fuelled by two very powerful motives: the first to make devices which will either advance human understanding or make life easier for us or both; and the second, among the most profound of all human impulses, identified by the Spanish thinker Miguel de Unamuno (1864–1935) as *el hambre de la inmortalidad personal*, the hunger for personal immortality. Perhaps one day we will make an artificial durable device with which in some sense a person can be identified and which will give them a sort of immortality: such visions have been the stuff of sci-fi for some time, as in this passage from Arthur C. Clarke's *2001: A Space Odyssey*:

> And now, out among the stars, evolution was driving towards new goals. The first explorers of Earth had long since come to the limits of flesh and blood; as soon as their machines were better than their bodies, it was time to move. First their brain, and then their thoughts alone, they transferred to shining new homes of metal and plastic.
>
> In these, they roamed among the stars. They no longer built spaceships. They *were* spaceships.
>
> (Clarke 1968, ch. 37)

Perhaps so: but I doubt if the artificial bodies will consist only of digital computers.

I want now to draw together the threads of argument we have looked at in this book, and to see what conclusions we can come to about the question we began with: What sort of thing is the mind, and how is it related to the body? We will do this by considering a philosophical essay which attempts to show why the mind–body problem is so difficult.

SUGGESTIONS FOR FURTHER READING

Bechtel, W. and Abrahamsen, A. (1991) *Connectionism and the Mind: An Introduction to Parallel Distributed Processing in Networks*, Oxford: Blackwell.

Copeland, B.J. (1993) *Artificial Intelligence: A Philosophical Introduction*, Oxford: Blackwell.

Crane, T. (1995) *The Mechanical Mind*, Harmondsworth: Penguin.

Searle, J. (1984) *Minds, Brains and Science (1984 Reith Lectures)*, Harmondsworth: Penguin.

5 Conclusion

OBJECTIVES

The overall aim of this chapter is to review the positions discussed in the preceding chapters from a new standpoint, by means of detailed consideration of an essay by the American philosopher Thomas Nagel. By the end of this chapter you should:

- have consolidated your understanding of the material already introduced in this book;
- understand Nagel's views on why the mind–body problem has proved so difficult;
- be able to give a reasoned answer to the question: What do I believe about the nature of the mind and its relation to the body?

In the course of this book we have investigated a number of views about the mind and its relation to the body, and we can begin our concluding review by restating some of the major points we have had cause to notice. Cartesian dualism does have the virtue of accommodating the point we noticed right at the start of our investigation, namely, that human consciousness, with its inherently subjective point of view, does not sit happily with a scientific worldview which strives for objectivity. It does this by claiming that mind just *is* radically different from body and – to use a spatial metaphor – exists outside the realm of the material universe. As we have seen, however, this approach is subject to serious philosophical criticism, notably in respect of one of the other basic features of the mental we have noticed, mental causation. Another point we have not so far mentioned is that the Cartesian version of dualism makes the very existence of consciousness even more puzzling than it might be, for how is this phenomenon to come into being? No *material* cause, the operation of the brain for example, can bring it into existence, since that would require causal interaction between the material and immaterial realms of a kind we have established to be impossible. Descartes' answer, of course, is that God creates minds, God being, like minds, immaterial in nature. It follows that Descartes needs God in order to complete his philosophy.

By contrast, materialist views of the mind do not have this requirement: since all there is is material in nature, then consciousness is material and can be caused by other causes in the realm of matter. The problem, however, as we have seen repeatedly, is that certain features of consciousness and its contents resolutely resist being construed as or reduced to features of the material world. For example, what in the objective material world can be equivalent to my qualia, the immediate qualities of my experiences experienced by me from my point of view? Or again: mental states have the property of aboutness, but does it even make sense to suppose that arrangements of matter can be *about* anything?

To repeat a point made earlier, we appear to be faced with a genuine, and very typical, example of a philosophical impasse generated by a real problem. We have a phenomenon in nature of central significance – the mind with all the properties we have discovered – which we cannot, seemingly, account for satisfactorily either as a radically different sort of thing from, or as the same sort of thing as, the rest of the universe.

I want as our last reading to look at a short paper by the American philosopher Thomas Nagel (b. 1937) which begins from this point and tries to work out why the mind–body problem is so intractable. Nagel's ideas are of great intrinsic interest; they also have the advantage of looking again at most of the ground we have covered in this book from another point of view, and so in reading him, we can also do some revision, and look at a number of philosophies of mind from a slightly different angle.

Reading
p. 217

Now read paragraphs 1–3 of Nagel's 'Consciousness and objective reality' (Reading 9).

Paragraph 1 opens with a dramatic statement of the point of view Nagel is in fact going to defend in the rest of his paper. What he means by the key term 'theory' will become clearer as we go along. In paragraphs 2 and 3, he produces an argument concerning some of the claims of AI.

EXERCISE 5.1

CONSCIOUSNESS AND INTENTIONALITY

Sum up the key assertions of these paragraphs in your own words, being careful to recast Nagel's assertion about the relationship of consciousness and intentionality in terms of necessary and sufficient conditions.

SPECIMEN ANSWER

Premise 1   Consciousness is a necessary but not a sufficient condition for intentionality. That is, there can be beings which are conscious but whose mental states are not about anything, but there cannot be beings whose mental states are about anything which lack consciousness.

Conclusion 1   If a computer lacks consciousness, whatever its internal states may be, they cannot have intentionality. A computer cannot *mean* anything by the symbols it manipulates.

DISCUSSION

1   You should notice that Nagel states explicitly that he cannot say exactly why Premise 1 is true: he cannot *prove* why consciousness should be necessary for intentionality.

2   You will no doubt have noticed also that Nagel's conclusion is similar to that of Searle's Chinese room argument. Both Searle and Nagel regard having intentional states as at least a necessary condition for having a mind.

3   Notice also that Nagel refuses even to speculate about whether there could be an artificial physical system which has a mind: since we know so little about why we have minds, such speculation is at present pointless.

EXERCISE 5.2

ARTIFICIAL INTELLIGENCE

If Nagel's contention is sound, which of the four versions of AI distinguished in Chapter 4 are ruled out in principle?

SPECIMEN ANSWER

Versions 1, 2 and 3.

Now read paragraph 4 of Nagel's 'Consciousness and objective reality' (Reading 9).

Reading
p. 218

Nagel here notes that what we would count as adequacy in a general theory of the mind is a *philosophical* question, not just a scientific one. This is because a general theory of the mind and its place in nature is not just an empirical theory, but one which has important conceptual aspects. What happens when the conceptual aspects of these questions are ignored can be seen with special clarity in some of the problems which beset AI. It is no use simply to assume that machines can think or be regarded as intelligent or that minds are programmes without a clear idea of what these claims mean; and to know what they mean, we have to be able to say what thinking is, and what intelligence is, and so on; and the answers to these questions are to a considerable extent conceptual.

Now read paragraphs 5 and 6 of Nagel's 'Consciousness and objective reality' (Reading 9).

Reading
p. 218

EXERCISE 5.3

FUNCTIONALISM AS A THEORY OF MIND

Using the terminology from our discussion of functionalism in Chapter 2, recast Nagel's argument in paragraph 6 concerning the adequacy of functionalism as a complete theory of the mind. (Note: the first premise of the argument should be your definition of functionalism.)

SPECIMEN ANSWER

Premise 1 — Functionalism is the view that mental states can be defined in terms of their causal role in the control of the organism;

Premise 2 — Conscious mental states have three types of property:

(i) functional properties, i.e. they form part of our explanations of behaviour;

(ii) a material basis in the physiochemistry of the brain;

(iii) qualia, i.e. mental states have specific looks and feels (etc.) of which the person experiencing them is immediately aware.

Premise 3 — The first and third types of property are not equivalent.

Premise 4 — The second and third types of property are not equivalent because descriptions of qualia cannot be analysed in terms of descriptions of physiochemical conditions.

Conclusion 1 — Therefore functionalism is an incomplete theory of the mind, because it leaves out qualia.

EXERCISE 5.4

Looking back to the arguments we encountered in our study of functionalism, can you see how Nagel might argue in support of Premise 3?

SPECIMEN ANSWER

He could use arguments of the inverted qualia or absent qualia type, i.e. he could argue that it is possible for mental states which involve different qualia to be functionally identical (i.e. bring about the same behaviour); or he could argue that mental states not involving qualia at all (the China brain) could be functionally identical to those involving qualia. In either case, these objections are designed to show that functionalism leaves out something central to mental experience, namely qualia.

DISCUSSION

Nagel also needs to be able to produce an argument in support of Premise 4. He could do this quite readily using concepts and ideas we have come across several times, as follows: descriptions of brain activity record events and properties which are in principle publicly observable and objective; descriptions of qualia record events and properties which are in principle private and subjective. Therefore, the two types of event have different properties. Therefore, different types of statement are true of each; therefore the statements describing the one sort of event are not logically equivalent to statements describing the other type of event.

The same sort of argument – such as the one we have just used concerning the asymmetry of properties obtaining between brain events and mental events – occurs in the context of more than one form of materialist theory of the mind, e.g. it is a problem for both functionalism and the identity theory. The problems over qualia and intentionality are central problems faced by all materialist theories of the mind, and are special cases of the general problem of consciousness with which Nagel is here concerned.

Now read paragraph 7 of Nagel's 'Consciousness and objective reality' (Reading 9).

Reading
p. 219

In paragraph 7, Nagel makes two assertions which are central to the argument of his essay as a whole. The first is a statement of what an adequate theory of the place of the mind in nature must do; the second is a statement of a major obstacle in the way of constructing such a theory.

EXERCISE 5.5

NAGEL'S REQUIREMENTS FOR A THEORY OF MIND

Pick out the two assertions just referred to.

SPECIMEN ANSWER

1   An adequate theory of the mind must relate systematically three disparate elements: first, functional organization (i.e. the way in which mental states function in bringing about human behaviour); second, physical constitution (i.e. the way in which mental events are related to

physical ones); and, third, subjective appearance (i.e. phenomena such as qualia and intentionality).

2   A major obstacle in the way of producing such a general theory is that the second of the three areas identified in number 1 above is unknown to us; we simply have not even the glimmerings of an idea at present how the workings of the brain produce the sort of conscious experience that they do.

DISCUSSION

This seems to me just true; at the time of writing, no one has the ghost of an idea about how the electrochemical activity of a neuronally organized brain generates the form of subjective consciousness which we all have. What is of specially philosophical interest, however, is what Nagel goes on to say. He has argued in an earlier paper (Nagel 1974) that the mind–body problem is unique in a logical way, and he now goes on, in the essay which we are studying, to say why that should be so.

Before we approach his argument, however, we need to master one of its key presuppositions, which is set out, not in this essay, but in the earlier piece just referred to. There Nagel proposes what has become a widely accepted analysis of what it means to say that something is conscious or has conscious mental experiences, as follows:

> the fact that an organism has conscious experience *at all* means, basically, that there is something that it is like to *be* that organism ... fundamentally an organism has conscious mental states if and only if there is something that it is like to *be* that organism – something it is like *for* the organism.
>
> (Nagel 1974, in Block 1980: 160)

Put another way, there is a conceptual link (Nagel contends) between being conscious and having a *subjective point of view* built into one's mental experience. To be conscious means to experience the world from the point of view of an individual subject. As Nagel puts it,

> the facts of experience ... are accessible only from one point of view.
>
> (ibid.: 163)

One further point has to be stressed before we go on. By saying that to have conscious experience involves viewing the world from a point of view, Nagel is not asserting that all conscious experience is, as ours is, *self*-conscious. From a conceptual point of view, to be self-conscious means essentially that not only do I have conscious mental experiences but that I am aware of them *as mine*, e.g. I not only experience pain but I experience it as a feature of myself. Having a point of view in Nagel's sense does not mean being self-conscious in this way. To have a point of view in this sense means having such awareness as we ascribe to cats, dogs, horses, and so on, all of which have a point of view but none of which can be said to be self-aware in the sense in which we are, though of course we also do have a point of view in the sense of which Nagel speaks. As we shall see, the assertion that to be conscious means to experience the world from a point of view has startling consequences for the philosophy of mind.

Now read paragraphs 8–13 of Nagel's 'Consciousness and objective reality' (Reading 9).

Reading
p. 219

In paragraphs 8–13, Nagel puts forward an argument designed to show why the mind–body problem which we have been studying is logically unique. The conclusion he wants to reach is stated in paragraph 13, namely that modern (i.e. since Descartes) physical science has built into itself a guarantee that it is incomplete, that it cannot in principle explain all there is.

EXERCISE 5.6

INCOMPLETENESS OF SCIENCE

Bearing in mind Nagel's analysis of what it means to be conscious, can you set out the major stages of his argument for this conclusion (i.e. that physical science has a built-in guarantee of incompleteness) in your own words?

SPECIMEN ANSWER

Premise 1	Modern physical science uses a method which seeks to discount the point of view of any particular type of mind, notably (of course) the human mind. In other words, science seeks a species-independent objectivity.
Conclusion 1	Therefore, if there is anything in the world which is by nature essentially subjective it cannot be investigated by using the methods of physical science.
Premise 2	Conscious experience, and therefore human conscious experience, by its nature involves a point of view or is by nature subjective.
Conclusion 2	Therefore, human conscious experience, which is subjective, cannot be accounted for by the methods of physical science.
Conclusion 3	Therefore, physical science cannot give a complete account of one class of things in the world, namely, our subjective experiences, and so science is in principle incomplete.

DISCUSSION

It can now be made explicit why it was appropriate to begin our investigations of the mind–body problem with Descartes. As Nagel points out (paragraph 9), it was Descartes who gave the problem its modern formulation – the one with which we have been wrestling – and it is no accident of history that this is so, but rather a matter of logic. Descartes was at the forefront of scientific progress in his day, both experimental and mathematical, and the way in which the mind–body problem presented itself to him arises from the logical considerations Nagel has set out. Once the goal of scientific method becomes objectivity in the sense Nagel explains in paragraphs 10–12, then the subjective aspects of our experience – consciousness, qualia, aboutness, and so on – become deeply problematic, and all the philosophies of mind we have looked at are in essence attempts to fit these things in different ways into a scientific world-picture. Descartes was perfectly aware of this, and that is one of the principal reasons why he felt compelled to put the mental into a quite separate realm, distinct from the material realm which can be successfully investigated by the methods of physical science.

Reading
p. 220

Now read paragraphs 14–16 of Nagel's 'Consciousness and objective reality' (Reading 9).

In paragraphs 14–16, Nagel goes on to draw out some consequences of this argument, in particular with regard to eliminativism, and we can now revisit that theory from a new perspective.

EXERCISE 5.7

REDUCTION

Looking back at what we learned in Chapter 3 of this book, what do you understand by the concept of reduction between theories?

SPECIMEN ANSWER

A theory can be reduced to another more general theory if all the phenomena explicable in terms of the first can also be explained in terms of the latter. The classic example is the reduction of thermodynamics to mechanics. (See the discussion of paragraph 3 of Shoemaker's essay on functionalism – Reading 6 'The mind–body problem'.)

EXERCISE 5.8

FP AND CONSCIOUSNESS

What do you understand by the term 'folk psychology' and how would you relate it to Nagel's concept of consciousness?

SPECIMEN ANSWER

Folk psychology or FP is the term used by eliminativists to refer to our ordinary way of describing, explaining and predicting both our own mental life and that of others. To use concepts such as hope, fear, desire, decision, memory, imagination, will, belief – i.e. the whole apparatus we use all the time in this context – is to use folk psychology. Nagel would agree that FP is the conceptual framework we use to articulate our mental lives, and would add that its concepts embody a point of view: hopes, fears, memories (etc.) are all *someone's* hopes, fears, memories (etc); this is the same as saying that all these concepts presuppose subjectivity, in Nagel's sense of the term.

EXERCISE 5.9

ELIMINATIVISM, FP AND NEUROSCIENCE

What do eliminativists contend on the question of whether folk psychology will be reducible to completed neuroscience, and what consequence do they draw from their answer to this first question?

SPECIMEN ANSWER

They predict, on the basis of arguments such as those advanced by Churchland which we have examined in Chapter 3, that folk psychology will *not* be reducible at all to neuroscience. From this they draw the conclusion that FP will be eliminated from our vocabulary when neuroscience is finally completed.

DISCUSSION

In order to draw this conclusion, eliminativists need to make a crucial assertion about the logical character of FP. They assert that FP is an empirical theory: that is, that it is a theory of the same logical kind as evolution, the theory of relativity or quantum theory. Theories of this kind have the logical property of falsifiability. These theories make predictions as to what phenomena will occur under given conditions, and these predictions can be checked by means of experiment. If the predictions made by the theory are not confirmed by the appropriate experiments, then the theories are regarded as having been proved false by the facts of the matter. A theory is also regarded as having been falsified if some significant area of the subject it is concerned with cannot be explained by the theory. Churchland argues that FP has always failed to account for large areas of our mental life, and in addition fails to cohere at all with the findings of neuroscience.

EXERCISE 5.10

NAGEL AND ELIMINATIVISM

In the light of what he has asserted about the nature of conscious awareness and the limitations of science, what do you think is Nagel's view of the assertion that FP is an empirical theory?

SPECIMEN ANSWER

That FP not only is not an empirical theory in the same sense as relativity (etc.) but in the nature of things cannot be one. This is because, for Nagel, FP is inevitably subjective, in the strong sense in which that term is used in the philosophy of mind, i.e. embodies the point of view of a subject. By contrast, empirical science strives to be objective. Therefore, for Nagel, this central contention of eliminativism is false.

EXERCISE 5.11

NAGEL AND ELIMINATIVISM

In paragraph 16, Nagel makes a further, explicit criticism of eliminativism. What is it?

SPECIMEN ANSWER

That by their own criteria, the eliminativists are being *un*scientific when they suggest that FP should be dropped because it does not cohere with science. The first rule of science is to respect the data, and the problematic features of mental life which constitute the stumbling blocks for materialism or physicalism in the philosophy of mind – qualia, intentionality, etc. – cannot just be wished away. They are real, and the solution of the mind–body problem, when it is found, will have to accommodate them.

Now read paragraphs 17–18 of Nagel's 'Consciousness and objective reality' (Reading 9).

Reading
p. 221

Where does Nagel's theory leave us? He gives an outline answer in these concluding paragraphs. If his analyses of consciousness and the limitations of science are correct, then a solution to the mind–body problem will not be just another bit of science, no matter how impressive or complex, but a theory of a kind we do not yet have. Such a theory must in some way combine the objective viewpoint which (one can assume) will inform neuroscience and the subjective viewpoint involved in consciousness. He refers in passing and speculatively to the philosophy of Benedict (or Baruch) Spinoza (1632–77), a major philosopher of the generation immediately after Descartes. We cannot here go into the ramifications of Spinoza's views, which are about as difficult as they are fascinating, but one can see why Nagel should feel attracted to them. Spinoza's fundamental contention is that the mental and the physical are modes or aspects of the same fundamental reality, appearing to us as it were in two seemingly different ways. Nagel speculates here (and he would put it no more strongly than that) that a solution to the mind–body problem will be somewhat of that kind, with the mental and the physical being construed as in some sense aspects of a reality more fundamental than them both.

SUMMARY

In this chapter we have reviewed from a new standpoint the proposed answers to the mind–body problem which have formed the principal subject-matter of this book. In his essay 'Consciousness and objective reality', Thomas Nagel has something to say about each of the points of view we have considered. In addition to putting forward some objections to these views, he adds a suggestion as to why it is that the mind–body problem is at the same time so difficult and so intriguing. This suggestion rests on his well-known analysis of what it is to be conscious: to be conscious, he argues, is to experience the world from a point of view. Put another way, for any conscious being, it makes sense to say that there is something that it is like to be that being. Since empirical science strives in principle to exclude unique points of view, it follows that it is likely to prove – as indeed it has proved – exceedingly hard to produce a scientific account of consciousness in terms of the concepts currently at our disposal.

CONCLUSION

I said right at the start of this book that it is characteristic of philosophical problems that they reveal their depth and significance only gradually, and one's understanding of them grows in much the same way. I would argue that the best description of this process is to be found in the works of the German philosopher Wilhelm Dilthey (1833–1911). Dilthey argues that understanding issues in the humanities works in a particular way: we begin with a relatively vague idea of the problem to be considered; then study some aspect of it, mastery of which changes the way we think of the whole problem; and this changed view of the problem affects the way we interpret the next element we master in detail, and so on. We oscillate back and forth between an understanding of the whole and an understanding of details, each modifying the other and deepening as the process continues. Dilthey's point is that this sort of understanding is not like just learning new propositions one after another: it isn't a simple additive process of that kind, but the subtler oscillation he describes. Understanding the mind–body problem seems to me to fit this description very well. Only now, I think, after a great deal of hard thinking and an examination of bits of the problem and proposed solutions to it, can we see why this question has proved so tough, at least in the modern post-Cartesian form in which we have been looking at it. Again, only now, I suspect, will what one can call the logical bite of the ideas with which we have become familiar – consciousness, subjectivity, aboutness, qualia, mental causation, and so forth – have become somewhat clearer. No one has yet invented a quick way of grasping these ideas. It is appropriate now to sum up what we have discovered, and see what conclusions we can come to.

We started out with a question which occurs to anyone who reflects on human nature, or on what is generally referred to as the human condition: what is the mind and how is it related to the body? We noted that the way in which you answer this question has a special role to play in the way in which we think of ourselves. For example, if you take the view that the phrase 'your mind' (a) refers to some sort of entity and (b) that this entity is of a radically different kind from your body, and (c) that other animals are not thus constituted but have no mind as we do, then you will think of human beings as having a special place in the order of things. By contrast, if you believe that the mind is some sort of effect or state of the brain or is at any rate brain-dependent, and that it will die when the brain dies, and you believe that many types of (let us say) higher mammals are consti-tuted in the same way, then you will take a different view of the place of humanity in the scheme of things: we may have one of the most highly developed brains which has so far evolved (and recall that evolution by natural selection has of course not stopped), but we are not constituted radically differently from many other life forms on this planet.

Yet while these questions and these implications of the broadly different answers are not too difficult to formulate, working out which possible answer is the true one has turned out to be anything but easy or quick. We have looked in some detail at two of the broad classes of answer, dualist and materialistic monist (these are not the only types of answer that are possible, but they are certainly the most widely canvassed). I suspect that most of the readers of this book began reading it with a sympathy for one or other of these points of view, perhaps not fully worked out, but with an intuition that minds are either very different sorts of things from bodies, or that minds are brain effects of some kind, and these are the outlooks hinted at in the two points of view set out at the opening of Chapter 1. Cartesian dualism has the virtue of doing justice to some of the beliefs which people often have about minds and their contents, and presents an answer to the mind–body problem which, in its major outlines, is easy to grasp; the mental and the physical constitute two discrete realms, composed of two types of substance very different in nature, and which interact only at one point, the pineal gland.

Moreover, though the mind interacts with the body and is intimately linked with it, yet it does not depend for its existence on the life of the body, and will survive the death of the latter. However, we have also seen that when you look at the details of this clear and simple outline, difficulties of no minor kind present themselves: first, how to give a convincing account in Cartesian terms of the bedrock intuition we all have that we are a unity of mind and body, not just two very different sorts of thing temporarily united; second, how to give a clear description of mental substance; and, most significantly, how to explain mind–body interaction. Just how can something which is non-spatial in nature causally interact with something spatial?

Occasionalism, which we looked at briefly, was (as a matter of history) the first response offered by two-substance dualists to this problem. Occasionalists solve the problem by denying that mind–body interaction occurs, and claiming that the mental and the physical are (as it were) two parallel realms which never touch, but which appear to do so thanks to the perfect synchronization of events in each which results from divine intervention. The occasionalist, like Descartes, needs a divinity to make this philosophy work: neither philosophy will work without God. We also looked briefly at two other forms of dualism, epiphenomenalism and property dualism, both fuelled by the same basic intuition that the mental is just too unlike the physical to be physical in nature itself, and we saw that each of these approaches involves conceptual problems of its own. None of the arguments against dualism we have considered shows that there is *no* form of dualism which will turn out to be acceptable; but they do tend to make dualism an unattractive option from the logical point of view.

We then looked at three views which are either explicitly materialist (the identity theory and eliminativism) or designed to be compatible with it (functionalism): both these views are supposed to account for the mind in terms of natural phenomena only and not to need any supernatural components to make them work. As we noted at the time, many philosophers and scientists approach the philosophy of mind with the conviction that some form of materialist account of the mind must be true because (they also hold) only this sort of view will be logically compatible with science. As with Cartesian dualism, the main outlines of these theories are not too difficult to grasp. The identity theorist contends that mental events and physical events are one and the same set of events referred to under two different sets of descriptions, but it is hard to see how this claim can be defended in the light of problems over the asymmetry of properties of mental and brain states. Again, the functionalist claims that what is distinctive about the mental is not what it is made of but what it does: the mental has a unique role to play in bringing about appropriate behaviour. Yet, once again when one examines the implications of this point of view, certain serious logical problems come to light, notably over qualia, and whatever the functionalists themselves may say, there is no agreement that these objections to functionalism have been met. Equally, eliminativism has a bold and clear central claim – that FP is a theory which will just be discarded, like the geocentric theory of the universe, when neuroscience finally gives us the full story on the nature of the mind–brain. This approach has the attraction of doing away with the most intractable problems which have so beset materialist theories of the mind at a stroke (qualia, aboutness and subjectivity), but, once again, the details of the theory are by no means free of problems of their own, e.g. over the central assertion that FP really is an empirical theory no different from other empirical theories. Once again, none of these problems shows that *no* form of materialism is acceptable; only that the versions we have considered involve some serious problems.

When the subject was first given its present name in the 1950s, AI seemed to promise great things both in respect of machines which could make life easier for us, and in respect of shedding light on the nature of the human mind. It seemed in those early days unproblematic to work on the assumption that the mind must operate as does a digital computer, and that thinking intelligent machines were just around the corner. A digital computer is a piece of hardware with a program, and since the brain was the hardware in this analogy, the mind had to be some form of program. As we have seen, however, the optimism concerning both the basic assumption and the creation of thinking machines has not been borne out by events. There are serious conceptual difficulties involved in the claim that human mental operations are computational in nature and so programmable into a digital computer. Nature turns out, as so often in the history of thought, to be subtler than our inventions and much more complex than the models, in this case computational, that we use to explain it. Perhaps one day we will, for example, make androids as sophisticated as Asimov's Daneel or the replicants of the *Blade Runner* film, but the technology on which they will operate is of a kind we have yet to glimpse. Indeed, at the time of writing this (February 1998) articles are beginning to appear in the reputable scientific press which suggest that the computer model of the mind–brain may well have had its day: this model has not delivered the goods after thirty years and the search is on for a replacement (cf. e.g. McCrone (1997) and the further references there given). However, it is necessary to stress that even if the mind–brain turns out not to operate like a von Neumann computer, it does not follow that no artificial device can be envisaged which we might one day wish to describe as having a mind. Some very interesting data is being assembled on devices which copy the connection patterns found in real neural networks, though whether in the end we would want to call a device with a mind just a machine, as opposed to an individual, is a point worth reflecting on.

Thomas Nagel, in the essay you have just read, puts his finger very firmly on the central problem in the relation of mind and body, and it lies in the seeming incompatibility of two facts: in the first place, that human experience is subjective – it has a point of view, and is always someone's experience; and, in the second place, that science – the most successful intellectual enterprise of the human race to date – seeks to provide an impersonal, objective account of all there is. Small wonder, then, that it has proved so hard for science to come up with an answer to the questions we began with at the start of this book.

So where does all this leave us? Not alas with a definitive and satisfying answer that can now be produced, as it were, out of a hat: at the time of writing this, and I suspect for some time to come, there is and will be no theory of the mind which has an accepted status in the intellectual community comparable to that of the general theory of relativity or the theory of evolution. My own hunch is that we are not going to solve the mind–body problem until neuroscience is rather more advanced than it presently is – and that is not just a disguised way of saying that some form of materialism will turn out to be true. Nature keeps surprising us and no one presently knows what concepts will be needed to describe the relationship of mind and brain when that relationship is finally sorted out to the general satisfaction. Many thinkers in this area currently turn to concepts from the science of complexity, an area we came across briefly in discussing Dennett's objection to the Chinese room argument in Chapter 4 (see the section in Chapter 4 on paragraphs 37–46 of Searle's essay). It is a fairly widely held view at the time of writing that the mind will turn out to be an emergent property of the brain, a property which emerges from this fantastically complex structure at a certain point (yet to be determined) as it evolves: if you would like to pursue this line of thought, see the works listed in the bibliography by Crick (1994), Damasio (1994), Kauffman (1995), Penrose (1989, 1994), Restak (1995) and Trefil (1997) (all scientists). Yet to say this is not to solve the problem: to say that the mind emerges from the brain does not tell us why or how, or precisely what sort of entity or property the mind will turn out to be, or how a complex arrangement of matter can be the basis for subjective awareness and intentional states. To repeat, we may need to find completely new concepts to answer these questions.

One of the things we have been doing in this book is to experience what it is like to deal with a major unsolved question about our nature and condition. What we have found ourselves faced with is a series of competing theories, each with their own advantages and difficulties, none of which commands absolute allegiance or enjoys the status of being the final answer to the question, and this situation is entirely typical of such circumstances. Equally, we have discovered that this question is not just an empirical one: it is – inescapably – one which involves the sort of conceptual considerations that are the central stuff of philosophy. To think seriously about the mind and its relation to the body you *have* to do some philosophy, whether you call yourself philosopher, theologian or scientist.

Finally, look back at your answer to the first question raised in the first chapter of this book: were you then specially sympathetic to one of the two points of view set out there, or were you unsure which view seemed most congenial to you? It would be worthwhile to ask yourself whether you are still of the same opinion, whether you have changed your view, and, if so, why. Philosophy, contrary to the opinion of those who have never done it, has an impact on what we believe and so on what we do. (The reason for the false belief, of course, is that most people assume that very general or abstract beliefs either do not or cannot make a difference to what they call 'the real world'. This assertion is just down-on-all-fours wrong: even if we do not know we are doing it, we orient our lives by reference to these 'abstractions'.) The investigation of the mind we have been engaged on is not a game: what you believe about this question matters, and will affect the way you conduct your life.

Readings

1 Meditations on the First Philosophy in which the Existence of God and the Distinction Between Mind and Body are Demonstrated

Meditation I

René Descartes

Descartes' first *Meditation* is given here. This text is *optional* reading: I have printed it simply because it is a short masterpiece of philosophical writing, and not difficult to read. If you do not wish to read it, please read my summary below, which covers the arguments.

In the first *Meditation*, Descartes states that he wishes to create a 'firm and permanent structure in the sciences', to 'build anew from the foundation', since he has recognized that much of what he once accepted as true is in fact false. The only way to construct a firm foundation is to accept as part of it only beliefs of which he can be absolutely certain. Hence he states that he will follow the rule 'no less carefully to withhold my assent from matters which are not entirely certain and indubitable than from those which appear to me manifestly to be false' (Haldane and Ross 1931, vol. I: 145). This statement is a rephrasing of the first of the four rules Descartes had set out some years earlier in the *Discourse on Method*. The earlier version goes as follows: 'The first of these [rules] was to accept nothing as true which I did not clearly recognise to be so: that is to say, carefully to avoid precipitation and prejudice in my judgements, and to accept in them nothing more than what was presented to my mind so clearly and distinctly that I could have no occasion to doubt it' (Haldane and Ross 1931, vol. I: 92). The key word here is 'doubt': Descartes will proceed to withhold assent from any belief he can find reason to doubt: if he can find any belief which is in some way immune to doubt, then he will have reached what he seeks, i.e. a starting point as certain as a Euclidean axiom on which he can base his revised belief structure.

The next question is: how can Descartes decide which beliefs are doubtful and which immune from doubt? As he himself says, if it were necessary to proceed by examining each belief in turn the project would have no end. Fortunately, it is not necessary to proceed in this piecemeal way. For most of the first Meditation, Descartes is concerned to set out two powerful sceptical arguments which will establish which beliefs are doubtful and which not. These famous arguments are always referred to respectively as the dream argument and the evil genius (or evil demon) argument.

The central premise of the dream argument is that I can never be certain that I am not dreaming. I often have dreams in which I believe firmly that I am awake, and am wrong in so doing. If that is so, then all the beliefs I have about the world derived from the experience of my senses can be doubted: if I can be wrong in any given case that I am not dreaming, then no case is beyond doubt. (It is of interest to note in passing that Descartes was not the first Western philosopher to feel the force of this line of thought: there is a similar passage in one of the later dialogues of Plato, the *Theaetetus*, 152.)

Yet, even if this is true (Descartes continues), must it not still be true that the illusions I entertain while dreaming are at least derived from counterparts in the real world? In other words, the dream argument leaves intact the belief that there *is* a real world, even if I am constantly deceived as to its nature. To show that this belief in the existence of a real world is open to doubt, Descartes uses a thought experiment in the form of the evil genius argument. It is possible that there is an evil genius whose pleasure it is to deceive me: he has so arranged matters that there is no external world at all, and all my experiences are illusions generated by him. Another way of stating the thought experiment is that it is logically possible that the entire universe – all there is – consists of the evil genius and myself, where the term 'myself' excludes my body, i.e. because I know of my body via sensations, and I can no longer assume that the sensations inform me of an external world. Descartes is not seriously suggesting that this is what is going on: but all he needs to make his point (that belief in an external world apart from myself is not immune to doubt) is the premise that it is *possible* that the evil genius scenario is true.

Within a few pages, Descartes has shown what he considers he can doubt: he can doubt not only that his sensations give him accurate information about the world, but also that there is a world at all. This is the point from which Meditation II begins. In it Descartes argues that there is a belief which he cannot doubt, and that this belief forms a suitable starting point for the reconstruction of all knowledge on a firm foundation. He also begins to set out his beliefs on the nature and relation of mind and body.

OF THE THINGS WHICH MAY BE BROUGHT WITHIN THE SPHERE OF THE DOUBTFUL

It is now some years since I detected how many were the false beliefs that I had from my earliest youth admitted as true, and how doubtful was everything I had since constructed on this basis; and from that time I was convinced that I must once and for all seriously undertake to rid myself of all the opinions which I had formerly accepted, and commence to build anew from the foundation, if I wanted to establish any firm and permanent structure in the sciences. But as this enterprise appeared to be a very great one, I waited until I had attained an age so mature that I could not hope that at any later date I should be better fitted to execute my design. This reason caused me to delay so long that I should feel that I was doing wrong were I to occupy in deliberation the time that yet remains to me for action. To-day, then, since very opportunely for the plan I have in view I have delivered my mind from every care [and am happily agitated by no passions] and since I have procured for myself an assured leisure in a peaceable retirement, I shall at last seriously and freely address myself to the general upheaval of all my former opinions.

Now for this object it is not necessary that I should show that all of these are false – I shall perhaps never arrive at this end. But inasmuch as reason already persuades me that I ought no less carefully to withhold my assent from matters which are not entirely certain and indubitable than from those which appear to me manifestly to be false, if I am able to find in each one some reason to doubt, this will suffice to justify my rejecting the whole. And for that end it will not be requisite that I should examine each in particular, which would be an endless undertaking; for owing to the fact that the destruction of the foundations of necessity brings with it the downfall of the rest of the edifice, I shall only in the first place attack those principles upon which all my former opinions rested.

All that up to the present time I have accepted as most true and certain I have learned either from the senses or through the senses; but it is sometimes proved to me that these senses are deceptive, and it is wiser not to trust entirely to any thing by which we have once been deceived.

But it may be that although the senses sometimes deceive us concerning things which are hardly perceptible, or very far away, there are yet many others to be met with as to which we cannot reasonably have any doubt, although we recognise them by their means. For example, there is the fact that I am here, seated by the fire, attired in a dressing gown, having this paper in my hands and other similar matters. And how could I deny that these hands and this body are mine, were it not perhaps that I compare myself to certain persons, devoid of sense, whose cerebella are so troubled and clouded by the violent vapours of black bile, that they constantly assure us that they think they are kings when they are really quite poor, or that they are clothed in purple when they are really without covering, or who imagine that they have an earthenware head or are nothing but pumpkins or are made of glass. But they are mad, and I should not be any the less insane were I to follow examples so extravagant.

At the same time I must remember that I am a man, and that consequently I am in the habit of sleeping, and in my dreams representing to myself the same things or sometimes even less probable things, than do those who are insane in their waking moments. How often has it happened to me that in the night I dreamt that I found myself in this particular place, that I was dressed and seated near the fire, whilst in reality I was lying undressed in bed! At this moment it does indeed seem to me that it is with eyes awake that I am looking at this paper;

that this head which I move is not asleep, that it is deliberately and of set purpose that I extend my hand and perceive it; what happens in sleep does not appear so clear nor so distinct as does all this. But in thinking over this I remind myself that on many occasions I have in sleep been deceived by similar illusions, and in dwelling carefully on this reflection I see so manifestly that there are no certain indications by which we may clearly distinguish wakefulness from sleep that I am lost in astonishment. And my astonishment is such that it is almost capable of persuading me that I now dream.

Now let us assume that we are asleep and that all these particulars, e.g. that we open our eyes, shake our head, extend our hands, and so on, are but false delusions; and let us reflect that possibly neither our hands nor our whole body are such as they appear to us to be. At the same time we must at least confess that the things which are represented to us in sleep are like painted representations which can only have been formed as the counterparts of something real and true, and that in this way those general things at least, i.e. eyes, a head, hands, and a whole body, are not imaginary things, but things really existent. For, as a matter of fact, painters, even when they study with the greatest skill to represent sirens and satyrs by forms the most strange and extraordinary, cannot give them natures which are entirely new, but merely make a certain medley of the members of different animals; or if their imagination is extravagant enough to invent something so novel that nothing similar has ever before been seen, and that then their work represents a thing purely fictitious and absolutely false, it is certain all the same that the colours of which this is composed are necessarily real. And for the same reason, although these general things, to wit, [a body], eyes, a head, hands, and such like, may be imaginary, we are bound at the same time to confess that there are at least some other objects yet more simple and more universal, which are real and true; and of these just in the same way as with certain real colours all these images of things which dwell in our thoughts, whether true and real or false and fantastic, are formed.

To such a class of things pertains corporeal nature in general, and its extension, the figure of extended things, their quantity or magnitude and number, as also the place in which they are, the time which measures their duration, and so on.

That is possibly why our reasoning is not unjust when we conclude from this that Physics, Astronomy, Medicine and all other sciences which have as their end the consideration of composite things, are very dubious and uncertain; but that Arithmetic, Geometry and other sciences of that kind which only treat of things that are very simple and very general, without taking great trouble to ascertain whether they are actually existent or not, contain some measure of certainty and an element of the indubitable. For whether I am awake or asleep, two and three together always form five, and the square can never have more than four sides, and it does not seem possible that truths so clear and apparent can be suspected of any falsity [or uncertainty].

Nevertheless I have long had fixed in my mind the belief that an all-powerful God existed by whom I have been created such as I am. But how do I know that He has not brought it to pass that there is no earth, no heaven, no extended body, no magnitude, no place, and that nevertheless [I possess the perceptions of all these things and that] they seem to me to exist just exactly as I now see them? And, besides, as I sometimes imagine that others deceive themselves in the things which they think they know best, how do I know that I am not deceived every time that I add two and three, or count the sides of a square, or judge of things yet simpler, if anything simpler can be imagined? But possibly God has not desired that I should be thus deceived, for He is said to be supremely good. If, however, it is contrary to His goodness to have made me such that I constantly deceive myself, it would also appear to be contrary to His goodness to permit me to be sometimes deceived, and nevertheless I cannot doubt that he does permit this.

There may indeed be those who would prefer to deny the existence of a God so powerful, rather than believe that all other things are uncertain. But let us not oppose them for the present, and grant that all that is here said of a God is a fable; nevertheless in whatever way they suppose that I have arrived at the state of being that I have reached — whether they attribute it to fate or to accident, or make out that it is by a continual succession of antecedents, or by some other method — since to err and deceive oneself is a defect, it is clear that the greater will be the probability of my being so imperfect as to deceive myself ever, as is the Author to whom they assign my origin the less powerful. To these reasons I have certainly nothing to reply, but at the end I feel constrained to confess that there is nothing in all that I formerly believed to be true, of which I cannot in some measure doubt, and that not merely through want of thought or through levity, but for reasons which are very powerful and maturely considered; so that henceforth I ought not the less carefully to refrain from giving credence to these opinions than to that which is manifestly false, if I desire to arrive at any certainty [in the sciences].

But it is not sufficient to have made these remarks, we must also be careful to keep them in mind. For these ancient and commonly held opinions still revert frequently to my mind, long and familiar custom having given them the right to occupy my mind against my inclination and rendered them almost masters of my belief; nor will I ever lose the habit of deferring to them or of placing my confidence in them, so long as I consider them as they really are, i.e. opinions in some measure doubtful, as I have just shown, and at the same time highly probable, so that there is much more reason to believe in than to deny them. That is why I consider that I shall not be acting amiss, if, taking of set purpose a contrary belief, I allow myself to be deceived, and for a certain time pretend that all these opinions are entirely false and imaginary, until at last, having thus balanced my former prejudices with my latter [so that they cannot divert my opinions more to one side than to the other], my judgement will no longer be dominated by bad usage or turned away from the right knowledge of the truth. For I am assured that there can be neither peril nor error in this course, and that I cannot at present yield too much to distrust, since I am not considering the question of action, but only of knowledge.

I shall then suppose, not that God who is supremely good and the fountain of truth, but some evil genius not less powerful than deceitful, has employed his whole energies in deceiving me; I shall consider that the heavens, the earth, colours, figures, sound, and all other external things are nought but the illusions and dreams of which this genius has availed himself in order to lay traps for my credulity; I shall consider myself as having no hands, no eyes, no flesh, no blood, nor any senses, yet falsely believing myself to possess all these things; I shall remain obstinately attached to this idea, and if by this means it is not in my power to arrive at the knowledge of any truth, I may at least do what is in my power [i.e. suspend my judgement], and with firm purpose avoid giving credence to any false thing, or being imposed upon by this arch deceiver, however powerful and deceptive he may be. But this task is a laborious one, and insensibly a certain lassitude leads me into the course of my ordinary life. And just as a captive who in sleep enjoys an imaginary liberty, when he begins to suspect that his liberty is but a dream, fears to awaken, and conspires with these agreeable illusions that the deception may be prolonged, so insensibly of my own accord I fall back into my former opinions, and I dread awakening from this slumber, lest the laborious wakefulness which would follow the tranquillity of this repose should have to be spent not in daylight, but in the excessive darkness of the difficulties which have just been discussed.

2 | Meditations on the First Philosophy in which the Existence of God and the Distinction Between Mind and Body are Demonstrated

Meditation II

René Descartes

OF THE NATURE OF THE HUMAN MIND; AND THAT IT IS MORE EASILY KNOWN THAN THE BODY

1 The Meditation of yesterday filled my mind with so many doubts that it is no longer in my power to forget them. And yet I do not see in what manner I can resolve them; and, just as if I had all of a sudden fallen into very deep water, I am so disconcerted that I can neither make certain of setting my feet on the bottom, nor can I swim and so support myself on the surface. I shall nevertheless make an effort and follow anew the same path as that on which I yesterday entered, i.e. I shall proceed by setting aside all that in which the least doubt could be supposed to exist, just as if I had discovered that it was absolutely false; and I shall ever follow in this road until I have met with something which is certain, or at least, if I can do nothing else, until I have learned for certain that there is nothing in the world that is certain. Archimedes, in order that he might draw the terrestrial globe out of its place, and transport it elsewhere, demanded only that one point should be fixed and immovable; in the same way I shall have the right to conceive high hopes if I am happy enough to discover one thing only which is certain and indubitable.

2 I suppose, then, that all the things that I see are false; I persuade myself that nothing has ever existed of all that my fallacious memory represents to me. I consider that I possess no senses; I imagine that body, figure, extension, movement and place are but the fictions of my mind. What, then, can be esteemed as true? Perhaps nothing at all, unless that there is nothing in the world that is certain.

3   But how can I know there is not something different from those things that I
have just considered, of which one cannot have the slightest doubt? Is there
not some God, or some other being by whatever name we call it, who puts
these reflections into my mind? That is not necessary, for is it not possible
that I am capable of producing them myself? I myself, am I not at least something? But I have already denied that I had senses and body. Yet I hesitate, for
what follows from that? Am I so dependent on body and senses that I cannot
exist without these? But I was persuaded that there was nothing in all the
world, that there was no heaven, no earth, that there were no minds, nor any
bodies: was I not then likewise persuaded that I did not exist? Not at all; of a
surety I myself did exist since I persuaded myself of something [or merely
because I thought of something]. But there is some deceiver or other, very
powerful and very cunning, who ever employs his ingenuity in deceiving me.
Then without doubt I exist also if he deceives me, and let him deceive me as
much as he will, he can never cause me to be nothing so long as I think that I
am something. So that after having reflected well and carefully examined all
things, we must come to the definite conclusion that this proposition: I am, I
exist, is necessarily true each time that I pronounce it, or that I mentally
conceive it.

4   But I do not yet know clearly enough what I am, I who am certain that I am;
and hence I must be careful to see that I do not imprudently take some other
object in place of myself, and thus that I do not go astray in respect of this
knowledge that I hold to be the most certain and most evident of all that I
have formerly learned. That is why I shall now consider anew what I believed
myself to be before I embarked upon these last reflections; and of my former
opinions I shall withdraw all that might even in a small degree be invalidated
by the reasons which I have just brought forward, in order that there may be
nothing at all left beyond what is absolutely certain and indubitable.

5   What then did I formerly believe myself to be? Undoubtedly I believed
myself to be a man. But what is a man? Shall I say a reasonable animal?
Certainly not; for then I should have to inquire what an animal is, and what is
reasonable; and thus from a single question I should insensibly fall into an
infinitude of others more difficult; and I should not wish to waste the little
time and leisure remaining to me in trying to unravel subtleties like these.
But I shall rather stop here to consider the thoughts which of themselves
spring up in my mind, and which were not inspired by anything beyond my
own nature alone when I applied myself to the consideration of my being. In
the first place, then, I considered myself as having a face, hands, arms, and all
that system of members composed of bones and flesh as seen in a corpse
which I designated by the name of body. In addition to this I considered that I
was nourished, that I walked, that I felt, and that I thought, and I referred all
these actions to the soul: but I did not stop to consider what the soul was, or
if I did stop, I imagined that it was something extremely rare and subtle like a
wind, a flame, or an ether, which was spread throughout my grosser parts. As
to body I had no manner of doubt about its nature, but thought I had a very
clear knowledge of it; and if I had desired to explain it according to the
notions that I had then formed of it, I should have described it thus: By the

body I understand all that which can be defined by a certain figure: something which can be confined in a certain place, and which can fill a given
space in such a way that every other body will be excluded from it; which
can be perceived either by touch, or by sight, or by hearing, or by taste, or
by smell: which can be moved in many ways not, in truth, by itself, but by
something which is foreign to it, by which it is touched [and from which it
receives impressions]: for to have the power of self-movement, as also of
feeling or of thinking, I did not consider to appertain to the nature of body:
on the contrary, I was rather astonished to find that faculties similar to them
existed in some bodies.

6   But what am I, now that I suppose that there is a certain genius which is
extremely powerful, and, if I may say so, malicious, who employs all his
powers in deceiving me? Can I affirm that I possess the least of all those
things which I have just said pertain to the nature of body? I pause to
consider, I revolve all these things in my mind, and I find none of which I can
say that it pertains to me. It would be tedious to stop to enumerate them.
Let us pass to the attributes of soul and see if there is any one which is in
me? What of nutrition or walking [the first mentioned]? But if it is so that I
have no body it is also true that I can neither walk nor take nourishment.
Another attribute is sensation. But one cannot feel without body, and besides
I have thought I perceived many things during sleep that I recognised in my
waking moments as not having been experienced at all. What of thinking? I
find here that thought is an attribute that belongs to me; it alone cannot be
separated from me. I am, I exist, that is certain. But how often? Just when I
think; for it might possibly be the case if I ceased entirely to think, that I
should likewise cease altogether to exist. I do not now admit anything which
is not necessarily true: to speak accurately I am not more than a thing which
thinks, that is to say a mind or a soul, or an understanding, or a reason,
which are terms whose significance was formerly unknown to me. I am,
however, a real thing and really exist; but what thing? I have answered: a
thing which thinks.

7   And what more? I shall exercise my imagination [in order to see if I am not
something more]. I am not a collection of members which we call the
human body: I am not a subtle air distributed through these members, I am
not a wind, a fire, a vapour, a breath, nor anything at all which I can imagine
or conceive; because I have assumed that all these were nothing. Without
changing that supposition I find that I only leave myself certain of the fact
that I am somewhat. But perhaps it is true that these same things which I
supposed were non-existent because they are unknown to me, are really not
different from the self which I know. I am not sure about this, I shall not
dispute about it now; I can only give judgement on things that are known to
me. I know that I exist, and I inquire what I am, I whom I know to exist. But
it is very certain that the knowledge of my existence taken in its precise
significance does not depend on things whose existence is not yet known to
me; consequently it does not depend on those which I can feign in imagination. And indeed the very term *feign* in imagination[1] proves to me my error,
for I really do this if I imagine myself a something, since to imagine is

nothing else than to contemplate the figure or image of a corporeal thing. But I already know for certain that I am, and that it may be that all these images, and, speaking generally, all things that relate to the nature of body are nothing but dreams [and chimeras]. For this reason I see clearly that I have as little reason to say, 'I shall stimulate my imagination in order to know more distinctly what I am,' than if I were to say, 'I am now awake, and I perceive somewhat that is real and true; but because I do not yet perceive it distinctly enough, I shall go to sleep of express purpose, so that my dreams may represent the perception with greatest truth and evidence.' And, thus, I know for certain that nothing of all that I can understand by means of my imagination belongs to this knowledge which I have of myself, and that it is necessary to recall the mind from this mode of thought with the utmost diligence in order that it may be able to know its own nature with perfect distinctness.

8 But what then am I? A thing which thinks. What is a thing which thinks? It is a thing which doubts, understands, [conceives], affirms, denies, wills, refuses, which also imagines and feels.

9 Certainly it is no small matter if all these things pertain to my nature. But why should they not so pertain? Am I not that being who now doubts nearly everything, who nevertheless understands certain things, who affirms that one only is true, who denies all the others, who desires to know more, is averse from being deceived, who imagines many things, sometimes indeed despite his will, and who perceives many likewise, as by the intervention of the bodily organs? Is there nothing in all this which is as true as it is certain that I exist, even though I should always sleep and though he who has given me being employed all his ingenuity in deceiving me? Is there likewise any one of these attributes which can be distinguished from my thought, or which might be said to be separated from myself? For it is so evident of itself that it is I who doubts, who understands, and who desires, that there is no reason here to add anything to explain it. And I have certainly the power of imagining likewise; for although it may happen (as I formerly supposed) that none of the things which I imagine are true, nevertheless this power of imagining does not cease to be really in use, and it forms part of my thought. Finally, I am the same who feels, that is to say, who perceives certain things, as by the organs of sense, since in truth I see light, I hear noise, I feel heat. But it will be said that these phenomena are false and that I am dreaming. Let it be so; still it is at least quite certain that it seems to me that I see light, that I hear noise and that I feel heat. That cannot be false; properly speaking it is what is in me called feeling;[2] and used in this precise sense that is no other thing than thinking.

10 From this time I begin to know what I am with a little more clearness and distinction than before; but nevertheless it still seems to me, and I cannot prevent myself from thinking, that corporeal things, whose images are framed by thought, which are tested by the senses, are much more distinctly known than that obscure part of me which does not come under the imagination. Although really it is very strange to say that I know and understand more distinctly these things whose existence seems to me dubious, which are

unknown to me, and which do not belong to me, than others of the truth of
which I am convinced, which are known to me and which pertain to my real
nature, in a word, than myself. But I see clearly how the case stands: my
mind loves to wander, and cannot yet suffer itself to be retained within the
just limits of truth. Very good, let us once more give it the freest rein, so
that, when afterwards we sense the proper occasion for pulling up, it may
the more easily be regulated and controlled.

11 Let us begin by considering the commonest matters, those which we believe
to be the most distinctly comprehended, to wit, the bodies which we touch
and see; not indeed bodies in general, for these general ideas are usually a
little more confused, but let us consider one body in particular. Let us take,
for example, this piece of wax: it has been taken quite freshly from the hive,
and it has not yet lost the sweetness of the honey which it contains; it still
retains somewhat of the odour of the flowers from which it has been culled;
its colour, its figure, its size are apparent; it is hard, cold, easily handled, and
if you strike it with the finger, it will emit a sound. Finally all the things
which are requisite to cause us distinctly to recognise a body, are met with in
it. But notice that while I speak and approach the fire what remained of the
taste is exhaled, the smell evaporates, the colour alters, the figure is
destroyed, the size increases, it becomes liquid, it heats, scarcely can one
handle it, and when one strikes it, no sound is emitted. Does the same wax
remain after this change? We must confess that it remains; none would judge
otherwise. What then did I know so distinctly in this piece of wax? It could
certainly be nothing of all that the senses brought to my notice, since all
these things which fall under taste, smell, sight, touch, and hearing, are
found to be changed, and yet the same wax remains.

12 Perhaps it was what I now think, viz. that this wax was not that sweetness of
honey, nor that agreeable scent of flowers, not that particular whiteness, nor
that figure, nor that sound, but simply a body which a little while before
appeared to me as perceptible under these forms, and which is now perceptible under others. But what, precisely, is it that I imagine when I form such
conceptions? Let us attentively consider this, and, abstracting from all that
does not belong to the wax, let us see what remains. Certainly nothing
remains excepting a certain extended thing which is flexible and movable.
But what is the meaning of flexible and movable? Is it not that I imagine that
this piece of wax being round is capable of becoming square and of passing
from a square to a triangular figure? No, certainly it is not that, since I
imagine it admits of an infinitude of similar changes, and I nevertheless do
not know how to compass the infinitude by my imagination, and consequently this conception which I have of the wax is not brought about by the
faculty of imagination. What now is this extension? Is it not also unknown?
For it becomes greater when the wax is melted, greater when it is boiled,
and greater still when the heat increases; and I should not conceive [clearly]
according to truth what wax is, if I did not think that even this piece that we
are considering is capable of receiving more variations in extension than I
have ever imagined. We must then grant that I could not even understand
through the imagination what this piece of wax is, and that it is my mind

alone which perceives it. I say this piece of wax in particular, for as to wax in general it is yet clearer. But what is this piece of wax which cannot be understood excepting by the [understanding or] mind? It is certainly the same that I see, touch, imagine, and finally it is the same which I have always believed it to be from the beginning. But what must particularly be observed is that its perception is neither an act of vision, nor of touch, nor of imagination, and has never been such although it may have appeared formerly to be so, but only an intuition of the mind, which may be imperfect and confused as it was formerly, or clear and distinct as it is at present, according as my attention is more or less directed to the elements which are found in it, and of which it is composed.

13   Yet in the meantime I am greatly astonished when I consider [the great feebleness of mind] and its proneness to fall [insensibly] into error; for although without giving expression to my thoughts I consider all this in my own mind, words often impede me and I am almost deceived by the terms of ordinary language. For we say that we see the same wax, if it is present, and not that we simply judge that it is the same from its having the same colour and figure. From this I should conclude that I knew the wax by means of vision and not simply by the intuition of the mind; unless by chance I remember that, when looking from a window and saying I see men who pass in the street, I really do not see them, but infer that what I see is men, just as I say that I see wax. And yet what do I see from the window but hats and coats which may cover automatic machines? Yet I judge these to be men. And similarly solely by the faculty of judgement which rests in my mind, I comprehend that which I believed I saw with my eyes.

14   A man who makes it his aim to raise his knowledge above the common should be ashamed to derive the occasion for doubting from the forms of speech invented by the vulgar; I prefer to pass on and consider whether I had a more evident and perfect conception of what the wax was when I first perceived it, and when I believed I knew it by means of the external senses or at least by the common sense as it is called, that is to say the imaginative faculty, or whether my present conception is clearer now that I have most carefully examined what it is, and in what way it can be known. It would certainly be absurd to doubt as to this. For what was there in this first perception which was distinct? What was there which might not as well have been perceived by any of the animals? But when I distinguish the wax from its external forms, and when, just as if I had taken from it its vestments, I consider it quite naked, it is certain that although some error may still be found in my judgement, I can nevertheless not perceive it thus without a human mind.

15   But finally what shall I say of this mind, that is, of myself, for up to this point I do not admit in myself anything but mind? What then, I who seem to perceive this piece of wax so distinctly, do I not know myself, not only with much more truth and certainty, but also with much more distinctness and clearness? For if I judge that the wax is or exists from the fact that I see it, it certainly follows much more clearly that I am or that I exist myself from the fact that I see it. For it may be that what I see is not really wax, it may also be

that I do not possess eyes with which to see anything; but it cannot be that when I see, or (for I no longer take account of the distinction) when I think I see, that I myself who think am nought. So if I judge that the wax exists from the fact that I touch it, the same thing will follow, to wit, that I am; and if I judge that my imagination, or some other cause, whatever it is, persuades me that the wax exists, I shall still conclude the same. And what I have here remarked of wax may be applied to all other things which are external to me [and which are met with outside of me]. And further, if the [notion or] perception of wax has seemed to me clearer and more distinct, not only after the sight or the touch, but also after many other causes have rendered it quite manifest to me, with how much more [evidence] and distinctness must it be said that I now know myself, since all the reasons which contribute to the knowledge of wax, or any other body whatever, are yet better proofs of the nature of my mind! And there are so many other things in the mind itself which may contribute to the elucidation of its nature, that those which depend on body such as these just mentioned, hardly merit being taken into account.

16 But finally here I am, having insensibly reverted to the point I desired, for, since it is now manifest to me that even bodies are not properly speaking known by the senses or by the faculty of imagination, but by the under-standing only, and since they are not known from the fact that they are seen or touched, but only because they are understood, I see clearly that there is nothing which is easier for me to know than my mind. But because it is diffi-cult to rid oneself so promptly of an opinion to which one was accustomed for so long, it will be well that I should halt a little at this point, so that by the length of my meditation I may more deeply imprint on my memory this new knowledge.

NOTES

1   Or 'form an image' (*effingo*).
2   *Sentire.*

3 Meditations on the First Philosophy in which the Existence of God and the Distinction Between Mind and Body are Demonstrated

Meditation VI

René Descartes

Since our focus of interest is on Descartes' philosophy of mind, it is not necessary for us to have a detailed knowledge of the contents of *Meditations III, IV* and *V*. However, it is useful to know the bare outline of the argument carried on in them: the *Meditations* as a whole constitute a single sustained and brilliantly conceived argument, and it is well worth knowing the thread of the whole.

In his attempt to reconstruct all human knowledge on a basis of mathematical certainty, Descartes has arrived at the end of *Meditation II* having established, in his view, two significant propositions: (1) that he exists and (2) that he is a thing that thinks. He begins *Meditation III* with the reflection that these propositions have the properties of clarity and distinctness, and he resolves to adopt these properties as his test or criterion of truth: whatever he perceives clearly and distinctly he will accept as true. He then goes on to use this criterion in the first of two arguments he uses to establish the third major conclusion in the *Meditations*, namely the existence of God. Once he has established this conclusion, he can proceed much more rapidly with his programme of the reconstruction of knowledge. This is because God is benevolent and so cannot be a deceiver, and Descartes can use this conclusion to refute the dream and evil genius arguments of the first *Meditation*. A benevolent God cannot allow me to be deceived in what I clearly and distinctly perceive.

The problem with this line of argument is that it might prove too much: if God is benevolent and wishes only my good, how is it that we can make mistakes at all? This issue is serious enough for Descartes to devote much of *Meditation IV* to it. There he argues that error arises from our misuse of our free will. What he says is exactly analogous to one of the major lines of response to the problem of evil.

In the fifth *Meditation*, Descartes offers a second argument for the existence of God. He also continues his reconstruction of knowledge by offering an analysis of the essence or nature of material things – not a proof of their *existence* (note: this has to wait for the final *Meditation*). He uses his clarity and distinctness criterion of truth to guarantee the assertion that the essence of material substance is what, using the standard vocabulary of his day, he calls extension: to be extended in this sense is simply to have length, breadth and depth in space.

Throughout *Meditation V* Descartes is careful *not* to assert that material things exist. At this point in the argument, the universe whose *existence* Descartes regards himself as having demonstrated with certainty consists of the I or *res cogitans* and God. However, the *res cogitans* now has quite a number of justified beliefs, including those concerning the essence of both mental and material substance, and the knowledge that the I actually exists. What now remains is to prove the existence of material things, and to complete his arguments concerning the nature of the mind, and its relation to the body.

OF THE EXISTENCE OF MATERIAL THINGS, AND OF THE REAL DISTINCTION BETWEEN THE SOUL AND BODY OF MAN

1   Nothing further now remains but to inquire whether material things exist. And certainly I at least know that these may exist in so far as they are considered as the objects of pure mathematics, since in this aspect I perceive them clearly and distinctly. For there is no doubt that God possesses the power to produce everything that I am capable of perceiving with distinctness, and I have never deemed that anything was impossible for Him, unless I found a contradiction in attempting to conceive it clearly. Further, the faculty of imagination which I possess, and of which, experience tells me, I make use when I apply myself to the consideration of material things, is capable of persuading me of their existence; for when I attentively consider what imagination is, I find that it is nothing but a certain application of the faculty of knowledge to the body which is immediately present to it, and which therefore exists.

2   And to render this quite clear, I remark in the first place the difference that exists between the imagination and pure intellection [or conception]. For example, when I imagine a triangle, I do not conceive it only as a figure comprehended by three lines, but I also apprehend these three lines as present by the power and inward vision of my mind, and this is what I call

READING 3: *MEDITATION VI*

165

imagining. But if I desire to think of a chiliagon, I certainly conceive truly that it is a figure composed of a thousand sides, just as easily as I conceive of a triangle that it is a figure of three sides only; but I cannot in any way imagine the thousand sides of a chiliagon [as I do the three sides of a triangle], nor do I, so to speak, regard them as present [with the eyes of my mind]. And although in accordance with the habit I have formed of always employing the aid of my imagination when I think of corporeal things, it may happen that in imagining a chiliagon I confusedly represent to myself some figure, yet it is very evident that this figure is not a chiliagon, since it in no way differs from that which I represent to myself when I think of a myriagon or any other many-sided figure; nor does it serve my purpose in discovering the properties which go to form the distinction between a chiliagon and other polygons. But if the question turns upon a pentagon, it is quite true that I can conceive its figure as well as that of a chiliagon without the help of my imagination; but I can also imagine it by applying the attention of my mind to each of its five sides, and at the same time to the space which they enclose. And thus I clearly recognise that I have need of a particular effort of mind in order to effect the act of imagination, such as I do not require in order to understand, and this particular effort of mind clearly manifests the difference which exists between imagination and pure intellection.

3   I remark besides that this power of imagination which is in one, inasmuch as it differs from the power of understanding, is in no wise a necessary element in my nature, or in [my essence, that is to say, in] the essence of my mind; for although I did not possess it I should doubtless ever remain the same as I now am, from which it appears that we might conclude that it depends on something which differs from me. And I easily conceive that if some body exists with which my mind is conjoined and united in such a way that it can apply itself to consider it when it pleases, it may be that by this means it can imagine corporeal objects; so that this mode of thinking differs from pure intellection only inasmuch as mind in its intellectual activity in some manner turns on itself, and considers some of the ideas which it possesses in itself; while in imagining it turns towards the body, and there beholds in it something conformable to the idea which it has either conceived of itself or perceived by the senses. I easily understand, I say, that the imagination could be thus constituted if it is true that body exists; and because I can discover no other convenient mode of explaining it, I conjecture with probability that body does exist; but this is only with probability, and although I examine all things with care, I nevertheless do not find that from this distinct idea of corporeal nature, which I have in my imagination, I can derive any argument from which there will necessarily be deduced the existence of body.

4   But I am in the habit of imagining many other things besides this corporeal nature which is the object of pure mathematics, to wit, the colours, sounds, scents, pain, and other such things, although less distinctly. And inasmuch as I perceive these things much better through the senses, by the medium of which, and by the memory, they seem to have reached my imagination, I believe that, in order to examine them more conveniently, it is right that I should at the same time investigate the nature of sense perception, and that I should see if

from the ideas which I apprehend by this mode of thought, which I call feeling, I cannot derive some certain proof of the existence of corporeal objects.

5   And first of all I shall recall to my memory those matters which I hitherto held to be true, as having perceived them through the senses, and the foundations on which my belief has rested; in the next place I shall examine the reasons which have since obliged me to place them in doubt; in the last place I shall consider which of them I must now believe.

6   First of all, then, I perceived that I had a head, hands, feet, and all other members of which this body – which I considered as a part, or possibly even as the whole, of myself – is composed. Further I was sensible that this body was placed amidst many others, from which it was capable of being affected in many different ways, beneficial and hurtful, and I remarked that a certain feeling of pleasure accompanied those that were beneficial, and pain those which were harmful. And in addition to this pleasure and pain, I also experienced hunger, thirst, and other similar appetites, as also certain corporeal inclinations towards joy, sadness, anger, and other similar passions. And outside myself, in addition to extension, figure, and motions of bodies, I remarked in them hardness, heat, and all other tactile qualities, and, further, light and colour, and scents and sounds, the variety of which gave me the means of distinguishing the sky, the earth, the sea, and generally all the other bodies, one from the other. And certainly, considering the ideas of all these qualities which presented themselves to my mind, and which alone I perceived properly or immediately, it was not without reason that I believed myself to perceive objects quite different from my thought, to wit, bodies from which those ideas proceeded; for I found by experience that these ideas presented themselves to me without my consent being requisite, so that I could not perceive any object, however desirous I might be, unless it were present to the organs of sense; and it was not in my power not to perceive it, when it was present. And because the ideas which I received through the senses were much more lively, more clear, and even, in their own way, more distinct than any of those which I could of myself frame in meditation, or than those I found impressed on my memory, it appeared as though they could not have proceeded from my mind, so that they must necessarily have been produced in me by some other things. And having no knowledge of those objects excepting the knowledge which the ideas themselves gave me, nothing was more likely to occur to my mind than that the objects were similar to the ideas which were caused. And because I likewise remembered that I had formerly made use of my senses rather than my reason, and recognised that the ideas which I formed of myself were not so distinct as those which I perceived through the senses, and that they were most frequently even composed of portions of these last, I persuaded myself easily that I had no idea in my mind which had not formerly come to me through the senses. Nor was it without some reason that I believed that this body (which by a certain special right I call my own) belonged to me more properly and more strictly than any other; for in fact I could never be separated from it as from other bodies; I experienced in it and on account of it all my appetites and

affections, and finally I was touched by the feeling of pain and the titillation of pleasure in its parts, and not in the parts of other bodies which were separated from it. But when I inquired, why, from some, I know not what, painful sensation, there follows sadness of mind, and from the pleasurable sensation there arises joy, or why this mysterious pinching of the stomach which I call hunger causes me to desire to eat, and dryness of throat causes a desire to drink, and so on, I could give no reason excepting that nature taught me so; for there is certainly no affinity (that I at least can understand) between the craving of the stomach and the desire to eat, any more than between the perception of whatever causes pain and the thought of sadness which arises from this perception. And in the same way it appeared to me that I had learned from nature all the other judgements which I formed regarding the objects of my senses, since I remarked that these judgements were formed in me before I had the leisure to weigh and consider any reasons which might oblige me to make them.

7 But afterwards many experiences little by little destroyed all the faith which I had rested in my senses; for I from time to time observed that those towers which from afar appeared to me to be round, more closely observed seemed square, and that colossal statues raised on the summit of these towers, appeared as quite tiny statues when viewed from the bottom; and so in an infinitude of other cases I found error in judgements founded on the external senses. And not only in those founded on the external senses, but even in those founded on the internal as well; for is there anything more intimate or more internal than pain? And yet I have learned from some persons whose arms or legs have been cut off, that they sometimes seemed to feel pain in the part which had been amputated, which made me think that I could not be quite certain that it was a certain member which pained me, even although I felt pain in it. And to those grounds of doubt I have largely added two others, which are very general; the first is that I never have believed myself to feel anything in waking moments which I cannot also sometimes believe myself to feel when I sleep, and as I do not think that these things which I seem to feel in sleep, proceed from objects outside of me, I do not see any reason why I should have this belief regarding objects which I seem to perceive while awake. The other was that being still ignorant, or rather supposing myself to be ignorant, of the author of my being, I saw nothing to prevent me from having been so constituted by nature that I might be deceived even in matters which seemed to me to be most certain. And as to the grounds on which I was formerly persuaded of the truth of sensible objects, I had not much trouble in replying to them. For since nature seemed to cause me to lean towards many things from which reason repelled me, I did not believe that I should trust much to the teachings of nature. And although the ideas which I receive by the senses do not depend on my will, I did not think that one should for that reason conclude that they proceeded from things different from myself, since possibly some faculty might be discovered in me – though hitherto unknown to me – which produced them.

8 But now that I begin to know myself better, and to discover more clearly the

author of my being, I do not in truth think that I should rashly admit all the matters which the senses seem to teach us, but, on the other hand, I do not think that I should doubt them all universally.

9　And first of all, because I know that all things which I apprehend clearly and distinctly can be created by God as I apprehend them, it suffices that I am able to apprehend one thing apart from another clearly and distinctly in order to be certain that the one is different from the other, since they may be made to exist in separation at least by the omnipotence of God; and it does not signify by what power this separation is made in order to compel me to judge them to be different; and, therefore, just because I know certainly that I exist, and that meanwhile I do not remark that any other thing necessarily pertains to my nature or essence, excepting that I am a thinking thing, I rightly conclude that my essence consists solely in the fact that I am a thinking thing [or a substance whose whole essence or nature is to think]. And although possibly (or rather certainly, as I shall say in a moment) I possess a body with which I am very intimately conjoined, yet because, on the one side, I have a clear and distinct idea of myself inasmuch as I am only a thinking and unextended thing, and as, on the other, I possess a distinct idea of body, inasmuch as it is only an extended and unthinking thing, it is certain that this I [that is to say, my soul by which I am what I am], is entirely and absolutely distinct from my body, and can exist without it.

10　I further find in myself faculties employing modes of thinking peculiar to themselves, to wit, the faculties of imagination and feeling, without which I can easily conceive myself clearly and distinctly as a complete being; while, on the other hand, they cannot be so conceived apart from me, that is without an intelligent substance in which they reside, for [in the notion we have of these faculties, or, to use the language of the Schools] in their formal concept, some kind of intellection is comprised, from which I infer that they are distinct from me as its modes are from a thing. I observe also in me some other faculties such as that of change of position, the assumption of different figures and such like, which cannot be conceived, any more than can the preceding, apart from some substance to which they are attached, and consequently cannot exist without it; but it is very clear that these faculties, if it be true that they exist, must be attached to some corporeal or extended substance, and not to an intelligent substance, since in the clear and distinct conception of these there is some sort of extension found to be present, but no intellection at all. There is certainly further in me a certain passive faculty of perception, that is, of receiving and recognising the ideas of sensible things, but this would be useless to me [and I could in no way avail myself of it], if there were not either in me or in some other thing another active faculty capable of forming and producing these ideas. But this active faculty cannot exist in me [inasmuch as I am a thing that thinks] seeing that it does not presuppose thought, and also that those ideas are often produced in me without my contributing in any way to the same, and often even against my will; it is thus necessarily the case that the faculty resides in some substance different from me in which all the reality which is objectively in the ideas that are produced by this faculty is formally or eminently contained, as I remarked before. And this substance is either a body, that is, a corporeal nature in which there is contained formally [and really] all that which is objectively [and by representation] in those ideas, or it is God Himself, or some other creature more noble than body in which that same is contained eminently. But, since God is no deceiver, it is very manifest that He does not communicate to me these ideas immediately and by Himself, nor yet by the intervention of some creature in which their reality is not formally, but only eminently, contained. For since He has given me no faculty to recognise that this is the case, but, on the other hand, a very great inclination to believe [that they are sent to me or] that they are conveyed to me by corporeal objects, I do not see how He could be defended from the accusation of deceit if these ideas were produced by causes other than corporeal objects. Hence we must allow that corporeal things exist. However, they are perhaps not exactly what we perceive by the senses, since this comprehension by the senses is in many instances very obscure and confused; but we must at least admit that all things which I conceive in them clearly and distinctly, that is to say, all things which, speaking generally, are comprehended in the object of pure mathematics, are truly to be recognised as external objects.

11　As to other things, however, which are either particular only, as, for example, that the sun is of such and such a figure, etc., or which are less clearly and distinctly conceived, such as light, sound, pain and the like, it is certain that although they are very dubious and uncertain, yet on the sole ground that God is not a deceiver, and that consequently He has not permitted any falsity to exist in my opinion which He has not likewise given me the faculty of correcting, I may assuredly hope to conclude that I have within me the means of arriving at the truth even here. And first of all there is no doubt that in all things which nature teaches me there is some truth contained; for by nature, considered in general, I now understand no other thing than either God Himself or else the order and disposition which God has established in created things; and by my nature in particular I understand no other thing than the complexus of all the things which God has given me.

12　But there is nothing which this nature teaches me more expressly [nor more sensibly] than that I have a body which is adversely affected when I feel pain, which has need of food or drink when I experience the feelings of hunger and thirst, and so on; nor can I doubt there being some truth in all this.

13　Nature also teaches me by these sensations of pain, hunger, thirst, etc., that I am not only lodged in my body as a pilot in a vessel, but that I am very closely united to it, and so to speak so intermingled with it that I seem to compose with it one whole. For if that were not the case, when my body is hurt, I, who am merely a thinking thing, should not feel pain, for I should perceive this wound by the understanding only, just as the sailor perceives by sight when something is damaged in his vessel; and when my body has need of drink or food, I should clearly understand the fact without being warned of it by confused feelings of hunger and thirst. For all these sensations of hunger, thirst, pain, etc. are in truth none other than certain confused modes of thought which are produced by the union and apparent intermingling of mind and body.

14   Moreover, nature teaches me that many other bodies exist around mine, of which some are to be avoided, and others sought after. And certainly from the fact that I am sensible of different sorts of colours, sounds, scents, tastes, heat, hardness, etc., I very easily conclude that there are in the bodies from which all these diverse sense-perceptions proceed certain variations which answer to them, although possibly these are not really at all similar to them. And also from the fact that amongst these different sense-perceptions some are very agreeable to me and others disagreeable, it is quite certain that my body (or rather myself in my entirety, inasmuch as I am formed of body and soul) may receive different impressions agreeable and disagreeable from the other bodies which surround it.

15   But there are many other things which nature seems to have taught me, but which at the same time I have never really received from her, but which have been brought about in my mind by a certain habit which I have of forming inconsiderate judgements on things; and thus it may easily happen that these judgements contain some error. Take, for example, the opinion which I hold that all space in which there is nothing that affects [or makes an impression on] my senses is void; that in a body which is warm there is something entirely similar to the idea of heat which is in me; that in a white or green body there is the same whiteness or greenness that I perceive; that in a bitter or sweet body there is the same taste, and so on in other instances; that the stars, the towers, and all other distant bodies are of the same figure and size as they appear from far off to our eyes, etc. But in order that in this there should be nothing which I do not conceive distinctly, I should define exactly what I really understand when I say that I am taught somewhat by nature. For here I take nature in a more limited signification than when I term it the sum of all the things given me by God, since in this sum many things are comprehended which only pertain to mind (and to these I do not refer in speaking of nature) such as the notion which I have of the fact that what has once been done cannot ever be undone and an infinitude of such things which I know by the light of nature [without the help of the body]; and seeing that it comprehends many other matters besides which only pertain to body, and are no longer here contained under the name of nature, such as the quality of weight which it possesses and the like, with which I also do not deal; for in talking of nature I only treat of those things given by God to me as a being composed of mind and body. But the nature here described truly teaches me to flee from things which cause the sensation of pain, and seek after the things which communicate to me the sentiment of pleasure and so forth; but I do not see that beyond this it teaches me that from those diverse sense-perceptions we should ever form any conclusion regarding things outside of us, without having [carefully and maturely] mentally examined them beforehand. For it seems to me that it is mind alone, and not mind and body in conjunction, that is requisite to a knowledge of the truth in regard to such things. Thus, although a star makes no larger an impression on my eye than the flame of a little candle there is yet in me no real or positive propensity impelling me to believe that it is not greater than that flame; but I have judged it to be so from my earliest years, without any rational foundation.

And although in approaching fire I feel heat, and in approaching it a little too near I even feel pain, there is at the same time no reason in this which could persuade me that there is in the fire something resembling this heat any more than there is in it something resembling the pain; all that I have any reason to believe from this is, that there is something in it, whatever it may be, which excites in me these sensations of heat or of pain. So also, although there are spaces in which I find nothing which excites my senses, I must not from that conclude that these spaces contain no body; for I see in this, as in other similar things, that I have been in the habit of perverting the order of nature, because these perceptions of sense having been placed within me by nature merely for the purpose of signifying to my mind what things are beneficial or hurtful to the composite whole of which it forms a part, and being up to that point sufficiently clear and distinct, I yet avail myself of them as though they were absolute rules by which I might immediately determine the essence of the bodies which are outside me, as to which, in fact, they can teach me nothing but what is most obscure and confused.

16 But I have already sufficiently considered how, notwithstanding the supreme goodness of God, falsity enters into the judgements I make. Only here a new difficulty is presented – one respecting those things the pursuit or avoidance of which is taught me by nature, and also respecting the internal sensations which I possess, and in which I seem to have sometimes detected error [and thus to be directly deceived by my own nature]. To take an example, the agreeable taste of some food in which poison has been intermingled may induce me to partake of the poison, and thus deceive me. It is true, at the same time, that in this case nature may be excused, for it only induces me to desire food in which I find a pleasant taste, and not to desire the poison which is unknown to it; and thus I can infer nothing from this fact, except that my nature is not omniscient, at which there is certainly no reason to be astonished, since man, being finite in nature, can only have knowledge the perfectness of which is limited.

17 But we not infrequently deceive ourselves even in those things to which we are directly impelled by nature, as happens with those who when they are sick desire to drink or eat things hurtful to them. It will perhaps be said here that the cause of their deceptiveness is that their nature is corrupt, but that does not remove the difficulty, because a sick man is none the less truly God's creature than he who is in health; and it is therefore as repugnant to God's goodness for the one to have a deceitful nature as it is for the other. And as a clock composed of wheels and counter-weights no less exactly observes the laws of nature when it is badly made, and does not show the time properly, than when it entirely satisfies the wishes of its maker, and as, if I consider the body of a man as being a sort of machine so built up and composed of nerves, muscles, veins, blood and skin, that though there were no mind in it at all, it would cease to have the same motions as at present, exception being made of those movements which are due to the direction of the will, and in consequence depend upon the mind [as opposed to those which operate by the disposition of its organs], I easily recognise that it would be as natural to this body, supposing it to be, for example, dropsical,

to suffer the parchedness of the throat which usually signifies to the mind the feeling of thirst, and to be disposed by this parched feeling to move the nerves and other parts in the way requisite for drinking, and thus to augment its malady and do harm to itself, as it is natural to it, when it has no indisposition, to be impelled to drink for its good by a similar cause. And although, considering the use to which the clock has been destined by its maker, I may say that it deflects from the order of its nature when it does not indicate the hours correctly; and as, in the same way, considering the machine of the human body as having been formed by God in order to have in itself all the movements usually manifested there, I have reason for thinking that it does not follow the order of nature when, if the throat is dry, drinking does harm to the conservation of health, nevertheless I recognise at the same time that this last mode of explaining nature is very different from the other. For this is but a purely verbal characterisation depending entirely on my thought, which compares a sick man and a badly constructed clock with the idea which I have of a healthy man and a well made clock, and it is hence extrinsic to the things to which it is applied; but according to the other interpretation of the term nature I understand something which is truly found in things and which is therefore not without some truth.

18 But certainly although in regard to the dropsical body it is only so to speak to apply an extrinsic term when we say that its nature is corrupted inasmuch as apart from the need to drink, the throat is parched; yet in regard to the composite whole, that is to say, to the mind or soul united to this body, it is not a purely verbal predicate, but a real error of nature, for it to have thirst when drinking would be hurtful to it. And thus it still remains to inquire how the goodness of God does not prevent the nature of man so regarded from being fallacious.

19 In order to begin this examination, then, I here say, in the first place, that there is a great difference between mind and body, inasmuch as body is by nature always divisible and the mind is entirely indivisible. For, as a matter of fact, when I consider the mind, that is to say, myself inasmuch as I am only a thinking thing, I cannot distinguish in myself any parts, but apprehend myself to be clearly one and entire; and although the whole mind seems to be united to the whole body, yet if a foot, or an arm, or some other part, is separated from my body, I am aware that nothing has been taken away from my mind. And the faculties of willing, feeling, conceiving, etc. cannot be properly speaking said to be its parts, for it is one and the same mind which employs itself in willing and in feeling and understanding. But it is quite otherwise with corporeal or extended objects, for there is not one of these imaginable by me which my mind cannot easily divide into parts, and which consequently I do not recognise as being divisible; this would be sufficient to teach me that the mind or soul of man is entirely different from the body, if I had not already learned it from other sources.

20 I further notice that the mind does not receive the impressions from all parts of the body immediately, but only from the brain, or perhaps even from one of its smallest parts, to wit, from that in which the common sense[1] is said to reside, which, whenever it is disposed in the same particular way, conveys

the same thing to the mind, although meanwhile the other portions of the body may be differently disposed, as is testified by innumerable experiments which it is unnecessary here to recount.

21　I notice, also, that the nature of body is such that none of its parts can be moved by another part a little way off which cannot also be moved in the same way by each one of the parts which are between the two, although this more remote part does not act at all. As, for example, in the cord *ABCD* [which is in tension] if we pull the last part *D*, the first part *A* will not be moved in any way differently from what would be the case if one of the intervening parts *B* or *C* were pulled, and the last part *D* were to remain unmoved. And in the same way, when I feel pain in my foot, my knowledge of physics teaches me that this sensation is communicated by means of nerves dispersed through the foot, which, being extended like cords from there to the brain, when they are contracted in the foot, at the same time contract the inmost portions of the brain which is their extremity and place of origin, and then excite a certain movement which nature has established in order to cause the mind to be affected by a sensation of pain represented as existing in the foot. But because these nerves must pass through the tibia, the thigh, the loins, the back and the neck, in order to reach from the leg to the brain, it may happen that although their extremities which are in the foot are not affected, but only certain ones of their intervening parts [which pass by the loins or the neck], this action will excite the same movement in the brain that might have been excited there by a hurt received in the foot, in consequence of which the mind will necessarily feel in the foot the same pain as if it had received a hurt. And the same holds good of all the other perceptions of our senses.

22　I notice finally that since each of the movements which are in the portion of the brain by which the mind is immediately affected brings about one partic-ular sensation only, we cannot under the circumstances imagine anything more likely than that this movement, amongst all the sensations which it is capable of impressing on it, causes mind to be affected by that one which is best fitted and most generally useful for the conservation of the human body when it is in health. But experience makes us aware that all the feelings with which nature inspires us are such as I have just spoken of; and there is there-fore nothing in them which does not give testimony to the power and goodness of the God [who has produced them]. Thus, for example, when the nerves which are in the feet are violently or more than usually moved, their movement, passing through the medulla of the spine to the inmost parts of the brain, gives a sign to the mind which makes it feel somewhat, to wit, pain, as though in the foot, by which the mind is excited to do its utmost to remove the cause of the evil as dangerous and hurtful to the foot. It is true that God could have constituted the nature of man in such a way that this same movement in the brain would have conveyed something quite different to the mind; for example, it might have produced consciousness of itself either in so far as it is in the brain, or it might finally have produced consciousness of anything else whatsoever; but none of all this would have contributed so well to the conservation of the body. Similarly, when we desire to drink, a certain dryness of the throat is produced which moves its nerves, and by their means the internal portions of the brain; and this movement causes in the mind the sensation of thirst, because in this case there is nothing more useful to us than to become aware that we have need to drink for the conservation of our health; and the same holds good in other instances.

23   From this it is quite clear that, notwithstanding the supreme goodness of God, the nature of man, inasmuch as it is composed of mind and body, cannot be otherwise than sometimes a source of deception. For if there is any cause which excites, not in the foot but in some part of the nerves which are extended between the foot and the brain, or even in the brain itself, the same movement which usually is produced when the foot is detrimentally affected, pain will be experienced as though it were in the foot, and the sense will thus naturally be deceived; for since the same movement in the brain is capable of causing but one sensation in the mind, and this sensation is much more frequently excited by a cause which hurts the foot than by another existing in some other quarter, it is reasonable that it should convey to the mind pain in the foot rather than in any other part of the body. And although the parchedness of the throat does not always proceed, as it usually does from the fact that drinking is necessary for the health of the body, but sometimes comes from quite a different cause, as is the case with dropsical patients, it is yet much better that it should mislead on this occasion than if, on the other hand, it were always to deceive us when the body is in good health; and so on in similar cases.

24   And certainly this consideration is of great service to me, not only in enabling me to recognise all the errors to which my nature is subject, but also in enabling me to avoid them or to correct them more easily. For knowing that all my senses more frequently indicate to me truth than falsehood respecting the things which concern that which is beneficial to the body, and being able almost always to avail myself of many of them in order to examine one particular thing, and, besides that, being able to make use of my memory in order to connect the present with the past, and of my understanding which already has discovered all the causes of my errors, I ought no longer to fear that falsity may be found in matters every day presented to me by my senses. And I ought to set aside all the doubts of these past days as hyperbolical and ridiculous, particularly that very common uncertainty respecting sleep, which I could not distinguish from the waking state; for at present I find a very notable difference between the two, inasmuch as our memory can never connect our dreams one with the other, or with the whole course of our lives, as it unites events which happen to us while we are awake. And, as a matter of fact, if someone, while I was awake, quite suddenly appeared to me and disappeared as fast as do the images which I see in sleep, so that I could not know from whence the form came nor whither it went, it would not be without reason that I should deem it a spectre or a phantom formed by my brain [and similar to those which I form in sleep], rather than a real man. But when I perceive things as to which I know distinctly both the place from which they proceed, and that in which they

are, and the time at which they appeared to me; and when, without any interruption, I can connect the perceptions which I have of them with the whole course of my life, I am perfectly assured that these perceptions occur while I am waking and not during sleep. And I ought in no wise to doubt the truth of such matters, if, after having called up all my senses, my memory, and my understanding, to examine them, nothing is brought to evidence by any one of them which is repugnant to what is set forth by the others. For because God is in no wise a deceiver, it follows that I am not deceived in this. But because the exigencies of action often oblige us to make up our minds before having leisure to examine matters carefully, we must confess that the life of man is very frequently subject to error in respect to individual objects, and we must in the end acknowledge the infirmity of our nature.

NOTE

1 *Sensus communis.*

4 'The passions of the soul'

Part I

René Descartes

ARTICLE 30

THAT THE SOUL IS UNITED TO ALL THE PORTIONS OF THE BODY CONJOINTLY

But in order to understand all these things more perfectly, we must know that the soul is really joined to the whole body, and that we cannot, properly speaking, say that it exists in any one of its parts to the exclusion of the others, because it is one and in some manner indivisible, owing to the disposition of its organs, which are so related to one another that when any one of them is removed, that renders the whole body defective; and because it is of a nature which has no relation to extension, nor dimensions, nor other properties of the matter of which the body is composed, but only to the whole conglomerate of its organs, as appears from the fact that we could not in any way conceive of the half or the third of a soul, nor of the space it occupies, and because it does not become smaller owing to the cutting off of some portion of the body, but separates itself from it entirely when the union of its assembled organs is dissolved.

ARTICLE 31

THAT THERE IS A SMALL GLAND IN THE BRAIN IN WHICH THE SOUL EXERCISES ITS FUNCTIONS MORE PARTICULARLY THAN IN THE OTHER PARTS

It is likewise necessary to know that although the soul is joined to the whole body, there is yet in that a certain part in which it exercises its functions more particularly than in all the others; and it is usually believed that this part is the brain, or possibly the heart: the brain, because it is with it that the organs of sense are connected, and the heart because it is apparently in it that we experience the passions. But, in examining the matter with care, it seems as though I had clearly ascertained that the part of the body in which the soul exercises its functions immediately is in no wise the heart, nor the whole of the brain, but merely the most inward of all its parts, to wit, a certain very small gland which is situated in the middle of its substance and so suspended above the duct whereby the animal spirits in its anterior cavities have communication with those in the posterior, that the slightest movements which take place in it may alter very greatly the course of these spirits; and reciprocally that the smallest changes which occur in the course of the spirits may do much to change the movements of this gland.

ARTICLE 32

HOW WE KNOW THAT THIS GLAND IS THE MAIN SEAT OF THE SOUL

The reason which persuades me that the soul cannot have any other seat in all the body than this gland wherein to exercise its functions immediately, is that I reflect that the other parts of our brain are all of them double, just as we have two eyes, two hands, two ears, and finally all the organs of our outside senses are double; and inasmuch as we have but one solitary and simple thought of one particular thing at one and the same moment, it must necessarily be the case that there must somewhere be a place where the two images which come to us by the two eyes, where the two other impressions which proceed from a single object by means of the double organs of the other senses, can unite before arriving at the soul, in order that they may not represent to it two objects instead of one. And it is easy to apprehend how these images or other impressions might unite in this gland by the intermission of the spirits which fill the cavities of the brain; but there is no other place in the body where they can be thus united unless they are so in this gland.

ARTICLE 34

HOW THE SOUL AND THE BODY ACT ON ONE ANOTHER

Let us then conceive here that the soul has its principal seat in the little gland which exists in the middle of the brain, from whence it radiates forth through all the remainder of the body by means of the animal spirits, nerves, and even the blood, which, participating in the impressions of the spirits, can carry them by the arteries into all the members. And recollecting what has been said above about the machine of our body, i.e. that the little filaments of our nerves are so distributed in all its parts, that on the occasion of the diverse movements which are there excited by sensible objects, they open in diverse ways the pores of the brain, which causes the animal spirits contained in these cavities to enter in diverse ways into the muscles, by which means they can move the members in all the different ways in which they are capable of being moved; and also that all the other causes which are capable of moving the spirits in diverse ways suffice to conduct them into diverse muscles; let us here add that the small gland which is the main seat of the soul is so suspended between the cavities which contain the spirits that it can be moved by them in as many different ways as there are sensible diversities in the object, but that it may also be moved in diverse ways by the soul, whose nature is such that it receives in itself as many diverse impressions, that is to say, that it possesses as many diverse perceptions as there are diverse movements in this gland. Reciprocally, likewise, the machine of the body is so formed that from the simple fact that this gland is diversely moved by the soul, or by such other cause, whatever it is, it thrusts the spirits which surround it towards the pores of the brain, which conduct them by the nerves into the muscles, by which means it causes them to move the limbs.

5 | 'Sensations and brain processes'

J.J.C. Smart

J.J.C. ('Jack') Smart was born in Cambridge (UK) in 1920, but spent his working life in Australia, and is noted for his interest in ethics as well as in the philosophy of mind. Tempted at first by behaviourism, Smart gave it up to develop the identity theory of which he is one of the most able and influential advocates. The following is a slightly shortened version of one of his now classic philosophical papers advocating this point of view.

1 Suppose that I report that I have at this moment a roundish, blurry-edged after-image which is yellowish towards its edge and is orange towards its centre. What is it that I am reporting? One answer to this question might be that I am not reporting anything, that when I say that it looks to me as though there is a roundish yellow-orange patch of light on the wall I am expressing some sort of *temptation*, the temptation to say that there is a roundish yellow-orange patch on the wall (though I may know that there is not such a patch on the wall). This is perhaps Wittgenstein's view in the *Philosophical Investigations* (see sections 367, 370). Similarly, when I 'report' a pain, I am not really reporting anything (or, if you like, I am reporting in a queer sense of 'reporting'), but am doing a sophisticated sort of wince. I prefer most of the time to discuss an after-image rather than a pain, because the word 'pain' brings in something which is irrelevant to my purpose: the notion of 'distress'. I think that 'he is in pain' entails 'he is in distress', that is, that he is in a certain agitation-condition.[1] Similarly, to say 'I am in pain' may be to do more than 'replace pain behaviour': it may be partly to report something, though this something is quite non-mysterious, being an agitation-condition, and so susceptible of behaviouristic analysis. The suggestion I wish if possible to avoid is a different one, namely that 'I am in pain' is a

genuine report, and that what it reports is an irreducibly psychical some-thing. And similarly the suggestion I wish to resist is also that to say 'I have a yellowish-orange after-image' is to report something irreducibly psychical.

2 Why do I wish to resist this suggestion? Mainly because of Occam's razor. It seems to me that science is increasingly giving us a viewpoint whereby organisms are able to be seen as physico-chemical mechanisms:[2] it seems that even the behaviour of man himself will one day be explicable in mecha-nistic terms. There does seem to be, so far as science is concerned, nothing in the world but increasingly complex arrangements of physical constituents. All except for one place: in consciousness. That is, for a full description of what is going on in a man you would have to mention not only the physical process in his tissues, glands, nervous system, and so forth, but also his states of consciousness: his visual, auditory, and tactual sensations, his aches and pains. That these should be *correlated* with brain processes does not help, for to say that they are *correlated* is to say that they are something 'over and above'. You cannot correlate something with itself. You correlate footprints with burglars, but not Bill Sikes the burglar with Bill Sikes the burglar. So sensations, states of consciousness, do seem to be the one sort of thing left outside the physicalist picture, and for various reasons I just cannot believe that this can be so. That everything should be explicable in terms of physics (together of course with descriptions of the ways in which the parts are put together – roughly, biology is to physics as radio-engineering is to electro-magnetism) except the occurrence of sensations seems to me to be frankly unbelievable. Such sensations would be 'nomological danglers', to use Feigl's expression.[3] It is not often realised how odd would be the laws whereby these nomological danglers would dangle. It is sometimes asked, 'Why can't there be psycho-physical laws which are of a novel sort, just as the laws of electricity and magnetism were novelties from the standpoint of Newtonian mechanics?' Certainly we are pretty sure in the future to come across new ultimate laws of a novel type, but I expect them to relate simple constituents: for example, whatever ultimate particles are then in vogue. I cannot believe that ultimate laws of nature could relate simple constituents to configurations consisting of perhaps billions of neurones (and goodness knows how many billion billions of ultimate particles) all put together for all the world as though their main purpose in life was to be a negative feedback mechanism of a complicated sort. Such ultimate laws would be like nothing so far known in science. They have a queer 'smell' to them. I am just unable to believe in the nomological danglers themselves, or in the laws whereby they would dangle. If any philosophical arguments seemed to compel us to believe in such things, I would suspect a catch in the argument. In any case it is the object of this paper to show that there are no philosophical arguments which compel us to be dualists.

3 Let me first try to state more accurately the thesis that sensations are brain processes. It is not the thesis that, for example, 'after-image' or 'ache' means the same as 'brain process of sort X' (where 'X' is replaced by a description of a certain sort of brain process). It is that in so far as 'after-image' or 'ache' is a report of a process, it is a report of a process that *happens to be a* brain

process. It follows that the thesis does not claim that sensation statements can be *translated* into statements about brain processes.[4] Nor does it claim that the logic of a sensation statement is the same as that of a brain-process statement. All it claims is that in so far as a sensation statement is a report of something, that something is in fact a brain process. Sensations are nothing over and above brain processes. Nations are nothing 'over and above' citizens, but this does not prevent the logic of nation statements being very different from the logic of citizen statements, nor does it ensure the translatability of nation statements into citizen statements. (I do not, however, wish to assert that the relation of sensation statements to brain-process statements is very like that of nation statements to citizen statements. Nations do not just happen to be nothing over and above citizens, for example. I bring in the 'nations' example merely to make a negative point: that the fact that the logic of A-statements is different from that of B-statements does not ensure that A's are anything above B's.)

REMARKS ON IDENTITY

4   When I say that a sensation is a brain process or that lightning is an electric discharge, I am using 'is' in the sense of strict identity. (Just as in the – in this case necessary – proposition '7 is identical with the smallest prime number greater than 5'). When I say that a sensation is a brain process or that lightning is an electric discharge I do not mean just that the sensation is somehow spatially or temporally continuous with the brain process or that the lightning is just spatially or temporally continuous with the discharge. When on the other hand I say that the successful general is the same person as the small boy who stole the apples I mean only that the successful general I see before me is a time slice[5] of the same four-dimensional object of which the small boy stealing apples is an earlier time slice. However, the four-dimensional object which has the general-I-see-before-me for its late time slice is identical in the strict sense with the four-dimensional object which has the small-boy-stealing-apples for an early time slice. I distinguish these two senses of 'is identical with' because I wish to make it clear that the brain-process doctrine asserts identity in the *strict* sense.

5   I shall now discuss various possible objections to the view that the processes reported in sensation statements are in fact processes in the brain. Most of us have met some of these objections in our first year as philosophy students. All the more reason to take a good look at them. Others of the objections will be more recondite and subtle.

OBJECTION I

6   Any illiterate peasant can talk perfectly well about his after-images, or how things look or feel to him, or about his aches and pains, and yet he may know nothing whatever about neurophysiology. A man may, like Aristotle, believe

that the brain is an organ for cooling the body without any impairment of his ability to make true statements about his sensations. Hence the things we are talking about when we describe our sensations cannot be processes in the brain.

REPLY

7   You might as well say that a nation of slugabeds, who never saw the Morning Star or knew of its existence, or who had never thought of the expression 'the Morning Star', but who used the expression 'the Evening Star' perfectly well, could not use this expression to refer to the same entity as we refer to (and describe as) 'the Morning Star'.[6]

8   You may object that the Morning Star is in a sense not the very same thing as the Evening Star, but only something spatio-temporally continuous with it. That is, you may say that the Morning Star is not the Evening Star in the strict sense of 'identity' that I distinguished earlier.

9   There is, however, a more plausible example. Consider lightning.[7] Modern physical science tells us that lightning is a certain kind of electrical discharge due to ionisation of clouds of water vapour in the atmosphere. This, it is now believed, is what the true nature of lightning is. Note that there are not two things: flash of lightning and an electrical discharge. There is one thing, a flash of lightning, which is described scientifically as an electrical discharge to the earth from a cloud of ionised water molecules. The case is not at all like that of explaining a footprint by reference to a burglar. We say that what lightning really is, what its true nature as revealed by science is, is an electrical discharge. (It is not the true nature of a footprint to be a burglar).

10   To forestall irrelevant objections, I should like to make it clear that by 'lightning' I mean the publicly observable physical object lightning, not a visual sense-datum of lightning. I say that the publicly observable physical object lightning is in fact the electrical discharge, not just a correlate of it. The sense-datum, or rather the having of the sense-datum, the 'look' of lightning, may well in my view be a correlate of the electrical discharge. For in my view it is a brain state caused by the lightning. But we should no more confuse sensations of lightning with lightning than we confuse sensations of a table with the table.

11   In short, the reply to Objection 1 is that there can be contingent statements of the form, 'A is identical with B', and a person may well know that something is an A without knowing that it is a B. An illiterate peasant might well be able to talk about his sensations without knowing about his brain processes, just as he can talk about lightning through he knows nothing of electricity.

OBJECTION 2

12   It is only a contingent fact (if it is a fact) that when we have a certain kind of sensation there is a certain kind of process in our brain. Indeed it is possible,

though perhaps in the highest degree unlikely, that our present physiological theories will be as out of date as the ancient theory connecting mental processes with goings on in the heart. It follows that when we report a sensation we are not reporting a brain process.

REPLY

13 The objection certainly proves that when we say 'I have an after-image' we cannot *mean* something of the form 'I have such and such a brain process.' But this does not show that what we report (having an after-image) is not *in fact* a brain process. 'I see lightning' does not *mean* 'I see an electrical discharge.' Indeed, it is logically possible (though highly unlikely) that the electrical discharge account of lightning might one day be given up. Again, 'I see the Evening Star' does not *mean* the same as 'I see the Morning Star', and yet 'the Evening Star and the Morning Star are one and the same thing' is a contingent proposition. Possibly Objection 2 derives some of its apparent strength from a 'Fido' – Fido theory of meaning. If the meaning of an expression were what the expression named, then of course it *would* follow from the fact that 'sensation' and 'brain process' have different meanings, that they cannot name one and the same thing.

OBJECTION 3[8]

14 Even if Objections 1 and 2 do not prove that sensations are something over and above brain processes, they do prove that the qualities of sensations are something over and above the qualities of brain processes. That is, it may be possible to get out of asserting the existence of irreducibly psychic processes, but not out of asserting the existence of irreducibly psychic *properties*. For suppose we identify the Morning Star with the Evening Star. Then there must be some properties which logically imply that of being the Morning Star, and quite distinct properties which entail that of being the Evening Star. Again, there must be some properties (for example, that of being a yellow flash) which are logically distinct from those in the physicalist story.

15 Indeed, it might be thought that the objection succeeds at one jump. For consider the property of 'being a yellow flash'. It might seem that this property lies inevitably outside the physicalist framework within which I am trying to work (either by 'yellow' being an objective emergent property of physical objects, or else by being a power to produce yellow sense-data, where 'yellow' in this second instantiation of the word, refers to a purely phenomenal or introspectible quality). I must therefore digress for a moment and indicate how I deal with secondary qualities. I shall concentrate on colour.

16 First of all, let me introduce the concept of a normal percipient. One person is more a normal percipient than another if he can make colour discriminations

that the other cannot. For example, if A can pick a lettuce leaf out of a heap of cabbage leaves, whereas B cannot though he can pick a lettuce leaf out of a heap of beetroot leaves, then A is more normal than B. (I am assuming that A and B are not given time to distinguish the leaves by their slight difference in shape, and so forth.) From the concept of 'more normal than' it is easy to see how we can introduce the concept of 'normal'. Of course, Eskimos may make the finest discriminations at the blue end of the spectrum, Hottentots at the red end. In this case the concept of a normal percipient is a slightly idealised one, rather like that of 'the mean sun' in astronomical chronology. There is no need to go into such subtleties now. I say that 'This is red' means something roughly like 'A normal percipient would not easily pick this out of a clump of geranium petals though he would pick it out of a clump of lettuce leaves'. Of course it does not exactly mean this: a person might know the meaning of 'red' without knowing anything about geraniums, or even about normal percipients. But the point is that a person can be trained to say 'This is red' of objects which would not easily be picked out of geranium petals by a normal percipient, and so on. (Note that even a colour-blind person can reasonably assert that something is red, though of course he needs to use another human being, not just himself, as his 'colour meter'.) This account of secondary qualities explains their unimportance in physics. For obviously the discriminations and lack of discriminations made by a very complex neurophysiological mechanism are hardly likely to correspond to simple and non-arbitrary distinctions in nature.

17 I therefore elucidate colours as powers, in Locke's sense, to evoke certain sorts of discriminatory responses in human beings. They are also, of course, powers to cause sensations in human beings (an account still nearer Locke's). But these sensations, I am arguing, are identifiable with brain processes.

18 Now how do I get over the objection that a sensation can be identified with a brain process only if it has some phenomenal property, not possessed by brain processes, whereby one half of the identification may be, so to speak, pinned down?

REPLY

19 My suggestion is as follows. When a person says, 'I see a yellowish-orange after-image', he is saying something like this: '*There is something going on which is like what is going on when* I have my eyes open, am awake, and there is an orange illuminated in good light in front of me, that is, when I really see an orange.' (And there is no reason why a person should not say the same thing when he is having a veridical sense datum, so long as we construe 'like' in the last sentence in such a sense that something can be like itself.) Notice that the italicised words, namely 'there is something going on which is like what is going on when', are all quasi-logical or topic-neutral words. This explains why the ancient Greek peasant's reports about his sensations can be neutral between dualistic metaphysics or my materialistic metaphysics. It explains how sensations can be brain processes and yet how a man who reports them need know nothing about brain processes. For he reports them

only very abstractly as 'something going on which is like what is going on when ....' Similarly, a person may say 'someone is in the room', thus reporting truly that the doctor is in the room, even though he has never heard of doctors. (There are not two people in the room 'someone' *and* the doctor.) This account of sensation statements also explains the singular elusiveness of 'raw feels' – why no one seems to be able to pin any properties on them.[9] Raw feels, in my view, are colourless for the very same reason that *something* is colourless. This does not mean that sensations do not have plenty of properties, for if they are brain processes they certainly have lots of neurological properties. It only means that in speaking of them as being like or unlike one another we need not know or mention these properties.

20 This, then, is how I would reply to objection 3. The strength of my reply depends on the possibility of our being able to report that one thing is like another without being able to state the respect in which it is like. I do not see why this should not be so. If we think cybernetically about the nervous system we can envisage it as able to respond to certain likenesses of its internal process without being able to do more. It would be easier to build a machine which would tell us, say on a punched tape, whether or not two objects were similar, than it would be to build a machine which would report wherein the similarities consisted.

OBJECTION 4

21 The after-image is not in physical space. The brain process is. So the after-image is not a brain process.

REPLY

22 This is an *ignoratio elenchi*. I am not arguing that the after-image is a brain process, but that the experience of having an after-image is a brain process. It is the *experience* which is reported in the introspective report. Similarly, if it is objected that the after-image is yellowy-orange my reply is that it is the experience of seeing yellowy-orange that is being described, and this experience is not a yellowy-orange something. So to say that a brain process cannot be yellowy-orange is not to say that a brain process cannot in fact be the experience of having a yellowy-orange after image. There is, in a sense, no such thing as an after-image or a sense-datum, though there is such a thing as the experience of having an image, and this experience is described indirectly in material object language, not in phenomenal language, for there is no such thing.[10] We describe the experience by saying, in effect, that it is like the experience we have when, for example, we really see a yellowy-orange patch on the wall. Trees and wallpaper can be green, but not the experience of seeing or imagining a tree or wallpaper. (Or if they are described as green or yellow this can only be in a derived sense).

OBJECTION 5

23 It would make sense to say of a molecular movement in the brain that it is swift or slow, straight or circular, but it makes no sense to say this of the experience of seeing something yellow.

REPLY

24 So far we have not given sense to talk of experiences as swift or slow, straight or circular. But I am not claiming that 'experience' and 'brain process' mean the same or even that they have the same logic. 'Somebody' and 'the doctor' do not have the same logic, but this does not lead us to suppose that talking about somebody telephoning is talking about someone over and above, say, the doctor. The ordinary man when he reports an experience is reporting that something is going on, but he leaves it open as to what sort of thing is going on, whether in a material solid medium or perhaps in some sort of gaseous medium, or even perhaps in some sort of non-spatial medium (if this makes sense). All that I am saying is that 'experience' and 'brain process' may in fact refer to the same thing, and if so we may easily adopt a convention (which is not a change in our present rules for the use of experience words but an addition to them) whereby it would make sense to talk of an experience in terms appropriate to physical processes.

OBJECTION 6

25 Sensations are private, brain processes are *public*. If I sincerely say 'I see a yellowish-orange after-image', and I am not making a verbal mistake, then I cannot be wrong. But I can be wrong about a brain process. The scientist looking into my brain might be having an illusion. Moreover, it makes sense to say that two or more people are observing the same brain process but not that two or more people are reporting the same inner experience.

REPLY

26 This shows that the language of introspective reports has a different logic from the language of material processes. It is obvious that until the brain-process theory is much improved and widely accepted there will be no *criteria* for saying 'Smith has an experience of such-and-such a sort' *except* Smith's introspective reports. So we have adopted a rule of language that (normally) what Smith says goes.

OBJECTION 7

27 I can imagine myself turned to stone and yet having images, aches, pains, and so on.

REPLY

28 I can imagine that the electrical theory of lightning is false, that lightning is some sort of purely optical phenomenon. I can imagine that lightning is not an electrical discharge. I can imagine that the Evening Star is not the Morning Star. But it is. All the objection shows is that 'experience' and 'brain process' do not have the same meaning. It does not show that an experience is not in fact a brain process.

29 This objection is perhaps much the same as one which can be summed up by the slogan: 'What can be composed of nothing cannot be composed of anything.'[11] The argument goes as follows: on the brain-process thesis the identity between the brain process and the experience is a contingent one. So it is logically possible that there should be no brain process, and no process of any other sort either (no heart process, no kidney, no liver process). There would be the experience but no 'corresponding' physiological process with which we might be able to identify it empirically.

30 I suspect that the objector is thinking of the experience as a ghostly entity. So it is composed of something, not of nothing, after all. On his view it is composed of ghost stuff, and on mine it is composed of brain stuff. Perhaps the counter-reply will be that the experience is simple and uncompounded,[12] and so it is not composed of anything after all. This seems to be a quibble, for, if it were taken seriously, the remark 'What can be composed of nothing cannot be composed of anything' could be recast as an *a priori* argument against Democritus and atomism and for Descartes and infinite divisibility. And it seems odd that a question of this sort could be settled *a priori*. We must therefore construe the word 'composed' in a very weak sense, which would allow us to say that even an indivisible atom is composed of something (namely, itself). The dualist cannot really say that an experience can be composed of nothing. For he holds that experiences are something over and above material processes, that is, that they are a sort of ghost stuff. (Or perhaps ripples in an underlying ghost stuff.) I say that the dualist's hypothesis is a perfectly intelligible one. But I say that experiences are not to be identified with ghost stuff but with brain stuff. This is another hypothesis, and in my view a very plausible one. The present argument cannot knock it down *a priori*.

OBJECTION 8

31 The 'beetle in the box' objection (see Wittgenstein, *Philosophical*

Investigations, section 293). How could descriptions of experiences, if these are genuine reports, get a foothold in language? For any rule of language must have public criteria for its correct application.

REPLY

32   The change from describing how things are to describing how we feel is just a change from uninhibitedly saying 'this is so' to saying 'this looks so'. That is, when the naïve person might be tempted to say 'There is a patch of light on the wall which moves whenever I move my eyes' or 'A pin is being stuck into me', we have learned how to resist this temptation and say 'It *looks as though* there is a patch of light on the wallpaper' or 'It *feels as though* someone were sticking a pin into me'. The introspective account tells us about the individual's state of consciousness in the same way as does 'I see a patch of light' or 'I feel a pin being stuck into me': it differs from the corresponding perception statement in so far as it withdraws any claim about what is actually going on in the external world. From the point of view of the psychologist, the change from talking about the environment to talking about one's perceptual sensations is simply a matter of disinhibiting certain reactions. These are reactions which one normally suppresses because one has learned that in the prevailing circumstances they are unlikely to provide a good indication of the state of the environment.[13] To say that that something looks green to me is simply to say that my experience is like the experience I get when I see something that really is green. In my reply to Objection 3, I pointed out the extreme openness or generality of statements which report experiences. This explains why there is no language of private qualities. (Just as 'someone', unlike 'the doctor', is a colourless word.)[14]

33   If it is asked what is the difference between those brain processes which, in my view, are experiences and those brain processes which are not, I can only reply that it is at present unknown. I have been tempted to conjecture that the difference may in part be that between perception and reception (in D.M. Mackay's terminology) and that the type of brain process which is an experience might be identifiable with Mackay's active 'matching response'.[15] This, however, cannot be the whole story, because sometimes I can perceive something unconsciously, as when I take a handkerchief out of a drawer without being aware that I am doing so. But at the very least we can classify the brain processes which are experiences as those brain processes which are, or might have been, causal conditions of those pieces of verbal behaviour which we call reports of immediate experience.

34   I have considered a number of objections to the brain-process thesis. I wish now to conclude with some remarks on the logical status of the thesis itself. U.T. Place seems to hold that it is a straight-out scientific hypothesis. If so, he is partly right and partly wrong. If the issue is between (say) a brain-process thesis and a heart thesis, or a liver thesis, or a kidney thesis, then the issue is a purely empirical one, and the verdict is overwhelmingly in favour of the brain. The right sorts of things don't go on in the heart, liver, or

kidney, nor do these organs possess the right sort of complexity of structure. On the other hand, if the issue is between a brain-or-liver-or-kidney thesis (that is, some form of materialism) on the one hand and epiphenomenalism on the other hand, then the issue is not an empirical one. For there is no conceivable experiment which could decide between materialism and epiphenomenalism. This latter issue is not like the average straight-out empirical issue in science, but like the issue between the nineteenth-century English naturalist Philip Gosse[16] and the orthodox geologists and palaeontologists of his day. According to Gosse, the earth was created about 4000 B.C. exactly as described in Genesis, with twisted rock strata, 'evidence' of erosion, and so forth, and all sorts of fossils, all in their appropriate strata, just as if the usual evolutionist story had been true. Clearly this theory is in a sense irrefutable: no evidence can possibly tell against it. Let us ignore the theological setting, in which Philip Gosse's hypothesis had been placed, thus ruling out objections of a theological kind, such as 'what a queer God who would go to such elaborate lengths to deceive us'. Let us suppose that it is held that the universe just began in 4004 B.C. with the initial conditions just everywhere as they were in 4004 B.C., and in particular that our own planet began with sediment in the rivers, eroded cliffs, fossils in the rocks, and so on. No scientist would ever entertain this as a serious hypothesis, consistent though it is with all possible evidence. The hypothesis offends against the principles of parsimony and simplicity. There would be far too many brute and inexplicable facts. Why are pterodactyl bones just as they are? No explanation in terms of the evolution of pterodactyls from earlier forms of life would any longer be possible. We would have millions of facts about the world as it was in 4004 B.C. that just have to be *accepted*.

35   The issue between the brain-process theory and epiphenomenalism seems to be of the above sort. (Assuming that a behaviouristic reduction of introspective reports is not possible.) If it be agreed that there are no cogent philosophical arguments which force us into accepting dualism, and if the brain-process theory and dualism are equally consistent with the facts, then the principles of parsimony and simplicity seem to me to decide overwhelmingly in favour of the brain-process theory. As I pointed out earlier, dualism involves a large number of irreducible psycho-physical laws (whereby the 'nomological danglers' dangle) of a queer sort, that just have to be taken on trust, and are just as difficult to swallow as the irreducible facts about the palaeontology of the earth with which we are faced on Philip Gosse's theory.

NOTES

(1) See Ryle, *The Concept of Mind*, p. 93.

(2) On this point, see Paul Oppenheim and Hilary Putnam, 'Unity of Science as a Working Hypothesis', in *Minnesota Studies in the Philosophy of Science*, pp. 3–36.

(3) Feigl, ibid., p. 428. Feigl uses the expression 'nomological danglers' for the laws whereby the entities dangle: I have used the expression to refer to the dangling entities themselves.

(4) See Feigl, in *Minnesota Studies in the Philosophy of Science*, II, p. 390.

(5) See J.H. Woodger, *Theory Construction, International Encyclopaedia of Unified Science*, II No.5 (Chicago, 1939) p. 38. I here permit myself to speak loosely. For warnings against possible ways of going wrong with this sort of talk, see my note 'Spatialising Time', *Mind*, LXIV (1955) pp. 239–41.

(6) Cf. Feigl in *Minnesota Studies in the Philosophy of Science*, II, p. 439.

(7) See Place, p. 47, above; also Feigl in *Minnesota Studies in the Philosophy of Science*, II, p. 438.

(8) I think this objection was first put to me by Professor Max Black. I think it is the most subtle of any of those I have considered, and the one which I am least confident of having satisfactorily met.

(9) See B.A. Farrell, Experience, *Mind*, LIX (1950) 170–98, especially p. 174.

(10) Dr J.R. Smythies claims that a sense-datum language could be taught independently of the material object language ('A Note on the Fallacy of "Phenomenological Fallacy', *British Journal of Psychology*, XLVIII (1957) pp. 141–4). I am not so sure of this: there must be some public criteria for a person having got a rule wrong before we can teach him the rule. I suppose someone might accidentally learn colour words by Dr Smythies' procedure. I am not, of course, denying that we can learn a sense-datum language in the sense that we can learn to report our experience. Nor would Place deny it.

(11) I owe this objection to Dr C.B. Martin. I gather that he no longer wishes to maintain this objection, at any rate in its present form.

(12) Martin did not make this reply, but one of his students did.

(13) I owe this point to Place, in correspondence.

(14) The 'beetle in the box' objection is, if it is sound, an objection to any view, and in particular the Cartesian one, that introspective reports are genuine reports. So it is no objection to a weaker thesis that I would be concerned to uphold, namely, that if introspective reports of 'experiences' are genuinely reports, then the things they are reports of are in fact brain-processes.

(15) See his article 'Towards an Information-Flow Model of Human Behaviour', *British Journal of Psychology*, XLVIII (1956) pp. 30–43.

(16) See the entertaining account of Gosse's book *Omphalos* by Martin Gardner in *Fads and Fallacies in the Name of Science*, 2nd edn (New York 1957), pp. 124–7.

6 The mind–body problem

Sydney Shoemaker

Sydney Shoemaker (b. 1931) is one of the most distinguished American philosophers of his generation, and has held posts at many American universities including Harvard, Cornell, Columbia and Stanford (among others). In the earlier part of his career he wrote extensively on the concept of personal identity, producing a number of much discussed papers on that subject. Later in his career, the focus of his interest turned to the defence of functionalism, for which he is perhaps best known. The following essay[1] begins with a summary of his functionalist point of view, which he follows by a statement of the leading objections to functionalism as a philosophy of mind, and his replies to them.

1   In common with many other contemporary philosophers, I see the mind–body problem, not as the problem of how a nonphysical mind can interact with a physical body, but rather as the problem of how minds can be part of a fundamentally physical reality. In part this is the problem of how certain widespread 'Cartesian' intuitions about mind can be either explained away, i.e. shown to be illusions, or else shorn of their apparent dualist implications. More generally, it is the problem of how distinctive features of the mental – intentionality, consciousness, subjectivity, etc. – can have a place in a naturalistic worldview which sees minds as a product of biological evolution and as having a physico-chemical substrate in just the way other biological phenomena do.

2   I see these issues as most fruitfully approached within the framework of the view that has come to be known as 'functionalism': the view that mental

states are defined, or individuated, in terms of their causal relations to 'inputs' (sensory stimuli and the like), outputs (behavior), and one another. Thus, for example, what makes a state the belief that it is raining is that it has certain characteristic causes (including rain and, more proximally, experiences of rain), that in combination with certain other states (e.g. the desire to keep dry) it gives rise to certain behavior (e.g. taking an umbrella), that in combination with certain mental states (e.g. the belief that rain makes the streets wet) it gives rise to yet other mental states (e.g. the belief that the streets are wet), and so on. Such a view is clearly compatible with materialism, for such a functionally defined state can be realized in, or implemented in, the states of a physical (normally biological) mechanism in much the sense in which a computer program can be realized or implemented in the hardware of a computer. But this view is compatible with the Cartesian intuition that such a mental state cannot be identical with any specific physical state; there will be no such identity if, as seems plausible, such functional states are 'multiply realizable,' i.e. can be physically realized or implemented in any of a variety of different ways ...

3   The view I favor is ... a radically 'nonreductive' version of materialism. Neither in the case of properties and states nor in the case of particulars will it hold that there is any neat mapping of our commonsense mentalistic taxonomy on to the taxonomies of the physical sciences. In this it agrees with Cartesian intuitions. But the sense in which psychology (whether it be commonsense psychology or scientific psychology) does not reduce to chemistry and physics is the same as the sense in which biology and geology do not reduce to chemistry and physics, and in which chemistry does not reduce to physics. No one doubts that the entities and phenomena that are the subject matter of geology, biology, and chemistry are ultimately composed of entities and phenomena that are the subject matter of physics. There is good reason to think that the same is true of mental phenomena. The philosophical task here is not to carry out a reduction but to make it intelligible that there is this compositional relationship.

4   There is still a great deal to be explained. One of the most active areas of research in contemporary philosophy of mind is that which concerns 'intentionality' or (what I here equate with this) mental representation. Given that mental states are realized in neurophysiological states of the brain, how can they have intentional representational content; how can they be thoughts about Iraq, beliefs that the Cold War is over, hopes that global warming can be arrested? If functional characterizations of mental states are construed 'narrowly,' i.e. as referring only to causal relations between what goes on 'inside the head' (and at its periphery), it seems clear that they will be insufficient to bestow representational content. It seems pretty clear that in some way or other relations to things outside our heads, to things in our environments, enter into bestowing on our mental states the contents they have. The aim of those who want to 'naturalize' intentionality is to show that these relations consist ultimately in relations, e.g. causal ones, for which there is room in a materialist ontology. Various proposals have been put forward about how mental representation can be naturalized, and each of these has

met with a variety of objections. All that can be said with confidence is that the problem is far from being solved.

5   Another main area of research in contemporary philosophy of mind concerns the nature of consciousness and subjectivity. This has been the primary focus of my own recent work. This is an area rife with Cartesian intuitions. To begin with, people seem to have a 'privileged access' to their own mental states which, on the face of it, it is difficult to reconcile with materialist views about the nature of such states. One knows what one is thinking and feeling, and, normally, what one believes, desires, etc., without having to ground this knowledge on evidence about one's behavior and bodily circumstances. And in being aware of one's own mental states one certainly is not aware of them *as* functional states, i.e. as states defined by functional or causal roles. And sometimes we seem to know the nature of our mental states in a way that seems incompatible with that nature being what materialist and functionalist accounts say it is.

6   This last seems true in the case of what have come to be known as 'qualia,' and are also referred to as the 'phenomenal features' of feelings, sensations, and perceptual states: the felt features of pains and itches that make them (so one wants to say) the kinds of sensations they are, the distinctive feature of a visual experience of redness that determines 'what it is like' to see red and distinguishes this from what it is like to see green, blue, yellow, and so on. It is natural to say that in being aware of these features of an experience one is aware of its 'intrinsic nature,' and aware of something whose nature cannot consist in its aptness for playing a certain causal role. Moreover, there are arguments that purport to show that qualia cannot be physical properties and cannot be functionally defined. Frank Jackson's 'knowledge argument' points out that someone could know all of the relevant physical facts about the seeing of red without knowing what it is like to see red, and concludes that there is something the physical facts leave out, and that physicalism is false (see Jackson 1982). Similar ideas are expressed by Thomas Nagel in his well-known paper 'What is it like to be a bat?' (1974). And the conceiv-ability of 'spectrum inversion' (red things looking to one person the way green things look to another, and vice versa), and more generally 'qualia inversion,' has been used to argue that qualia are not functionally definable. For, allowing the conceivability of this, it seems possible that there should be creatures who are functionally exactly alike (at the psychological level of description) but who differ in the qualitative character of their experiences … I think we can give an account of qualia which answers to most, if not all, of the intuitions that motivate the use of the term, and which allows materi-alists and functionalists to acknowledge their existence.

7   Briefly, I allow that the inverted qualia argument shows that individual qualia (e.g. the one that characterizes my experiences of red) cannot be function-ally defined, but I hold that the notion of a quale is nonetheless a functional concept. The key notion here is that of qualitative similarity. This can be functionally defined in terms of its role in perceptual discrimination and recognition, and in the fixation of perceptual beliefs. In terms of this we can define a notion of qualitative identity, and in terms of that we can explain

what it is for a property to be a quale. Having this much of a functional account allows us to speak of qualia as being physically realized or implemented (in the sense in which any functional property can be physically realized or implemented), and makes their existence compatible with materialism (Shoemaker 1975, 1982). I think that the Jackson–Nagel 'knowledge argument' can likewise be answered, but shall not attempt to give my answer here.

8   Returning to the more general question of consciousness and self-knowledge, I think that a promising way of taming Cartesian intuitions about our special access to our own mental states is to show that some of them, at least, are consequences of a plausible functionalist account of the nature of such states (and are compatible with materialism because functionalism is). A common view about 'introspective' self-knowledge, due largely to D.M. Armstrong, is that awareness of one's mental states is basically a matter of having higher-order beliefs about one's own mental states that are produced, via a reliable mechanism in the mind–brain, by the very states they are about (see Armstrong 1968). What I would add to this is that in many cases it belongs to the very essence of a mental state (its functional nature) that, normally, its existence results, under certain circumstances, in there being such awareness of it. It should be noted that much of the explanatory role of some mental states *vis-à-vis* behavior is a role they can play only via their subject's higher-order beliefs about them (the beliefs which if true count as awareness of them). This is true of the role of pain in explaining such behavior as seeking medical treatment … What these considerations suggest is that a functionalist account of mind can accept a version of the Cartesian intuition that (some) mental states are 'self-intimating.'

9   Much of what I have just said is controversial, and would be disputed by many philosophers who share my general outlook. What I have tried to do is to suggest ways in which Cartesian intuitions can be accommodated within a functionalist–materialist framework. As I said at the outset, for a materialist a large part of solving the mind–body problem will consist in either 'explaining away' Cartesian intuitions or, what is my preference, showing how they can be accommodated within a materialist account.

NOTE

1   This essay is taken from Warner, R. and Szubka, T. (eds) (1994) *The Mind–body Problem: A Guide to the Current Debate*, Oxford: Blackwell, pp. 55–60. The essay was specially written for this anthology and was not previously published.

REFERENCES

Armstrong, D.M. (1968) *A Materialist Theory of the Mind*, London: Routledge & Kegan Paul.
Dennett, D. (1988) 'Quining qualia,' in A. J. Marcel and E. Bisiach (eds) *Consciousness in Contemporary Science*, Oxford: Clarendon Press, pp. 42–77.
Harman, G. (1990) 'The intrinsic quality of experience,' *Philosophical Perspectives* 4: 31–52.
Jackson, F. (1982) 'Epiphenomenal qualia,' *Philosophical Quarterly* 32: 127–33.
Nagel, T. (1974) 'What is it like to be a bat?' *Philosophical Review* 83: 435–50.
Shoemaker, S. (1975) 'Functionalism and qualia,' *Philosophical Studies* 27: 291–315, reprinted 1984 in *Identity, Cause and Mind: Philosophical Essays*, Cambridge: Cambridge University Press.

Shoemaker, S. (1982) 'The inverted spectrum,' *Journal of Philosophy* 79: 357–81; reprinted 1984 in *Identity, Cause and Mind, Philosophical Essays*, Cambridge: Cambridge University Press.
Shoemaker, S. (1988) 'On knowing one's own mind,' *Philosophical Perspectives* 2: 183–209.
Shoemaker, S. (1990) 'First-person access,' *Philosophical Perspectives* 4: 187–214.

7 | 'Eliminative materialism and the propositional attitudes'

Paul M. Churchland

Paul M. Churchland (b. 1942) is a Canadian-born philosopher who has worked in both Canada and the USA. He and his wife Patricia S. Churchland are the leading advocates of eliminative materialism at the present time. The following sections are taken from one of Churchland's most important essays advocating the eliminativist point of view.[1] In contrast to holders of the mind–brain identity theory (for example), he denies that mental processes are identical to brain processes, since he denies that mental processes (as traditionally conceived) exist at all.

1   Eliminative materialism is the thesis that our common-sense conception of psychological phenomena constitutes a radically false theory, a theory so fundamentally defective that both the principles and the ontology of that theory will eventually be displaced, rather than smoothly reduced, by completed neuroscience. Our mutual understanding and even our introspection may then be reconstituted within the conceptual framework of completed neuroscience, a theory we may expect to be more powerful by far than the common-sense psychology it displaces, and more substantially integrated within physical science generally. My purpose in this paper is to explore these projections, especially as they bear on (1) the principal elements of common-sense psychology: the propositional attitudes (beliefs, desires, etc.), and (2) the conception of rationality in which these elements figure.

2   This focus represents a change in the fortunes of materialism. Twenty years ago, emotions, qualia, and 'raw feels' were held to be the principal stumbling blocks for the materialist program. With these barriers dissolving, the locus of opposition has shifted. Now it is the realm of the intentional, the realm of

the propositional attitude, that is most commonly held up as being both irre-ducible to and ineliminable in favor of anything from within a materialist framework. Whether and why this is so, we must examine.

3   Such an examination will make little sense, however, unless it is first appreci-ated that the relevant network of common-sense concepts does indeed constitute an empirical theory, with all the functions, virtues, *and perils* entailed by that status. I shall therefore begin with a brief sketch of this view and a summary rehearsal of its rationale. The resistance it encounters still surprises me. After all, common sense has yielded up many theories. Recall the view that space has a preferred direction in which all things fall; that weight is an intrinsic feature of a body; that a force-free moving object will promptly return to rest; that the sphere of the heavens turns daily; and so on. These examples are clear, perhaps, but people seem willing to concede a theoretical component within common sense only if (1) the theory and the common sense involved are safely located in antiquity, and (2) the relevant theory is now so clearly false that its speculative nature is inescapable. Theories are indeed easier to discern under these circumstances. But the vision of hindsight is always 20/20. Let us aspire to some foresight for a change.

I   WHY FOLK PSYCHOLOGY IS A THEORY

4   Seeing our common-sense conceptual framework for mental phenomena as a theory brings a simple and unifying organization to most of the major topics in the philosophy of mind, including the explanation and prediction of behaviour, the semantics of mental predicates, action theory, the other-minds problem, the intentionality of mental states, the nature of introspection, and the mind–body problem. Any view that can pull this lot together deserves careful consideration.

5   Let us begin with the explanation of human (and animal) behavior. The fact is that the average person is able to explain, and even predict, the behavior of other persons with a facility and success that is remarkable. Such explana-tions and predictions standardly make reference to the desires, beliefs, fears, intentions, perceptions, and so forth, to which the agents are presumed subject. But explanations presuppose laws – rough and ready ones, at least – that connect the explanatory conditions with the behavior explained. The same is true for the making of predictions ... Reassuringly, a rich network of common-sense laws can indeed be reconstructed from this quotidian commerce of explanation and anticipation; its principles are familiar homi-lies; and their sundry functions are transparent. Each of us understands others, as well as we do, because we share a tacit command of an integrated body of lore concerning the law-like relations holding among external circumstances, internal states, and overt behavior. Given its nature and func-tions, this body of lore may quite aptly be called 'folk psychology.'

6   This approach entails that the semantics of the terms in our familiar mental-istic vocabulary is to be understood in the same manner as the semantics of

theoretical terms generally; the meaning of any theoretical term is fixed or constituted by the network of laws in which it figures.

7   More importantly, the recognition that folk psychology is a theory provides a simple and decisive solution to an old sceptical problem, the problem of other minds. The problematic conviction that another individual is the subject of certain mental states is not inferred deductively from his behavior, nor is it inferred by inductive analogy from the perilously isolated instance of one's own case. Rather, that conviction is a singular *explanatory hypothesis* of a perfectly straightforward kind. Its function, in conjunction with the background laws of folk psychology, is to provide explanations/predictions/understanding of the individual's continuing behavior, and it is credible to the degree that it is successful in this regard over competing hypotheses. In the main, such hypotheses are successful, and so the belief that others enjoy the internal states comprehended by folk psychology is a reasonable belief ...

8   Finally, the realization that folk psychology is a theory puts a new light on the mind–body problem. The issue becomes a matter of how the ontology of one theory (folk psychology) is, or is not, going to be related to the ontology of another theory (completed neuroscience); and the major philosophical positions on the mind–body problem emerge as so many different anticipations of what future research will reveal about the intertheoretic status and integrity of folk psychology.

9   The identity theorist optimistically expects that folk psychology will be smoothly *reduced* by completed neuroscience, and its ontology preserved by dint of transtheoretic identities. The dualist expects that it will prove irreducible to completed neuroscience, by dint of being a nonredundant description of an autonomous, nonphysical domain of natural phenomena. The functionalist also expects that it will prove irreducible, but on the quite different grounds that the internal economy characterized by folk psychology is not, in the last analysis, a law-governed economy of natural states, but an abstract organization of functional states, an organization instantiable in a variety of quite different material substrates. It is therefore irreducible to the principles peculiar to any of them.

10 Finally, the eliminative materialist is also pessimistic about the prospects of reduction, but his reason is that folk psychology is a radically inadequate account of our internal activities, too confused and too defective to win survival through intertheoretic reduction. On his view it will simply be displaced by a better theory of those activities.

11 Which of these fates is the real destiny of folk psychology, we shall attempt to divine presently. For now, the point to keep in mind is that we shall be exploring the fate of a theory, a systematic, corrigible, speculative *theory*.

II   WHY FOLK PSYCHOLOGY MIGHT (REALLY) BE FALSE

12 Given that folk psychology is an empirical theory, it is at least an abstract possibility that its principles are radically false and that its ontology is an

illusion. With the exception of eliminative materialism, however, none of the major positions takes this possibility seriously. None of them doubts the basic integrity or truth of folk psychology (hereafter, 'FP'), and all of them anticipate a future in which its laws and categories are conserved. This conservatism is not without some foundation. After all, FP does enjoy a substantial amount of explanatory and predictive success. And what better grounds than this for confidence in the integrity of its categories?

13 What better grounds indeed? Even so, the presumption in FP's favor is spurious, born of innocence and tunnel vision. A more searching examination reveals a different picture. First, we must reckon not only with FP's successes, but with its explanatory failures, and with their extent and seriousness. Second, we must consider the long-term history of FP, its growth, fertility, and current promise of future development. And third, we must consider what sorts of theories are *likely* to be true of the etiology of our behavior, given what else we have learned about ourselves in recent history. That is, we must evaluate FP with regard to its coherence and continuity with fertile and well-established theories in adjacent and overlapping domains – with evolutionary theory, biology, and neuroscience, for example – because active coherence with the rest of what we presume to know is perhaps the final measure of any hypothesis.

14 A serious inventory of this sort reveals a very troubled situation, one which would evoke open scepticism in the case of any theory less familiar and dear to us. Let me sketch some relevant detail. When one centres one's attention not on what FP can explain, but on what it cannot explain or fails even to address, one discovers that there is a very great deal. As examples of central and important mental phenomena that remain largely or wholly mysterious within the framework of FP, consider the nature and dynamics of mental illness, the faculty of creative imagination, or the ground of intelligence differences between individuals. Consider our utter ignorance of the nature and psychological functions of sleep, that curious state in which a third of one's life is spent. Reflect on the common ability to catch an outfield fly ball on the run, or hit a moving car with a snowball. Consider the internal construction of a 3-D visual image from subtle differences in the 2-D array of stimulations in our respective retinas. Consider the rich variety of perceptual illusions, visual and otherwise. Or consider the miracle of memory, with its lightning capacity for relevant retrieval. On these and many other mental phenomena, FP sheds negligible light.

15 One particularly outstanding mystery is the nature of the learning process itself, especially where it involves large-scale conceptual change, and especially as it appears in its pre-linguistic or entirely non-linguistic form (as in infants and animals), which is by far the most common form in nature. FP is faced with special difficulties here, since its conception of learning as the manipulation and storage of propositional attitudes founders on the fact that how to formulate, manipulate, and store a rich fabric of propositional attitudes is itself something that is learned, and is only one among many acquired cognitive skills. FP would thus appear constitutionally incapable of even addressing this most basic of mysteries.

16   Failures on such a large scale do not (yet) show that FP is a false theory, but they do move that prospect well into the range of real possibility, and they do show decisively that FP is *at best* a highly superficial theory, a partial and unpenetrating gloss on a deeper and more complex reality. Having reached this opinion, we may be forgiven for exploring the possibility that FP provides a positively misleading sketch of our internal kinematics and dynamics, one whose success is owed more to selective application and forced interpretation on our part than to genuine theoretical insight on FP's part.

17   A look at the history of FP does little to allay such fears, once raised. The story is one of retreat, infertility, and decadence. The presumed domain of FP used to be much larger than it is now. In primitive cultures, the behavior of most of the elements of nature were understood in intentional terms. The wind could know anger, the moon jealousy, the river generosity, the sea fury, and so forth. These were not metaphors. Sacrifices were made and auguries undertaken to placate or divine the changing passions of the gods. Despite its sterility, this animistic approach to nature has dominated our history, and it is only in the last two or three thousand years that we have restricted FP's literal application to the domain of the higher animals.

18   Even in this preferred domain, however, both the content and the success of FP have not advanced sensibly in two or three thousand years. The FP of the Greeks is essentially the FP we use today, and we are negligibly better at explaining human behavior in its terms that was Sophocles. This is a very long period of stagnation and infertility for any theory to display, especially when faced with such an enormous backlog of anomalies and mysteries in its own explanatory domain. Perfect theories, perhaps, have no need to evolve. But FP is profoundly imperfect. Its failure to develop its resources and extend its range of success is therefore darkly curious, and one must query the integrity of its basic categories. To use Imre Lakatos' terms, FP is a stagnant or degenerating research program, and has been for millennia.

19   Explanatory success to date is of course not the only dimension in which a theory can display virtue or promise. A troubled or stagnant theory may merit patience and solicitude on other grounds; for example, on grounds that it is the only theory or theoretical approach that fits well with other theories about adjacent subject matters, or the only one that promises to reduce to or be explained by some established background theory whose domain encompasses the domain of the theory at issue. In sum, it may rate credence because it holds promise of theoretical integration. How does FP rate in this dimension?

20   It is just here, perhaps, that FP fares poorest of all. If we approach *homo sapiens* from the perspective of natural history and the physical sciences, we can tell a coherent story of his constitution, development, and behavioural capacities which encompasses particle physics, atomic and molecular theory, organic chemistry, evolutionary theory, biology, physiology, and materialistic neuroscience. That story, though still radically incomplete, is already extremely powerful, outperforming FP at many points even in its own domain. And it is deliberately and self-consciously coherent with the rest of

our developing world picture. In short, the greatest theoretical synthesis in the history of the human race is currently in our hands, and parts of it already provide searching descriptions and explanations of human sensory input, neural activity, and motor control.

21   But FP is no part of this growing synthesis. Its intentional categories stand magnificently alone, without visible prospect of reduction to that larger corpus. A successful reduction cannot be ruled out, in my view, but FP's explanatory impotence and long stagnation inspire little faith that its categories will find themselves neatly reflected in the framework of neuroscience. On the contrary, one is reminded of how alchemy must have looked as elemental chemistry was taking form, how Aristotelian cosmology must have looked as classical mechanics was being articulated, or how the vitalist conception of life must have looked as organic chemistry marched forward.

22   In sketching a fair summary of this situation, we must make a special effort to abstract from the fact that FP is a central part of our current *lebenswelt*, and serves as the principal vehicle of our interpersonal commerce. For these facts provide FP with a conceptual inertia that goes far beyond its purely theoretical virtues. Restricting ourselves to this latter dimension, what we must say is that FP suffers explanatory failures on an epic scale, that it has been stagnant for at least twenty-five centuries, and that its categories appear (so far) to be incommensurable with or orthogonal to the categories of the background physical science whose long-term claim to explain human behavior seems undeniable. Any theory that meets this description must be allowed a serious candidate for outright elimination.

23   We can of course insist on no stronger conclusion at this stage. Nor is it my concern to do so. We are here exploring a possibility, and the facts demand no more, and no less, than it be taken seriously. The distinguishing feature of the eliminative materialist is that he takes it very seriously indeed.

NOTE

1   The article from which these extracts are taken is 'Eliminative materialism and the propositional attitudes', *Journal of Philosophy* (Feb. 1981) 78(2): 67–90.

8 'Is the brain's mind a computer program?'

No. A program merely manipulates symbols, whereas a brain attaches meaning to them

John R. Searle

The American philosopher John Rogers Searle (b. 1932) began his very distin-guished philosophical career as a writer on the philosophy of language, producing some widely respected work on the concept of speech acts. Later, he changed the focus of his interest to the philosophy of mind, and in particular the notion of intentionality. It is accordingly no surprise that the Chinese room argu-ment should make use of the idea that one of the most important properties of minds is that they have semantic contents. The bare bones of the argument are easy to set out:

Premise 1	programs are formal (syntactical);
Premise 2	minds have contents (semantics);
Premise 3	syntax is not sufficient for semantics;
Conclusion 1	therefore programs are not sufficient for minds (*cf.* Searle in Guttenplan 1994: 546).

This argument, which Searle has refined and modified over the years, is in all probability the most discussed argument to date concerning AI, attracting attention both from within and outside the philosophical world. The version given below is from Searle (1990)[1] and is a later one, in which he takes account both of developments in parallel distributed processing and of the objections raised against earlier versions of his argument first presented in 1980.

1   Can a machine think? Can a machine have conscious thoughts in exactly the same sense that you and I have? If by 'machine' one means a physical system

capable of performing certain functions (and what else can one mean?), then humans are machines of a special biological kind, and humans can think, and so of course machines can think. And, for all we know, it might be possible to produce a thinking machine out of different materials altogether – say, out of silicon chips or vacuum tubes. Maybe it will turn out to be impossible, but we certainly do not know that yet.

2   In recent decades, however, the question of whether a machine can think has been given a different interpretation entirely. The question that has been posed in its place is, Could a machine think just by virtue of implementing a computer program? Is the program by itself constitutive of thinking? This is a completely different question because it is not about the physical, causal properties of actual or possible physical systems but rather about the abstract, computational properties of formal computer programs that can be implemented in any sort of substance at all, provided only that the substance is able to carry the program.

3   A fair number of researchers in artificial intelligence (AI) believe the answer to the second question is yes; that is, they believe that by designing the right programs with the right inputs and outputs, they are literally creating minds. They believe furthermore that they have a scientific test for determining success or failure: the Turing test devised by Alan M. Turing, the founding father of artificial intelligence. The Turing test, as currently understood, is simply this: if a computer can perform in such a way that an expert cannot distinguish its performance from that of a human who has a certain cognitive ability – say, the ability to do addition or to understand Chinese – then the computer also has that ability. So the goal is to design programs that will simulate human cognition in such a way as to pass the Turing test. What is more, such a program would not merely be a model of the mind; it would literally be a mind, in the same sense that a human mind is a mind.

4   By no means does every worker in artificial intelligence accept so extreme a view. A more cautious approach is to think of computer models as being useful in studying the mind in the same way that they are useful in studying the weather, economics or molecular biology. To distinguish these two approaches, I call the first strong AI and the second weak AI. It is important to see just how bold an approach strong AI is. Strong AI claims that thinking is merely the manipulation of formal symbols, and that is exactly what the computer does: manipulate formal symbols. This view is often summarized by saying, 'The mind is to the brain as the program is to the hardware.'

5   Strong AI is unusual among theories of the mind in at least two respects: it can be stated clearly, and it admits of a simple and decisive refutation. The refutation is one that any person can try for himself or herself. Here is how it goes. Consider a language you don't understand. In my case, I do not under- stand Chinese. To me Chinese writing looks like so many meaningless squiggles. Now suppose I am placed in a room containing baskets full of Chinese symbols. Suppose also that I am given a rule book in English for matching Chinese symbols with other Chinese symbols. The rules identify the symbols entirely by their shapes and do not require that I understand any of them. The rules might say such things as, 'Take a squiggle-squiggle sign

from basket number one and put it next to a squoggle-squoggle sign from basket number two.'

6   Imagine that people outside the room who understand Chinese hand in small bunches of symbols and that in response I manipulate the symbols according to the rule book and hand back more small bunches of symbols. Now, the rule book is the 'computer program.' The people who wrote it are 'programmers,' and I am the 'computer.' The baskets full of symbols are the 'data base,' the small bunches that are handed in to me are 'questions' and the bunches I then hand out are 'answers.'

7   Now suppose that the rule book is written in such a way that my 'answers' to the 'questions' are indistinguishable from those of a native Chinese speaker. For example, the people outside might hand me some symbols that unknown to me mean, 'What's your favourite colour?' and I might after going through the rules give back symbols that, also unknown to me, mean, 'My favourite is blue, but I also like green a lot.' I satisfy the Turing test for understanding Chinese. All the same, I am totally ignorant of Chinese. And there is no way I could come to understand Chinese in the system as described, since there is no way that I can learn the meanings of any of the symbols. Like a computer, I manipulate symbols, but I attach no meaning to the symbols.

8   The point of the thought experiment is this: if I do not understand Chinese solely on the basis of running a computer program for understanding Chinese, then neither does any other digital computer solely on that basis. Digital computers merely manipulate formal symbols according to rules in the program.

9   What goes for Chinese goes for other forms of cognition as well. Just manipulating the symbols is not by itself enough to guarantee cognition, perception, understanding, thinking and so forth. And since computers, *qua* computers, are symbol-manipulating devices, merely running the computer program is not enough to guarantee cognition.

10 This simple argument is decisive against the claims of strong AI. The first premise of the argument simply states the formal character of a computer program. Programs are defined in terms of symbol manipulations, and the symbols are purely formal, or 'syntactic.' The formal character of the program, by the way, is what makes computers so powerful. The same program can be run on an indefinite variety of hardwares, and one hardware system can run an indefinite range of computer programs. Let me abbreviate this 'axiom' as

Axiom 1.   Computer programs are formal (syntactic).

11 This point is so crucial that it is worth explaining in more detail. A digital computer processes information by first encoding it in the symbolism that the computer uses and then manipulating the symbols through a set of precisely stated rules. These rules constitute the program. For example, in Turing's early theory of computers, the symbols were simply 0's and 1's, and the rules of the program said such things as, 'Print a 0 on the tape, move one

square to the left and erase a 1.' The astonishing thing about computers is that any information that can be stated in a language can be encoded in such a system, and any information-processing task that can be solved by explicit rules can be programmed.

12 Two further points are important. First, symbols and programs are purely abstract notions: they have no essential physical properties to define them and can be implemented in any physical medium whatsoever. The 0's and 1's, *qua* symbols, have no essential physical properties and *a fortiori* have no physical, causal properties. I emphasize this point because it is tempting to identify computers with some specific technology – say, silicon chips – and to think that the issues are about the physics of silicon chips or to think that syntax identifies some physical phenomenon that might have as yet unknown causal powers, in the way that actual physical phenomena such as electromagnetic radiation or hydrogen atoms have physical, causal properties. The second point is that symbols are manipulated without reference to any meanings. The symbols of the program can stand for anything the programmer or user wants. In this sense the program has syntax but no semantics.

13 The next axiom is just a reminder of the obvious fact that thoughts, perceptions, understandings and so forth have a mental content. By virtue of their content they can be about objects and states of affairs in the world. If the content involves language, there will be syntax in addition to semantics, but linguistic understanding requires at least a semantic framework. If, for example, I am thinking about the last presidential election, certain words will go through my mind, but the words are about the election only because I attach specific meanings to these words, in accordance with my knowledge of English. In this respect they are unlike Chinese symbols for me. Let me abbreviate this axiom as

Axiom 2.   Human minds have mental contents (semantics).

14 Now let me add the point that the Chinese room demonstrated. Having the symbols by themselves – just having the syntax – is not sufficient for having the semantics. Merely manipulating symbols is not enough to guarantee knowledge of what they mean. I shall abbreviate this as

Axiom 3.   Syntax by itself is neither constitutive of nor sufficient for semantics.

15 At one level this principle is true by definition. One might, of course, define the terms syntax and semantics differently. The point is that there is a distinction between formal elements, which have no intrinsic meaning or content, and those phenomena that have intrinsic content. From these premises it follows that

Conclusion 1.   Programs are neither constitutive of nor sufficient for minds.

16 And that is just another way of saying that strong AI is false.

17 It is important to see what is proved and not proved by this argument.

18 First, I have not tried to prove that 'a computer cannot think.' Since anything that can be simulated computationally can be described as a computer, and since our brains can at some levels be simulated, it follows trivially that our brains are computers and they can certainly think. But from the fact that a system can be simulated by symbol manipulation and the fact that it is thinking, it does not follow that thinking is equivalent to formal symbol manipulation.

19 Second, I have not tried to show that only biologically based systems like our brains can think. Right now those are the only systems we know for a fact can think, but we might find other systems in the universe that can produce conscious thoughts, and we might even come to be able to create thinking systems artificially. I regard the issue as up for grabs.

20 Third, strong AI's thesis is not that, for all we know, computers with the right programs might be thinking, that they might have some as yet undetected psychological properties; rather it is that they must be thinking because that is all there is to thinking.

21 Fourth, I have tried to refute strong AI so defined. I have tried to demonstrate that the program by itself is not constitutive of thinking because the program is purely a matter of formal symbol manipulation – and we know independently that symbol manipulations by themselves are not sufficient to guarantee the presence of meanings. That is the principle on which the Chinese room argument works.

22 I emphasize these points here partly because it seems to me the Churchlands [see Churchland and Churchland 1990: 26] have not quite understood the issues. They think that strong AI is claiming that computers might turn out to think and that I am denying this possibility on commonsense grounds. But that is not the claim of strong AI, and my argument against it has nothing to do with common sense.

23 I will have more to say about their objections later. Meanwhile I should point out that, contrary to what the Churchlands suggest, the Chinese room argument also refutes any strong-AI claims made for the new parallel technologies that are inspired by and modelled on neural networks. Unlike the traditional von Neumann computer, which proceeds in a step-by-step fashion, these systems have many computational elements that operate in parallel and interact with one another according to rules inspired by neurobiology. Although the results are still modest, these 'parallel distributed processing' models raise useful questions about how complex, parallel network systems like those in brains might actually function in the production of intelligent behaviour.

24 The parallel, 'brainlike' character of the processing, however, is irrelevant to the purely computational aspects of the process. Any function that can be computed on a parallel machine can also be computed on a serial machine. Indeed, because parallel machines are still rare, connectionist programs are usually run on traditional serial machines. Parallel processing, then, does not afford a way around the Chinese room argument.

25 What is more, the connectionist system is subject even on its own terms to a variant of the objection presented by the original Chinese room argument. Imagine that instead of a Chinese room, I have a Chinese gym: a hall containing many monolingual, English-speaking men. These men would carry out the same operations as the nodes and synapses in a connectionist architecture as described by the Churchlands, and the outcome would be the same as having one man manipulate symbols according to a rule book. No one in the gym speaks a word of Chinese, and there is no way for the system as a whole to learn the meanings of any Chinese words. Yet with appropriate adjustments, the system could give the correct answers to Chinese questions.

26 There are, as I suggested earlier, interesting properties of connectionist nets that enable them to simulate brain processes more accurately than traditional serial architecture does. But the advantages of parallel architecture for weak AI are quite irrelevant to the issues between the Chinese room argument and strong AI.

27 The Churchlands miss this point when they say that a big enough Chinese gym might have higher-level mental features that emerge from the size and complexity of the system, just as whole brains have mental features that are not had by individual neurones. That is, of course, a possibility, but it has nothing to do with computation. Computationally, serial and parallel systems are equivalent: any computation that can be done in parallel can be done in serial. If the man in the Chinese room is computationally equivalent to both, then if he does not understand Chinese solely by virtue of doing the computations, neither do they. The Churchlands are correct in saying that the original Chinese room argument was designed with traditional AI in mind but wrong in thinking that connectionism is immune to the argument. It applies to any computational system. You can't get semantically loaded thought contents from formal computations alone, whether they are done in serial or in parallel; that is why the Chinese room argument refutes strong AI in any form.

28 Many people who are impressed by this argument are nonetheless puzzled about the differences between people and computers. If humans are, at least in a trivial sense, computers, and if humans have a semantics, then why couldn't we give semantics to other computers? Why couldn't we program a Vax or a Cray so that it too would have thoughts and feelings? Or why couldn't some new computer technology overcome the gulf between form and content, between syntax and semantics? What, in fact, are the differences between animal brains and computer systems that enable the Chinese room argument to work against computers but not against brains?

29 The most obvious difference is that the processes that define something as a computer – computational processes – are completely independent of any reference to a specific type of hardware implementation. One could in principle make a computer out of old beer cans strung together with wires and powered by windmills.

30 But when it comes to brains, although science is largely ignorant of how brains function to produce mental states, one is struck by the extreme specificity of the anatomy and the physiology. Where some understanding exists of

how brain processes produce mental phenomena – for example, pain, thirst, vision, smell – it is clear that specific neurobiological processes are involved. Thirst, at least of certain kinds, is caused by certain types of neurone firings in the hypothalamus, which in turn are caused by the action of a specific peptide, angio-tensin II. The causation is from the 'bottom up' in the sense that lower-level neuronal processes cause higher-level mental phenomena. Indeed, as far as we know, every 'mental' event, ranging from feelings of thirst to thoughts of mathematical theorems and memories of childhood, is caused by specific neurones firing in specific neural architectures.

31   But why should this specificity matter? After all, neurone firings could be simulated on computers that had a completely different physics and chemistry from that of the brain. The answer is that the brain does not merely instantiate a formal pattern or program (it does that, too), but it also *causes* mental events by virtue of specific neurobiological processes. Brains are specific biological organs, and their specific biochemical properties enable them to cause consciousness and other sorts of mental phenomena. Computer simulations of brain processes provide models of the formal aspects of these processes. But the simulation should not be confused with duplication. The computational model of mental processes is no more real than the computational model of any other natural phenomenon.

32   One can imagine a computer simulation of the action of peptides in the hypothalamus that is accurate down to the last synapse. But equally one can imagine a computer simulation of the oxidation of hydrocarbons in a car engine or the action of digestive processes in a stomach when it is digesting pizza. And the simulation is no more the real thing in the case of the brain than it is in the case of the car or the stomach. Barring miracles, you could not run your car by doing a computer simulation of the oxidation of gasoline, and you could not digest pizza by running the program that simulates such digestion. It seems obvious that a simulation of cognition will similarly not produce the effects of the neurobiology of cognition.

33   All mental phenomena, then, are caused by nerophysiological processes in the brain. Hence.

Axiom 4.   Brains cause minds.

34   In conjunction with my earlier derivation, I immediately derive, trivially,

Conclusion 2.   Any other system capable of causing minds would have to have causal powers (at least) equivalent to those of brains.

35   This is like saying that if an electrical engine is to be able to run a car as fast as a gas engine, it must have (at least) an equivalent power output. This conclusion says nothing about the mechanisms. As a matter of fact, cognition is a biological phenomenon: mental states and processes are caused by brain processes. This does not imply that only a biological system could think, but it does imply that any alternative system, whether made of silicon, beer cans

or whatever, would have to have the relevant causal capacities equivalent to those of brains. So now I can derive

Conclusion 3.   Any artefact that produced mental phenomena, any artificial brain, would have to be able to duplicate the specific causal powers of brains, and it could not do that just by running a formal program.

36 Furthermore, I can derive an important conclusion about human brains:

Conclusion 4.   The way that human brains actually produce mental phenomena cannot be solely by virtue of running a computer program.

37 I first presented the Chinese room parable in the pages of *Behavioural and Brain Sciences* in 1980, where it appeared, as is the practice of the journal, along with peer commentary, in this case 26 commentaries. Frankly, I think the point it makes is rather obvious, but to my surprise the publication was followed by a further flood of objections that – more surprisingly – continues to the present day. The Chinese room argument clearly touched some sensitive nerve.

38 The thesis of strong AI is that any system whatsoever – whether it is made of beer cans, silicon chips or toilet paper – not only might have thoughts and feelings but *must* have thoughts and feelings, provided only that it implements the right program, with the right inputs and outputs. Now, that is a profoundly antibiological view, and one would think that people in AI would be glad to abandon it. Many of them, especially the younger generation, agree with me, but I am amazed at the number and vehemence of the defenders. Here are some of the common objections.

(a) In the Chinese room you really do understand Chinese, even though you don't know it. It is, after all, possible to understand something without knowing that one understands it.

(b) You don't understand Chinese, but there is an (unconscious) subsystem in you that does. It is, after all, possible to have unconscious mental states, and there is no reason why your understanding of Chinese should not be wholly unconscious.

(c) You don't understand Chinese, but the whole room does. You are like a single neurone in the brain, and just as such a single neurone by itself cannot understand but only contributes to the understanding of the whole system, you don't understand, but the whole system does.

(d) Semantics doesn't exist anyway; there is only syntax. It is a kind of prescientific illusion to suppose that there exist in the brain some mysterious 'mental contents,' 'thought processes' or 'semantics.' All that exists in the brain is the same sort of syntactic symbol manipulation that goes on in computers. Nothing more.

(e) You are not really running the computer program – you only think you are. Once you have a conscious agent going through the steps of the program, it ceases to be a case of implementing a program at all.

(f) Computers would have semantics and not just syntax if their inputs and outputs were put in appropriate causal relation to the rest of the world. Imagine that we put the computer into a robot, attached television cameras to the robot's head, installed transducers connecting the television messages to the computer and had the computer output operate the robot's arms and legs. Then the whole system would have a semantics.

(g) If the program simulated the operation of the brain of a Chinese speaker, then it would understand Chinese. Suppose that we simulated the brain of a Chinese person at the level of neurones. Then surely such a system would understand Chinese as well as any Chinese person's brain.

And so on.

39 All of these arguments share a common feature: they are all inadequate because they fail to come to grips with the actual Chinese room argument. That argument rests on the distinction between the formal symbol manipulation that is done by the computer and the mental contents biologically produced by the brain, a distinction I have abbreviated – I hope not misleadingly – as the distinction between syntax and semantics. I will not repeat my answers to all of these objections, but it will help to clarify the issues if I explain the weaknesses of the most widely held objection, argument (c) – what I call the systems reply. (The brain simulator reply, argument (g), is another popular one, but I have already addressed that one in the previous section.)

40 The systems reply asserts that of course *you* don't understand Chinese but the whole system – you, the room, the rule book, the bushel baskets full of symbols – does. When I first heard this explanation, I asked one of its proponents, 'Do you mean the room understands Chinese?' His answer was yes. It is a daring move, but aside from its implausibility, it will not work on purely logical grounds. The point of the original argument was that symbol shuffling by itself does not give any access to the meanings of the symbols. But this is as much true of the whole room as it is of the person inside. One can see this point by extending the thought experiment. Imagine that I memorize the contents of the baskets and the rule book, and I do all the calculations in my head. You can even imagine that I work out in the open. There is nothing in the 'system' that is not in me, and since I don't understand Chinese, neither does the system.

41 The Churchlands in their companion piece produce a variant of the systems reply by imagining an amusing analogy. Suppose that someone said that light could not be electromagnetic because if you shake a bar magnet in a dark room, the system still will not give off visible light. Now, the Churchlands ask, is not the Chinese room argument just like that? Does it not merely say that if you shake Chinese symbols in a semantically dark room, they will not give off the light of Chinese understanding? But just as later investigation showed that light was entirely constituted by electromagnetic radiation,

could not later investigation also show that semantics are entirely constituted of syntax? Is this not a question for further scientific investigation?

42   Arguments from analogy are notoriously weak, because before one can make the argument work, one has to establish that the two cases are truly analogous. And here I think they are not. The account of light in terms of electromagnetic radiation is a causal story right down to the ground. It is a causal account of the physics of electromagnetic radiation. But the analogy with formal symbols fails because formal symbols have no physical, causal powers. The only power that symbols have, qua symbols, is the power to cause the next step in the program when the machine is running. And there is no question of waiting on further research to reveal the physical, causal properties of 0's and 1's. The only relevant properties of 0's and 1's are abstract computational properties, and they are already well known.

43   The Churchlands complain that I am 'begging the question' when I say that uninterpreted formal symbols are not identical to mental contents. Well, I certainly did not spend much time arguing for it, because I take it as a logical truth. As with any logical truth, one can quickly see that it is true, because one gets inconsistencies if one tries to imagine the converse. So let us try it. Suppose that in the Chinese room some undetectable Chinese thinking really is going on. What exactly is supposed to make the manipulation of the syntactic elements into specifically Chinese thought contents? Well, after all, I am assuming that the programmers were Chinese speakers, programming the system to process Chinese information.

44   Fine. But now imagine that as I am sitting in the Chinese room shuffling the Chinese symbols, I get bored with just shuffling the – to me – meaningless symbols. So, suppose that I decide to interpret the symbols as standing for moves in a chess game. Which semantics is the system giving off now? Is it giving off a Chinese semantics or a chess semantics, or both simultaneously? Suppose there is a third person looking in through the window, and she decides that the symbol manipulations can all be interpreted as stock-market predictions. And so on. There is no limit to the number of semantic interpretations that can be assigned to the symbols because, to repeat, the symbols are purely formal. They have no intrinsic semantics.

45   Is there any way to rescue the Churchlands' analogy from incoherence? I said above that formal symbols do not have causal properties. But of course the program will always be implemented in some hardware or another, and the hardware will have specific physical, causal powers. And any real computer will give off various phenomena. My computers, for example, give off heat, and they make a humming noise and sometimes crunching sounds. So is there some logically compelling reason why they could not also give off consciousness? No. Scientifically, the idea is out of the question, but it is not something the Chinese room argument is supposed to refute, and it is not something that an adherent of strong AI would wish to defend, because any such giving off would have to derive from the physical features of the implementing medium. But the basic premise of strong AI is that the physical features of the implementing medium are totally irrelevant. What matters are programs, and programs are purely formal.

46   The Churchlands' analogy between syntax and electromagnetism, then, is confronted with a dilemma; either the syntax is construed purely formally in terms of its abstract mathematical properties, or it is not. If it is, then the analogy breaks down, because syntax so construed has no physical powers and hence no physical, causal powers. If, on the other hand, one is supposed to think in terms of the physics of the implementing medium, then there is indeed an analogy, but it is not one that is relevant to strong AI.

47   Because the points I have been making are rather obvious – syntax is not the same as semantics, brain processes cause mental phenomena – the question arises, How did we get into this mess? How could anyone have supposed that a computer simulation of a mental process must be the real thing? After all, the whole point of models is that they contain only certain features of the modelled domain and leave out the rest. No one expects to get wet in a pool filled with Ping-Pong-ball models of water molecules. So why would anyone think a computer model of thought processes would actually think?

48   Part of the answer is that people have inherited a residue of behaviorist psychological theories of the past generation. The Turing test enshrines the temptation to think that if something behaves as if it had certain mental processes, then it must actually have those mental processes. And this is part of the behaviorists' mistaken assumption that in order to be scientific, psychology must confine its study to externally observable behaviour. Paradoxically, this residual behaviorism is tied to a residual dualism. Nobody thinks that a computer simulation of digestion would actually digest anything, but where cognition is concerned, people are willing to believe in such a miracle because they fail to recognize that the mind is just as much a biological phenomenon as digestion. The mind, they suppose, is something formal and abstract, not a part of the wet and slimy stuff in our heads. The polemical literature in AI usually contains attacks on something the authors call dualism, but what they fail to see is that they themselves display dualism in a strong form, for unless one accepts the idea that the mind is completely independent of the brain or of any other physically specific system, one could not possibly hope to create minds just by designing programs.

49   Historically, scientific developments in the West that have treated humans as just a part of the ordinary physical, biological order have often been opposed by various rearguard actions. Copernicus and Galileo were opposed because they denied that the earth was the centre of the universe: Darwin was opposed because he claimed that humans had descended from the lower animals. It is best to see strong AI as one of the last gasps of this antiscientific tradition, for it denies that there is anything essentially physical and biological about the human mind. The mind according to strong AI is independent of the brain. It is a computer program and as such has no essential connection to any specific hardware.

50   Many people who have doubts about the psychological significance of AI think that computers might be able to understand Chinese and think about numbers but cannot do the crucially human things, namely – and then follows their favourite human specialty – falling in love, having a sense of humor, feeling the angst of post-industrial society under late capitalism, or

whatever. But workers in AI complain — correctly — that this is a case of moving the goal posts. As soon as an AI simulation succeeds, it ceases to be of psychological importance. In this debate both sides fail to see the distinction between simulation and duplication. As far as simulation is concerned, there is no difficulty in programming my computer so that it prints out, 'I love you, Suzy'; 'Ha ha'; or 'I am suffering the angst of post-industrial society under late capitalism.' The important point is that simulation is not the same as duplication, and that fact holds as much import for thinking about arithmetic as it does for feeling angst. The point is not that the computer gets only to the 40-yard line and not all the way to the goal line. The computer doesn't even get started. It is not playing that game.

NOTE

1   From Searle, J. R. (1990) 'Is the brain's mind a computer program', *Scientific American*, January, pp. 20–5.

9 'Consciousness and objective reality'

Thomas Nagel

Thomas Nagel, born in Belgrade in 1937, is one of the leading philosophers working in America. He has devoted a great deal of effort to analysing the concept of the self, and to elaborating and reconciling two ways in which we view the world, the subjective and the objective. It is this latter distinction which he sees at the heart of the mind–body problem. In the essay printed below he argues that it is precisely the subjectivity of mental states which makes them so difficult to include in a scientific, objective account of the world.[1]

1 We do not at present have even the outline of an adequate theory of the place of mind in the natural order. We know that conscious mental processes occur as part of animal life, and that they are intimately connected with behavior and with the physical activity of our nervous systems and those of other animals. But at the more general, one might say cosmological, level, we know essentially nothing, for we do not understand why those particular connections exist. Our knowledge is entirely empirical and *ad hoc*, not theoretical.

2 Much discussion in the philosophy of mind is concerned with the problem of intentionality: what it means to attribute content to mental states like belief, desire, thought, perception, and so forth. This topic also links discussion of the relation between the mind and the brain with discussion of the relation between natural and artificial intelligence, and of the possibility of ascribing mental states to computers, in some distant future stage of their development. However, I believe that the most fundamental problem in the area is that of consciousness. While consciousness in the form of pure sensation does not in itself guarantee intentionality, I believe true intentionality cannot occur in a being incapable of consciousness. The nature of this relation is

very unclear to me, but its truth seems evident. We may assign meaning to the operations and output of an unconscious computer, as we can assign meaning to words in a book, but the computer can't mean or intend anything itself by what it says or does.

3   For this reason I believe it is at present not possible to speculate fruitfully about the question whether artificially created physical systems could have minds. We can say nothing interesting about this when we know so little about why *we* have minds, or why the other natural organisms to which we find it natural to attribute mental states have them. What is it about a system constructed as we are that explains why it can feel, perceive, want, believe, and think? Until we can begin to answer that question at some level of generality, we are unlikely to say anything useful about whether systems of a radically different physical type could do those things.

4   Ultimately, a person's opinion concerning this question will depend not merely on his scientific beliefs but on his philosophical beliefs about the mind–body problem. That is because it is a philosophical question, what a general theory of mind would have to account for to be adequate.

5   There are those who believe, for example, that mental states can be defined in terms of their causal role in the control of the organism. When this definition refers to a system of interacting states, definable entirely in terms of their relations to physical inputs, behavioral outputs, and to one another, the view is called functionalism. If functionalism were correct as an account of what it is for a being to have a mind, or to be the subject of mental states, then nothing more would be required for a general theory of the physical conditions of mind than an account of how physical materials can be put together to construct systems whose functional organization was of the right type. To explain this would be a stupendous task; and it is not at all obvious that the same functional organization that characterizes a mouse, let alone a human, could be embodied in a completely different type of physical system, in the way that much simpler functions like addition can be carried out by different physical machines. But at least we can understand the general character of the question. The possibility of an alternative physical realization of visual perception, for example, would depend both on the functional analysis of that mental faculty and on the possibility of replicating that type of functional operation in a structure physically quite different from the standard biological model. Such a theory would enable us to consider the possibility of the eventual construction of artificial minds, through the creation of systems which mimic the behavior and functional organization of human and other animal organisms.

6   I believe, however, that functionalism, though part of the truth, is not an adequate theory of mind, and that the complete truth is much more complicated and more resistant to understanding. In addition to their functional role in the explanation of behavior and their concrete physiological basis, conscious mental states have characteristics of a third type, familiar to us all, namely their subjective experiential quality: how they are or how they appear or feel from the point of view of their subjects. However true it may be that mental states and processes play a functional role in the behavioral

life of the organism, these experiential or phenomenological qualities of conscious experience are not simply *equivalent* to those functional roles. And however closely tied these phenomenological qualities may be to specific neurophysiological conditions, they are quite clearly not analyzable in terms of the physical description of those conditions.

7   If this is correct, then an adequate general theory of the place of mind in the natural order must systematically relate three seemingly disparate things: functional organization, physical constitution, and subjective appearance. We know a certain amount about how these three are related in human sensory perception, and perhaps more generally in mammalian perception. We know parts of the story about other aspects of mind, in ourselves and other animals. But we have not even the glimmerings of a general theory which explains *why* the particular physical operation of the human central nervous system gives rise to the sort of conscious life that it does – though we understand a bit more in certain respects about how it makes possible the organism's behavior in dealing with its environment. But unless our theory of mind includes a theory of consciousness, it cannot give us any basis for speculating either positively or negatively about the possibility of alternative physical bases of mind, different from the familiar biological examples. And at present we have simply no idea what *in general* the occurrence of conscious processes depends on.

8   We have increasing knowledge of a fascinating character about the physical conditions of particular types of conscious states, but these correlations, even if substantially multiplied, do not amount to a general explanatory theory. In order to achieve a real understanding of these matters, we would have to make progress of a fundamental kind with the mind–body problem: progress which constituted a conceptual advance, rather than merely more empirically ascertainable information, however interesting. A theory which succeeded in explaining the relation between behavior, consciousness, and the brain would have to be of a fundamentally different kind from theories about other things; it cannot be generated by the application of already existing methods of explanation.

9   The reason for this is simple. The mind–body problem is a natural outgrowth or by-product of the overwhelmingly successful methods of physical science which have driven the permanent scientific revolution of our era since the seventeenth century. That is why the problem received its essential modern formulation from Descartes, who participated in the beginnings of that revolution.

10   What has made modern physical science possible is the method of investigating the observable physical world not with respect to the way it appears to our senses – to the species-specific view of human perceivers – but rather as an objective realm existing independently of our minds. (I realize that this description may be thought not to fit certain developments of contemporary physics, but that is a complication I leave aside, as it is not relevant to the present issue.) In order to do this, it was necessary to find ways of detecting and measuring and describing features of the physical world which were not inextricably tied to the ways things looked, sounded, and felt to us; and this

resulted in the discovery of objective, essentially spatiotemporal properties of the physical world which could be mathematically described and related by general laws of extraordinary power and universality, thus enabling us to transcend the rough and particular associations available at the level of merely human appearances. The result is an understanding of objective physical reality almost unrecognizably different from the familiar world of our theoretically unaided experience.

11   But it was a condition of this remarkable advance that the subjective appearances of things be excluded from what had to be explained and described by our physical theories. And what was done with those appearances instead was that they were detached from the physical world and relocated in our minds. The whole idea of objective physical reality depends on excluding the subjective appearances from the external world and consigning them to the mind instead.

12   But it follows inexorably from this strategy that the same methods of objective physical understanding cannot be successfully applied to the subjective contents of the mind themselves. The method can be used on the body, including its central nervous system, and on the relation of neural activity to observable behavioral functioning, because these are all aspects of objective physical reality. But for the subjective qualities of experience themselves, we need a different form of understanding. We cannot hope to understand them completely as an aspect of objective physical reality, because the concept of objective physical reality depends on excluding them from what has to be understood. They are excluded, because they are tied to a species-specific point of view that the objectivity of physical science requires us to leave behind.

13   So when science turns to the effort to explain the subjective quality of experience, there is no further place for these features to escape to. And since the traditional, enormously successful method of modern physical understanding cannot be extended to this aspect of the world, that form of understanding has built into it a guarantee of its own essential incompleteness – its intrinsic incapacity to account for everything.

14   One consequence is that the traditional form of scientific explanation, reduction of familiar substances and processes to their more basic and in general imperceptibly small component parts, is not available as a solution to the analysis of mind. Reductionism within the objective domain is essentially simple to understand, for it uses the uncomplicated geometrical idea of the part–whole relation. Geometry is the basic imaginative tool which made possible the formulation of atomic theory, and in more and more sophisticated versions it has allowed physical understanding to expand. But it depends on first stripping familiar objects of all but their spatiotemporal, or primary, qualities and relations. That makes possible their reduction to more basic and law-governed objective phenomena from which the familiar properties can be seen to arise by necessity, as the mass and hardness of a diamond can be seen to result from the combined mass and structural arrangement of its carbon atoms, or the liquidity of water can be seen to result from the relations of its molecules to one another.

15 No correspondingly straightforward psychophysical reduction is imaginable, because it would not have the simple character of a relation between one objective level of description and another. We at present lack the conception of a complete analysis of subjective, phenomenological features of mental reality in terms of an objective, physical basis, and there is no reason to believe that such a thing is possible.

16 Surprisingly, there are some who believe this is a reason to deny the reality of the third, subjective aspect of the mental; they call themselves eliminative materialists. But this is an irrational and, I might add, unscientific attitude. The first role of science is not to ignore the data, and the existence of phenomenological features of mental life is one of the most obvious and unavoidable categories of data with which we are presented. To regard it as unreal because it cannot be accounted for by the methods of current physical science is to get things backwards. The data are not determined by our methods; rather the adequacy of our methods is determined by whether they can account for the data. To admit to reality only what can be understood by current methods is a sure recipe for stagnation.

17 The limits of the classical methods of objective physical science are not surprising, since those methods were developed to deal with a definite, though universal, type of subject matter. If we are to take the next great step, to a truly theoretical understanding of the mental, we must proceed by regarding this limitation as a challenge to develop a new form of under-standing appropriate to a subject whose exclusion from physical science was essential to its progress. This is in my view the most interesting and difficult scientific challenge we now face, and I have no idea how it might be met. My own instincts are in the direction of a Spinozistic monism, which will reveal both the mental and the physical as incomplete descriptions of a more funda-mental reality and explains them both, as well as their necessary connection – but of which we have at present no conception. The possibility of the development of conscious organisms must have been built into the world from the beginning: it cannot be an accident. (Nor can it be explained through the theory of evolution, in terms of the survival value of conscious-ness. Evolution can explain only why a trait has survived and not been extinguished, not how it is possible in the first place.) But such speculation is at this point idle.

18 Machines won't have minds unless they have points of view, and at present we know practically nothing about the general conditions under which subjective points of view arise out of the activities of the physical world. In some respects we understand quite well how that world works, and we are making significant progress in extending this physical form of understanding to biology, including neurophysiology. But until we discover a way to stand theoretically astride the boundary between objective spatiotemporal physical reality and the subjective contents of experience, we cannot claim to be in possession of the basic intellectual tools needed for a comprehensive under-standing of conscious life. This may be unattainable, but without it we cannot have a general cosmology.

NOTE

1   This essay is taken from Warner, R. and Szubka, T. (eds) (1994) *The Mind–body Problem: A Guide to the Current Debate*, Blackwell, pp. 63–8.

Revision test

This test is designed to help you revise the main points and techniques covered in this book. Try working through the questions without using your notes or referring back to the text of the book. Then compare your answers to those given on page 228.

CHAPTER 1

1   Which of the following, if any, are true?
    When philosophers of mind speak of the subjectivity of individual experience, they mean that:

    (a) we have a special mode of awareness of our own experiences;
    (b) we can be aware of everyone's experiences in the same way;
    (c) we can only have opinions about this matter: no definite truth can be reached about it;
    (d) experience always involves a unique and private point of view.

CHAPTER 2

2   Which, if any, of the following statements are true?
    Descartes contends that:

    (a) minds are non-material properties of bodies;
    (b) minds are a different type of substance from bodies;
    (c) the essence of mind is thought;
    (d) imagination is part of the essence of the mind;
    (e) the essence of matter is extension.

3   Which, if any, of the following statements are true?
    Descartes contends that:

(a) mind and body are intimately related;

(b) mind and body constitute parallel universes which do not interact;

(c) mind and body interact at one point in the brain.

4   Which, if any, of the following statements would Malebranche regard as true?

(a) minds are a special type of property of bodies;

(b) minds and bodies are different types of substance;

(c) minds and bodies interact at one point in the brain;

(d) minds and bodies never interact;

(e) minds and bodies appear to interact thanks to divine intervention.

5   If you are an epiphenomenalist, which, if any, of the following assertions would you regard as true?

(a) mental acts cause physical events, i.e. bodily movements;

(b) minds are an effect of bodies;

(c) the mental cannot be reduced to the physical;

(d) minds are a different type of substance from bodies;

(e) mental events play no causal role in the universe.

6   Which, if any, of the following statements is true of *all* forms of dualism?

(a) minds and bodies are different types of substances;

(b) minds are a special type of effect of bodies;

(c) minds and bodies mutually causally interact;

(d) minds are a special type of property of bodies;

(e) minds or mental properties are in some way irreducibly different from bodies or their properties.

CHAPTER 3

7   Which, if any, of the following statements would be accepted by Smart?

(a) sensations are an effect of brain processes;

(b) sensations stand to brain processes as lightning stands to an electrical discharge;

(c) s-statements and bp-statements refer to the same events;

(d) s-statements and bp-statements have the same meaning.

8   Which, if any, of the following statements would be accepted by a functionalist?

(a) what is distinctive about the mind is what it does;

(b) what is distinctive of the mind is what it is made of;

(c) an acceptable philosophy of mind only has to be true of human beings;

(d) an acceptable philosophy of mind has to allow for non-human and artificial beings to have minds;

(e) mental states are definable as functional states;
(f) mental states are identical to physical states;
(g) the mental can be reduced to the physical.

9   Which of the following, if any, is true?
    The claim that all mental states have intentionality means:

    (a) all mental states include intentions;
    (b) all mental states are about something;
    (c) we have privileged access to our mental states.

10 Which, if any, of the following statements are true?
    Objections to functionalism which make use of the concept of qualia are designed to show that:

    (a) functionalism is internally inconsistent;
    (b) functionalism is too liberal as a philosophy of mind;
    (c) functionalism is too chauvinistic as a philosophy of mind;
    (d) functionalism is an incomplete account of the mind because it misses out a key aspect of mental states.

11 Which, if any, of the following statements are true?
    Eliminativists believe that:

    (a) FP will one day be reduced to or in some way accommodated within completed neuroscience;
    (b) FP has a special status among the explanatory theories by means of which we seek to understand the world;
    (c) FP is an empirical theory like any of the others advanced by science;
    (d) FP has become progressively more sophisticated and inclusive over the centuries;
    (e) FP does not explain all that a theory of the mind should explain;
    (f) FP will one day be junked;
    (g) FP coheres well with scientific discoveries about the mind–brain.

12 Which, if any, of the following could be argued to be problems for any attempt to construct a materialist monist theory of the mind?

    (a) aboutness or intentionality;
    (b) mental causation;
    (c) subjectivity.

CHAPTER 4

13 Which, if any, of the following views is the Chinese room argument designed to prove?

    (a) that no computer can think (i.e. as humans can be said to 'think');
    (b) that no artificial device of any kind can think;

(c) that only biological systems can think;

(d) that running a computer program is not a sufficient condition for thinking.

14 In Searle's opinion, which of the following assertions states the dissimilarity between human thought and running a computer program which is most important from the philosophical point of view?

(a) the computer runs much faster than the brain;

(b) thought has semantic properties; the program has only syntactical properties;

(c) human thought is based on the parallel distributed processing system of the brain;

(d) the computer works using von Neumann architecture.

15 Which of the following, if any, is true?
The systems objection to the Chinese room argument is the objection that:

(a) in the Chinese room you really do understand Chinese but you don't know it;

(b) even if the operator in the room doesn't understand Chinese, it doesn't follow that the whole set up doesn't understand Chinese;

(c) there is no such thing as semantics; there is only syntax;

(d) if the program simulated the brain processes of a Chinese speaker, then it would understand Chinese.

16 Which, if any, of the following assertions are true?
Knowledge how, as distinct from knowledge that, is a problem for traditional AI because:

(a) anything that does not display knowledge how could not be described as intelligent in the same sense as humans;

(b) knowledge how or skills would need huge numbers of propositions to describe fully;

(c) knowledge how is not entirely propositional in nature, and so cannot be computed.

17 Which, if any, of the following constitute problems for traditional AI?

(a) the sheer number of propositions needed to simulate human knowledge strains the memory capacity of computers;

(b) it is very difficult to produce an agreed analysis of the ontology implicit in the common-sense view of the world;

(c) the number of propositions which a computer has to review in simulating human intelligence is so great that its operating speed is impaired;

(d) human experience has meanings, i.e. is experienced as meaningful, because it is embedded in and is a product of a complex culture;

(e) producing a program to copy the human ability to select the data relevant to any context currently presents insuperable difficulties.

CHAPTER 5

18 In the view of Nagel is consciousness:

  (a) a necessary condition for intentionality?
  (b) a sufficient condition for intentionality?

19 Why in Nagel's view must physical science be incomplete?

  (a) because brain physiology has turned out to be so fantastically complex;
  (b) because we have no idea how the brain generates consciousness;
  (c) because human consciousness is by nature subjective, whereas science is designed to handle only objective phenomena.

20 Which of the following assertions, if any, is true?
    Nagel criticizes eliminativism because:

  (a) it regards FP, wrongly, as just another empirical theory;
  (b) it is unscientific in its rejection of data.

Answers to revision test

1   (a) and (d)
2   (b), (c) and (e)
3   (a) and (c)
4   (b), (d) and (e)
5   (b), (c) and (e)
6   (e)
7   (b) and (c)
8   (a), (d) and (e)
9   (b)
10 (b) and (d)
11 (c), (e) and (f)
12 (a) and (c)
13 (d)
14 (b)
15 (b)
16 (a) and (c)
17 (b), (d) and (e)
18 (a)
19 (c)
20 (a) and (b)

Bibliography

Adam, C. and Tannery, P. (eds) (1964–76) *Oeuvres de Descartes*, 12 vols, Paris: Vrin/CNRS.

Armstrong, D.M. (1968) *A Materialist Theory of the Mind*, London: Routledge.

Baier, K. (1970) 'Smart on sensations', in C.V. Borst (ed.) *The Mind/Brain Identity Theory: A Collection of Papers,* London: Macmillan.

Blakemore, Colin (1977) *Mechanics of the Mind*, Cambridge: Cambridge University Press.

Block, N. (1978) *Troubles with Functionalism*, see Block (1980).

—— (ed.) (1980) *Readings in Philosophy of Psychology*, Vol. 1, London: Methuen (contains a reprint of Block (1978) and a number of other important pieces concerning functionalism).

Boden, M. (ed.) (1990) *The Philosophy of Artificial Intelligence*, Oxford: Oxford University Press.

Boehner, P. (ed.) (1957) *Ockham: Philosophical Writings*, London: Nelson.

Borst, C.V. (ed.) (1970) *The Mind/Brain Identity Theory: A Collection of Papers*, London: Macmillan.

Braddon-Mitchell, D. and Jackson, F. (1996) *Philosophy of Mind and Cognition*, Blackwell.

Brentano, F. (1995) [1874] *Psychology from an Empirical Standpoint*, ed. Oskar Kraus, London: Routledge.

Burks, A.W., Goldstine, H.H. and von Neumann, J. (1946) *Preliminary Discussion of the Logical Design of an Electronic Computing Instrument*, in Randell (1982) (shortened version).

Churchland, P.M. (1981) 'Eliminative materialism and the propositional attitudes', *Journal of Philosophy* 78(2): 67–76.

—— (1988) *Matter and Consciousness: A Contemporary Introduction to the Philosophy of Mind*, revised edn, Cambridge MA: MIT Press.

—— (1989) *A Neurocomputational Perspective: The Nature of Mind and the Structure of Science*, Cambridge MA: MIT Press.

—— (1990) 'Could a machine think?', *Scientific American* 262(1): 26–31.

—— (1994) *The Computer that Could: A Neurophilosophical Portrait*, Cambridge MA: MIT Press.

Clarke, A.C. (1968) *2001: A Space Odyssey*, Legend Books edn., 1990.

Clifford, W.K. (1879a) *Lectures and Essays*, 2 vols (ed. L. Stephen and F. Pollock), London: Macmillan.

—— (1879b) *Seeing and Thinking*, London: Macmillan.

Copeland, B.J. (1993) *Artificial Intelligence: A Philosophical Introduction*, Oxford: Blackwell.

Costilhes, J. (1962) see Malebranche, N. (1962a, b, c).

Cottingham, J.G. (ed. and trans.) (1976) *Descartes' Conversation with Burman*, Oxford: Clarendon Press.

—— (ed.) (1992) *The Cambridge Companion to Descartes*, Cambridge: Cambridge University Press.

Cottingham, J.G., Stoothoff, R., Kenny, A. and Murdoch, D. (1985–91) *The Philosophical Writings of Descartes*, 3 vols, Cambridge: Cambridge University Press.

Crane, T. (1995) *The Mechanical Mind*, Penguin.

Crick, F. (1994) *The Astonishing Hypothesis*, New York: Simon and Schuster.

Damasio, A.R. (1994) *Descartes' Error: Emotion, Reason and the Laws of Physics*, Avon Books.

Davidson, D. (1970) 'Mental events', reprinted in Davidson (1980).

—— (1980) *Essays on Actions and Events*, Oxford: Oxford University Press.

Dennett, D.C. (1981) 'Three kinds of intentionality', first published in Henley (1981); reprinted in Dennett (1987).

—— (1987) *The Intentional Stance*, Cambridge MA: MIT Press.

—— (1991) *Consciousness Explained*, Harmondsworth: Allen Lane (Penguin).

Dilthey, W. (1976) *Selected Writings*, ed. and tr. H.P. Rickman, Cambridge: Cambridge University Press.

Doney, W. (ed.) (1968) *Descartes: A Collection of Critical Essays*, London: Macmillan.

Dreyfus, H.L. (1992) *What Computers Still Can't Do*, Cambridge MA: MIT Press.

Feigl, H. (1958) *The 'Mental' and the 'Physical'*, see Feigl, Scriven and Maxwell (1958).

Feigl, H., Scriven, M. and Maxwell, G. (eds) (1958) *Minnesota Studies in the Philosophy of Science: Concepts, Theories and the Mind–Body Problem*, Minneapolis: University of Minnesota Press.

Feyerabend, P. (1963) 'Materialism and the mind–body problem', *Review of Metaphysics* XVII(1): 65 (Sept.).

Frege, G. (1980) [1892] 'On sense and reference' (Über Sinn und Bedeutung), in P. Geach and M. Black (eds and trans) *Translations from the Philosophical Writings of Gottlob Frege*, Oxford: Oxford University Press.

Garnham, A. (1998) *Artificial Intelligence*, London: Routledge.

Geach, P. and Black, M. (eds and trans) (1980) *Translations from the Philosophical Writings of Gottlob Frege*, Oxford: Oxford University Press.

Gewirth, A. (1943) 'Clearness and distinctness in Descartes' philosophy', *Philosophy* 18(69): 17–36, reprinted in Doney (1968).

Goldman, A. (1992) 'In defense of the simulation theory', *Mind and Language* 7: 104–19.

Gordon, R. (1986) 'Folk psychology as simulation', *Mind and Language* 1(2): 158–71.

Graubard, S.R. (ed.) (1990) *The Artificial Intelligence Debate*, Cambridge MA: MIT Press.

Guttenplan, S. (ed.) (1994) *A Companion to the Philosophy of Mind*, Oxford: Blackwell.

Haldane, E.S. and Ross, G.R.T. (1931) *The Philosophical Works of Descartes*, 2 vols, Cambridge: Cambridge University Press (corrected edn).

Haugeland, J. (1985) *Artificial Intelligence: The Very Idea*, Cambridge MA: MIT Press.

Henley, R. (ed.) (1981) *Reduction, Time and Reality*, Cambridge: Cambridge University Press.

Horgan, T. and Woodward, J. (1985) 'Folk psychology is here to stay', *Philosophical Review* 94: 197–225.

Jackson, F. (1982) 'Epiphenomenal qualia', *Philosophical Quarterly* 32: 127–36.

—— (1986) 'What Mary didn't know', *Journal of Philosophy* 83: 291–5.

Kauffman, S. (1995) *At Home in the Universe: The Search for the Laws of Self-organisation and Complexity*, Oxford: Oxford University Press.

Kenny, A. (1968) *Descartes: A Study of his Philosophy*, London: Random House (also later edns).

Leibniz, G.W. (1951a) [1685] 'The art of discovery', in P.P. Weiner (ed.) *Leibniz: Selections*, Scribners.

—— (1951b) [1695] 'New system of nature and of the communication of substances, as well as of the union of soul and body', in P.P. Weiner (ed.) *Leibniz: Selections*, Scribners.

—— (1969) *Philosophical Papers and Letters*, L.E. Loemker (ed.), The Hague: Reidel (contains Leibniz's 'Meditations on knowledge, truth and ideas').

Lepore, E. and Van Gulick, R. (eds) (1991) *John Searle and his Critics*, Oxford: Blackwell.

Lewis, D. (1990) 'What experience teaches', in W.G. Lycan (ed.) (1990) *Mind and Cognition: a Reader*, Oxford: Blackwell, pp. 499–519.

Loeb, L.E. (1992) 'The Cartesian circle' in J.G. Cottingham (ed.) *The Cambridge Companion to Descartes*, Cambridge: Cambridge University Press, pp. 200–35.

Lycan, W.G. (ed.) (1990) *Mind and Cognition: A Reader*, Oxford: Blackwell.

Malcolm, N. (1966) [1958] *Ludwig Wittgenstein: A Memoir*, rev. edn, Oxford: Oxford University Press.

Malebranche, N. (1962a) [1674–5] *De la Recherche de la Verité* (The Search for Truth), Vol. II, i, 5, J. Costilhes (ed.), Paris: Presses Universitaires de France.

—— (1962b) [1688] 'Entretiens sur la Metaphysique et sur la Religion' (Dialogues on Metaphysics and Religion), Vol. IX, in J. Costilhes (ed.) *Lumière et mouvement de l'esprit (Textes choisis)*, Paris: Presses Universitaires de France.

—— (1962c) *Lumière et mouvement de l'esprit (Textes choisis)*, (ed. Jean Costilhes), Paris: Presses Universitaires de France.

McCrone, J. (1997) 'Wild minds', *New Scientist* 2112: 26, 13 December.

Moyal, G.M.D. (ed.) (1991) *René Descartes: Critical Assessments*, 4 vols, London: Routledge.

Nagel, T. (1974) 'What is it like to be a bat?', *Philosophical Review* 83: 435–50 (also in Block (1980: 160)).

——(1979) *Mortal Questions*, Cambridge: Cambridge University Press.

—— (1986) *The View from Nowhere*, Oxford: Oxford University Press.

Newell, A. and Simon, H.A. (1958) 'Heuristic problem solving: the next advance in operations research', *Operations Research* 6: 1–10.

—— (1961) RAND Corporation P-2276, April 20.

Penelhum, T. (1970) *Survival and Disembodied Existence*, London: Routledge & Kegan Paul.

Penrose, R. (1989) *The Emperor's New Mind*, Oxford: Oxford University Press.

—— (1994) *Shadows of the Mind*, Oxford: Oxford University Press.

Ramakrishna R. (ed.) (1993) *Cultivating Consciousness*, Praeger.

Randell, B. (ed.) (1982) *The Origins of Digital Computers*, Berlin: Springer-Verlag (contains a shortened version of Burks *et al.*, 1946).

Restak, R.M. (1995) *Brainscapes*, Hyperion.

Rorty, R. (1965) 'Mind–body identity, privacy, and categories', *Review of Metaphysics* XIX(1): 73.

Rosenthal, D.M. (ed.) (1971) *Materialism and the Mind–body Problem*, Englewood Cliffs NJ: Prentice Hall.

Rumelhart, D.E. and McClelland, J.L. (1986) (eds) *Parallel Distributed Processing*, 2 vols, Cambridge MA: MIT Press.

Ryle, G. (1949) *The Concept of Mind*, London: Hutchinson; and many subsequent editions under various imprints.

Santayana, G. (1906) *Reason in Science*, repr. in the Triton Edn of G. Santayana (1936) *Works*, Vol. 5, New York: Scribners.

—— (1967) 'Comparison with other views of spirit', undated ms published in John Lachs (ed.) *Animal Faith and Spiritual Life*, New York: Appleton-Century-Crofts.

Searle, J.R. (1990) 'Is the brain's mind a computer program?', *Scientific American*, Jan.: 20–25.

—— (1992a) *Intentionality: An Essay in the Philosophy of Mind*, Cambridge: Cambridge University Press.

—— (1992b) *The Rediscovery of the Mind*, Cambridge MA: MIT Press.

Shoemaker, S. (1984) *Identity, Cause and Mind: Philosophical Essays*, Cambridge: Cambridge University Press.

Smart, J.J.C. (1970) *Sensations and Brain Processes*, first published in *Philosophical Review* LXVIII: 141–56, 1959; reprinted in many anthologies, e.g. Borst (1970).

Smith, P. and Jones, O.R. (1986) *The Philosophy of Mind*, Cambridge: Cambridge University Press.

Tart, C.T. (n.d.) 'Mind embodied: computer-generated virtual reality as a new, dualistic-interactive model for transpersonal psychology' in R. Ramakrishna (ed.) *Cultivating Consciousness*, Praeger.

Trefil, J. (1997) *Are We Unique?*, Chichester: Wiley.

Turing, A. (1950) 'Computing machinery and intelligence' *Mind* 59; 433–60, reprinted in Boden (1990).

Warburton, N. (1996) *Thinking from A to Z*, London: Routledge.

Warner, R. and Szubka, T. (eds) (1994) *The Mind–body Problem: A Guide to the Current Debate*, Oxford: Blackwell.

Weiner, P.P. (ed.) (1951) *Leibniz: Selections*, New York: Scribners.

Wilkes, K. (1981) 'Functionalism, psychology and the philosophy of mind', *Philosophical Topics* 12, pt 1.

—— (1984) 'Pragmatics in science and theory in common sense', *Inquiry* 27, pt 4.

Williams, B. (1978/1990) *Descartes: The Project of Pure Enquiry*, Harmondsworth: Penguin.

Wittgenstein, L. (1968) [1953] *Philosophical Investigations*, G.E.M. Anscombe (trans.), Oxford: Blackwell.

Index

Notes: AI = artificial intelligence; FP = folk psychology; figures are indicated by italicised page numbers.